ENGAGING
COMMUNICATION
IN CONFLICT

To the many conversation partners
who made this book possible

ENGAGING
COMMUNICATION
IN CONFLICT

SYSTEMIC PRACTICE

STEPHEN W. LITTLEJOHN
KATHY DOMENICI

 Sage Publications, Inc.
International Educational and Professional Publisher
Thousand Oaks ▪ London ▪ New Delhi

For information:

Sage Publications, Inc.
2455 Teller Road
Thousand Oaks, California 91320
E-mail: order@sagepub.com

SAGE Publications Ltd
1 Oliver's Yard
55 City Road
London EC1Y 1SP

SAGE Publications India Pvt Ltd
B-42, Panchsheel Enclave
Post Box 4109
New Delhi 110 017

Printed in the United States of America

Library of Congress Cataloging-in-Publication Data

Littlejohn, Stephen W.
Engaging communication in conflict: Systemic practice / by Stephen W. Littlejohn and Kathy Domenici.
p. cm.
Includes bibliographical references and index.
ISBN 0-7619-2186-9 (cloth: alk. paper) — ISBN 0-7619-2187-7
(paper: alk. paper)
1. Conflict management. 2. Communication. 3. Interpersonal conflict.
4. Interpersonal communication. I. Domenici, Kathy. II. Title.
HM1126 .L57 2000
303.6'9—dc21   00-009056

04 05 06 07 7 6 5 4 3 2

Acquisition Editor: Margaret H. Seawell
Editorial Assistant: Sandra Krumholz
Production Editor: Diane F. Foster
Editorial Assistant: Cindy Bear
Typesetter/Designer: Tina Hill
Cover Designer: Ravi Balasuriya

Contents

Preface
■■■■■■■■■

We met one another in 1993. Stephen had been a communication professor in California and had been researching and writing about conflict and mediation. Having explored these topics academically, he was increasingly drawn to the practice of conflict intervention. He eventually left his long-standing career as a professor, moved to New Mexico, and became a mediator and facilitator. Retaining a love of teaching, he began working part-time at the University of New Mexico and met Kathy there.

Kathy's first love was being a mother, and she had worked actively with others on parenting issues, teaching parents how to talk so children will listen and how to listen so children will talk. After returning to graduate school at the University of New Mexico in the early 1990s, Kathy learned about mediation and began an active practice. She taught regular courses in mediation, organized the Mediation Clinic at the University, and wrote a book on mediation.

We got to know one another when Stephen was a student in Kathy's mediation class. Since then we have worked on many projects together. Stephen has brought to the partnership a rich background in communication theory and years of teaching experience, and Kathy has contributed practical experience, a keen ability to organize, and an amazing appreciation for relationships, and sensitivity to human need. Our partnership has been enriching because of the diversity of contributions each of us makes and the things we share in common. This book is an expression of the things we have learned from one another and the commitments that have come to guide our work.

In our experience, human beings have trouble managing the very differences that make them human. This paradox intrigues us. The human condition is enriched by variation, and yet personal, group, and cultural differences make life a constant challenge. Our commitment to new, constructive methods of conflict management is one response to the struggle we see around us and, indeed, the struggle we ourselves experience in our own relationships and communities. Our work is dedicated to processes that can turn conflict from a destructive force into an enriching opportunity, and as mediators we have seen the power of careful, well-structured, and constructive forms of communication to transform potentially explosive situations.

Conflict intervention work can occur in many places, and we are fortunate to have had opportunities to participate in a variety of settings. Several years ago, Stephen helped to found a group called the Public Dialogue Consortium, which is dedicated to developing ways that communities can explore significant issues productively. The PDC has been involved in several exciting projects and experimented with a number of interesting new techniques. At about the same time, Kathy was introduced to Prosperity Games™, a fascinating and powerful technology originating at Sandia National Laboratories in Albuquerque. These Games are live, interactive, and collaborative strategic-planning events in which professionals negotiate and form partnerships. Kathy has since developed and facilitated many such Games.

Our work—in private, group, organizational, and public settings—has taught us that the qualities of good intervention remain essentially the same from one situation to another. Whether mediating a private dispute, facilitating a larger group, or intervening in complex systems, basic communication principles apply. In this book we present a host of methods that are helpful in various settings, but we also include the core themes, values, ethics, principles, and skills common to all situations.

One of our core themes is communication. Communication makes us who we are and shapes the worlds in which we live. In the academic literature, the theoretical orientation that guides our work is called *systemic social constructionism,* but we prefer the simpler moniker *the communication perspective.* This theory comes from a large and respectable body of literature in biology, sociology, communication, psychology, family therapy, and management. The communication perspective captures the idea that human beings are connected in complex webs of relationships, or patterns of interaction. The communication patterns that form our relationships, sometimes at home and sometimes across vast psychic and geographical territory, create our social worlds. Communication is the glue that holds the system together, and the character of communication determines the quality of these worlds.

This perspective has much to contribute to conflict intervention work. Conflicts are made by communication patterns in a system. Where conflict is destructive, we want to look at the communication patterns that made it so. Where conflict leads to growth and life, we want to study the forms of interaction that led to such outcomes. When we intervene in a conflict, we want to think about what new forms of communication might be developed within the system.

The title of this book, *Engaging Communication in Conflict: Systemic Practice*, reflects each of the above commitments. First, there is the commitment to *practice*, becoming directly involved with people in challenging situations. Second, there is the commitment to a *systems* view, the idea that conflicts are part of complex patterns of interaction among people, groups, and institutions. Third, there is the commitment to *communication*, which is the medium through which we work. Finally, there is commitment to working with *conflict*, the inevitable expression of human difference. We are certainly not alone in these commitments, and they will resonate with the experience of many readers.

We know that this book will be used as a text in college classes, and we hope that its applied approach will be appealing to students. To enhance the book as a text, we have added a theory appendix to help students and other interested readers understand the theoretical background of our work. We encourage students to make use of the multi-level structure of the book, so that they might compare conflict management across contexts such as personal, group, organizational, and public venues.

We have also written this book for practitioners and hope it will be of interest to anyone who faces the complex task of engaging conflict in a system. This certainly includes professionals in alternative dispute resolution, especially mediators and facilitators. The audience should also include individuals responsible for organizing and conducting meetings. Management and communication consultants are often called upon to work in conflict situations in organizations, and we hope these professionals will find our work informative. Because of our emphasis on method, we think Learning and Development and Organizational Development professionals and trainers may also find these pages helpful. Human Resources professionals and agencies concerned with such issues as equal employment opportunity may find here alternatives to the adversarial approaches common to employee relations systems. Any number of community organizations and agencies are interested in promoting constructive communication on difficult community issues, and we hope this book will be a reference for them as well.

We have organized this book in four simple parts. In Part I, we address the basic processes we use in all of our work. In Chapter 1, we talk in more detail about the communication perspective and system thinking. We explain our way of working and present a set of goals we often pursue. In Chapter 2, we describe the kind of communication we try to follow and engender in others. The term *dialogue* captures a certain quality of human relationship that we have repeatedly found to be healthy and productive in even the most difficult situations.

In Part II of the book, we begin to apply these basic ideas to small-system interventions. Chapter 3 addresses mediation in private settings, and Chapter 4 expands the purview to groups. In these chapters we present a number of techniques, some of which are relatively new to the field of conflict intervention.

Part III continues the discussion in terms of larger systems, including organizations, economic and social sectors, and communities. Chapter 5 covers conflict system design, or creating ongoing places and ways within existing systems that allow conflict to be worked through productively. Systemic Mediation systems are featured in this chapter. Chapter 6 covers gaming methodology and its many uses and forms. Chapter 7 deals with public-issue management and summarizes the insights we have gained from our work in communities.

Part IV is the conclusion. In Chapter 8 we present our vision of the world of communication as it might be. We entitled this chapter "Conversations with Friends" because it features the work and ideas of colleagues we greatly admire. We see this book as our "turn" in an ongoing "conversation," and the final chapter brings additional voices into the conversation.

We present this book as "our work," but it is not. What we do is based on the wisdom of the academic research and theories generated over many years by people who care deeply about the quality of ideas. Our practice would be impossible without the creative work of other practitioners, from whom we borrow shamelessly. And we certainly could not have written this book without the support and encouragement of our colleagues in many organizations. In this regard, we have adopted a writer's convention: For simplicity in the text, when we refer to "our work" or to what "we" have done, you should read this as work done individually, together, or with other colleagues.

A final note: We want this book to be easy and interesting to read, so we have limited our use of academic citations and references in the text itself. At the same time, we realize that you may wish to pursue our sources, so we have included in every chapter a list of resources you can use. Each list of references covers all of the citations in the chapter as well as additional sources of interest.

PART I

Basic Commitments

1

■■■■

Constructing Conflict

We hope you find the title of this chapter interesting. The construction metaphor can be a powerful way to understand and intervene in conflicts. If you look at this title twice, you will see a double meaning: Conflicts are constructed by those who engage in them, and in this book we as authors are constructing a way of working with conflicts.

We have chosen the construction metaphor because it draws our attention to how conflicts are made. This metaphor helps us think about who is involved, how they are engaged with one another, the resources they use, the way the conflict is built, and the kind of conflict that results. It also helps us with our intervention work, because it reminds us that no two conflicts are ever quite the same. They are made by different people in different ways using different materials. The metaphor reminds us too that conflicts can be remodeled, or remade in new ways that can have more positive results than the original construction. Like buildings, conflicts can be made and abandoned, occupied for a time, and reshaped, renewed, refurbished, and rebuilt. One of the things we most enjoy about being mediators is that we never know what will walk in the door. Every case is different, and every case presents a new hope that positive change might be achieved.

■ How Conflicts Are Made

Conflicts happen when human differences become an issue. Though they are always there, differences sometimes don't matter. They don't get in the way, they don't seem obvious or challenging, or they don't need to be

3

managed. Much of the time, however, differences do matter, and how we deal with them becomes important. Neighbors realize they have different opinions about pets. A developer and community members become aware of their different views of neighborhood traffic patterns. A married couple struggles with different ways of using money. Coworkers become irritated with one another because they have quite different ideas about how to organize the office.

When difference gets in the way, conflict results.

Talking About Difference

We once mediated a dispute between two neighbors who co-owned a large parcel of land. They had owned the land jointly for over 20 years and sold it off gradually and were now disputing about the last 5 acres. The investment was good, and both families had made a great deal of money. You can imagine our surprise, then, when we discovered that they had been fighting over who should pay the relatively low attorney's fees on this final deal, a deal that would net them nearly four million dollars.

As we explored the problem with the parties, they revealed that the relationship had gone sour from the beginning. Virtually every decision had been contested. The families got angrily stuck on what decisions should be made, how the decisions should be made, and who should make them. They never agreed on how the land should be managed, and now some 20 years into the deal, they found themselves in court once again.

By the time of this mediation, these families had lost thousands of dollars in attorney's fees fighting each another; they had no trust; they could think of nothing good to say about the other party; they were so angry they could not listen or speak coherently during the mediation, and—to our great surprise—they could not imagine how their lives would be different once this final parcel of land was sold. In other words, they had become so self-identified with the conflict that they could not imagine living without it.

This mediation seemed unsuccessful in every way. There was no positive communication, no new information learned, no relationship building, and no agreement. Each party left convinced that the judge would see it their way.

As we drove home that night, we thought a lot about difference, how differences can be managed badly or well, and how the way we construct a conflict can add to or detract from the quality of life. Ironically, that case was not discouraging to us but steeled our commitment to continue our search for ways to manage conflict humanely, constructively, and productively.

A key to the constructive management of difference can be found in how we *talk about our differences*. In many North American cultures, as in other parts of the world, people are accustomed to thinking about difference in polarized, blame-oriented ways. Because we tend to think in individualized terms, our worlds too often end at our skin, so that the values, ideas, language, customs, opinions, and actions of other people seem foreign. We are naturally ego involved in our own ways of doing things and we get very protective of our own interests. So when our ideas are threatened, we sometimes go into a defensive stance and talk in terms of *fighting for our rights, prevailing, winning, being right, knowing the truth, not submitting to what is obviously wrong*, and many other polarized frames.

Why Talk Matters

After the cold war, there was a concerted effort at the national defense laboratories to think of ways to use war technology for peace. Pace VanDevender at Sandia National Laboratory had the idea that the war game concept could be modified to achieve peaceful ends. Instead of talking about strategies for defeating the enemy, teams could talk about strategies for collaborating to create forces for a prosperity-oriented future. Instead of playing the game in a war theater, we might play it in a socioeconomic sector where representatives from a variety of stakeholder groups would spend time together involved in healthy competition, collaboration, and complementation. If played well, many new policy recommendations would emerge.

We will have much more to say about gaming methodology in Chapter 6. For now, the important thing is that this exciting technology shows that how we talk about difference is important. In these games, participants are encouraged to speak of difference as a positive resource on which new ideas and ways of thinking can be built.

The conflict management business is a communication enterprise, and the essential question is, "How can we talk about our differences effectively?" All of the methods covered in this book address this question. Although we acknowledge the importance of nonverbal communication as a part of talk, we cannot overemphasize the importance of language in human life. Perhaps the biggest distinction between human beings and other animals is our huge cerebral cortex, our ability to process symbols, and the fact that our worlds are made largely by how we use language.

Our Conflict Worlds

We sometimes begin our trainings with a simple exercise. Trainees are divided into pairs and given roles. One partner is told that he or she has just moved into a new house with a hideous and huge tree in the front yard. The tree blocks the light and is an eyesore. Our role player is instructed to get rid of the tree immediately. The other partner is asked to play the role of the neighbor across the street, a person who loves the tree and sees it as an asset to the neighborhood. The role players discover their difference of opinion when the old neighbor crosses the street to welcome the new neighbor to the community.

It is interesting to see how different students handle the tree problem. Some avoid the topic and talk about other things. Some try to work it out and maybe negotiate some kind of a solution. Some end by exclaiming, "You can't do this. See you in court!" This little exercise illustrates quite a few things about conflict. One of the most eye-opening results is that no matter how many pairs of trainees you have, they never deal with the problem in exactly the same way. In a very real sense, each pair makes a somewhat different conflict world. We never predict the outcome at the beginning of a mediation because we just can't tell how things will end. One of the most fascinating aspects of this work is that every case unfolds differently.

Still, there are some general ways that people react to important differences. Let's look at some of these:

Living With It: The World of Avoidance. People are sometimes painfully aware of their differences and even find them quite a challenge without ever being direct and open about these differences. This is a common pattern in conflicts, and it can be the very best way to react. Avoidance can relieve the tension of "talking it out;" it can buy time to think; it can allow us to work on more important problems; it can be a way to save the relationship; it can avoid the collateral damage that direct confrontation might cause. In reality, most of us live with continual conflict much of our lives. We agree to disagree, acknowledge the difference, and work around it. A married couple that never had to live with significant differences would be the ideal subject of a Disney movie. In many ways, learning to live with difference while working together productively is a high skill.

At the same time, avoidance can sometimes hurt. It can leave problems unsolved, cause conflicts to escalate, preclude potentially creative and productive discussion, and even increase emotional stress. The challenge is to decide when avoidance is appropriate, how the difference should be managed, and when to try a new way.

Working It Out: The World of Negotiation. Negotiation has always been an important part of life in the United States. In the commercial world, negotiation is de rigueur. The Harvard Program on Negotiation has become world famous for teaching win-win methods, or principled negotiation. International diplomacy largely consists of negotiation. Labor and management avoid strikes by negotiating. Workers negotiate for pay raises. Kids negotiate with their parents for privileges. Negotiation is almost always tried in lawsuits, and it is common in criminal cases as well. Although there are many types of negotiation, all are distinguished by the fact that disputants talk to one another directly to strike a deal.

Unfortunately, negotiation frequently fails. If we cannot work out our differences, what comes next? There are myriad possibilities, and one of the most common is the intervention of a third party.

Expanding the Conversation by Intervention. Intervention is not always sought, of course. Sometimes it is forced on the parties. Sometimes it is recommended or strongly suggested. Bringing in a third party is too often viewed as a difficult or threatening thing to do, but when you consider the alternatives of litigation and war, it looks pretty good to many disputants. Because this entire book is about intervention, we will not say much about it here. Important to mention now is that intervention is a way of changing the pattern of communication between parties, to alter their interaction in some way, and to open an opportunity for new ways of thinking about the situation in which they are embroiled. We think the various intervention forms discussed in this book have much potential for doing just these things.

Going to Battle: The World of Litigation. An amazing colleague of ours tells about beginning her career as a trial attorney and later becoming a professor of law specializing in trial practice. She says that two things changed her life and the course of her career. The first was becoming a Buddhist, where she learned new ways of understanding human relationships. The second was getting sued. When she became the victim of the "justice system" and experienced some of the very techniques she had been teaching for years, she realized how personally damaging and stressful litigation can be and how much it causes parties to lose control over the course of their lives.

We are not opposed to litigation, of course. It is a necessary part of our society's system of conflict resolution. Without belaboring the obvious, people need a way to have difficult, contentious disputes settled nonviolently. They need an avenue for seeking redress and a way to stop immoral or dangerous practices, and litigation also provides a way to challenge the law itself. As conflict management professionals, however, we have observed two things about litigation.

First, while it should be the course (or court) of last resort, it is too often the first thing we think of when we face a serious conflict. Call the cops and hire an attorney! With the potential of a vast system of conflict resolution strategies, in the United States we most often limit our thinking to litigation. Our second observation is that as a society we devote considerable attention to the justice system and litigation methods. There is no end to the resources devoted to this entire enterprise. Creative forms of conflict management have received much less attention, so that's where we want our commitment to be.

We had a good chuckle the other day with an attorney friend of ours who runs the city's Alternative Dispute Resolution Program, which consists of only two employees housed in a huge city attorney's office. After smirking at the sign on the entry door saying "Litigation Office," we walked down a long corridor past numerous offices of trial attorneys and finally arrived at our friend's ADR office adjacent to the back door. We laughed when she said that she hoped for a day when the entry door would say Alternative Dispute Resolution, and there would be one small office near the back door saying "Litigation."

A student of ours recently asked, "Shouldn't you have to be a lawyer to mediate? Mediation includes so many legal issues." We explained that yes, there can be many legal issues, but people tend to narrow their thinking about conflicts to the legal aspect without considering the many other factors that are also involved. Often, emotional issues are central, so maybe only psychologists should be mediators. Often, financial issues are at stake, so maybe only CPAs and financial planners should be allowed to mediate. Issues related to families, businesses, community concerns, and the environment may be at stake. We do not mean to be facetious, but there is no end to the number of professions that have something important to contribute to mediation and other conflict resolution forms.

This is why we believe that professional background is not as important as skill in working with conflicts in creative and constructive ways. You can always bring in attorneys, CPAs, and others as needed. Of course, many attorneys are excellent mediators. They are good at it because they show sensitivity to a range of factors beyond legal ones. Our colleagues who work in the world of conflict intervention come from many different walks of life, but all share the goal of helping parties manage their conflicts constructively.

Going to War: The World of Violence. Litigation can provide a way to settle conflict without physical damage to the parties (sometimes!). Violence is an all-too-common way by which human beings try to manage their differences. We think that violence at every level is a response to frustration. When people do not feel heard, when they are unable to get redress in other ways, when their goals are impeded, when they feel threatened, when anger becomes uncontrollable, violence may result.

People tend to think of war as something that happens between nations or groups. But any time one party tries to prevail over another by the use of force, it is declaring a kind of war. This happens in families, at work, between neighbors, between communities, as well as internationally between nations.

With few exceptions, violence is probably the worst way to manage human differences, and this is the last we'll mention it in this book, which is about the very best ways of managing conflict that we have found in our practice.

▪ A Conversation of Opportunity

We began this chapter with the construction metaphor, and now we would like to share another way of thinking that has shaped our work. This is the *metaphor of conversation.* We like to think that human life is like having many conversations, in which we take turns talking and listening. Everything you say responds in some way to something that happened before and leads to other things that will happen in the future. Even your first statement to another person, "Hi, how are you?" is a response to having learned throughout your life how to greet someone. And the last statement, "Bye. See ya later," leads to the possibility of ongoing talk in the future.

So life itself is like a network of connected conversations. What you say and do now is linked to other conversations you have had before and those you will have in the future. Because we make our social worlds by talk, conversations are a way of structuring reality. *How we converse* is important, for it structures what we think is going on, how we define the situation, where we think we are going, and what seems to be the right thing to do.

This metaphor has been immensely helpful in our work. If we think of a conflict as having a certain kind of conversation, we can consider ways of changing the conversation to lead to more positive outcomes. A mediator or facilitator enters a conversation and affects that conversation in some way. We hope that what we say and do when we intervene is a positive turn and will contribute to a salutary outcome.

In various trainings and courses, you may have been asked to list things that come to your mind when you think of a certain word. This is a good exercise, and we use it frequently ourselves. Offer the word *conflict* and see what comes to mind. Put these word associations on a flip chart and watch it fill up.

When we do this exercise, we are really listing ways that conflict conversations can be characterized. The words *emotionally draining* describe a conversation that saps energy. *Fight* connotes a conversation of struggle. *Avoidable* suggests a conversation you don't have to have. *Damaged relationship* says that the conversation led to a bad result. If you have done this exercise, you know that within a few minutes a group of trainees can literally fill a couple of flip chart pages with these "conversational descriptions." Most of these will be negative, but a few will be positive. When we do this exercise, we like to ask, "What is needed to turn these negative conflict conversations into something positive?"

Our practice of conflict intervention, then, is a turn in an ongoing conversation brought to us by the clients. Our goal in this conversation is to establish a basis of respect and understanding on which clients together can build a positive future. In this conversation, we invite participants to share the stories they consider important and to listen carefully to the stories others tell. In these conversations, taking turns at listening is as important as taking turns at speaking.

This kind of telling and hearing is sometimes difficult, so we work to help the parties establish a comfortable atmosphere of trust in which the conversation might take new and healthy directions. We look for certain kinds of openings to enter the conversation. We are interested in responding in a way that helps participants feel that their stories are being heard and honored by us. Getting stuck on the negative, however, can reproduce and even accentuate the very pattern that the clients want to overcome. So we invite new stories, especially positive, future-oriented ones. We are interested in learning about the constructive resources of the system, we look for the truth embedded in all stories, and we ask questions that can help participants think of new ideas. It is never our job to suggest what new directions should be taken but to listen carefully and ask good questions that invite the participants themselves to imagine their own futures.

We consider the practice of conflict intervention to be an art, the art of making transformative conversation. Like any artist, we work creatively with media and tools. We do not exclude any technique and are at moments quite traditional in our approach, but we see every intervention—traditional or innovative—as a move in an ongoing conversation in which a social world is being made.

We like to think of this type of communication as a conversation of opportunity. The opportunities that conflict affords are several. We feature three below.

Finding New Ways of Exploring Differences

In the early 1990s, the Public Conversations Project began a remarkable series of dialogues on abortion. The public "conversations" on this controversial topic had not been very positive since the *Roe v. Wade* decision in 1972. They tended to be conversations of struggle, debate, and resistance. And these conversations were stuck, going around in circles like a hamster on a wheel, and getting us nowhere as a society. Laura Chasin and her colleagues, however, were certain that the moral difference between pro-life and pro-choice representatives could be explored in a productive way. Looking to family therapy for guidance, these practitioners developed just such a way. They decided to try having these conversations in private rather than in public, to build a safe environment, and to provide sufficient time to explore the issue in personal terms and in depth. There were perhaps 20 of these dialogues, and they were amazingly successful. Hardly anyone changed his or her mind in these discussions, but these dialogues weren't designed to change minds. What did happen is that a greater level of understanding and respect grew out of this new form of communication. We'll have more to say about the Public Conversations Project and everything we have learned from it in Chapter 2.

Conflict can be an opportunity to learn more about yourself and others, a forum for learning significant new things about differences and common ground, a place to explore and see what happens. This can only result, though, when you think of conflict as a conversation of opportunity. We stress this with our mediation clients. Mediation at its best is an opportunity to get new information, think critically and creatively, and even change your mind about a few things. And for most of the people with whom we work, mediation is a new experience. When it works well, it shows participants that duking it out is not the only way of "doing conflict."

Building Relationships

Lately, we have been helping high-performance teams learn constructive methods for managing the inevitable conflicts that arise in the workplace. In this kind of environment, teams make decisions as a group; they establish many of their own work processes; they are jointly responsible for high productivity, and sometimes, incentive pay is even linked to team performance. Consequently, the quality of relationships among team members is crucial in this kind of organization. Teams must manage their differences effectively, or team management just won't work.

In Chapter 4, we describe some effective ways for team members to deal with conflict, but one thing is clear: Conflict cannot be avoided and must be thought of as an opportunity to build rather than destroy relationships. For many participants, this is a foreign concept. For them, conflict by definition threatens relationships. How can you confront a coworker about being consistently late from breaks without risking your working relationship with this person? How can you openly reveal an opinion that runs counter to the majority of your coworkers without risking personal loss of respect and esteem? How can you move toward a group commitment in an area that you already find very distasteful? These are not easy questions, but they do have workable answers, if people are willing to see these conflicts as opportunities to build relationships.

Actually, working through a difficult problem with another person can help a relationship. We have done many mediations in which there is a clear sense at the end that something important was accomplished. "We didn't think we could do this, but we have. Wow!" One of our favorite mediation stories involves a women's band and a disagreement the members had about how to split up the band's assets and instruments. They did a fine job, signed an agreement, and went out for a beer afterward. When a mediation ends with a hug, we feel pretty satisfied, but that usually doesn't happen. If the parties understand one another a little more, have enough respect to hear one another out, and establish a way to work together productively, they have accomplished important relationship work.

Working through a conflict can have a positive relationship effect, but how parties actually do this is more important than reaching an agreement. We have been involved in several disputes in which the parties did solve the problem and sign an agreement, but at the cost of harming the relationship in some way. There are never guarantees, but you are ahead if you at least see conflict as an opportunity for relationship building and work through the conflict with that goal in mind.

Creating Positive Futures

A few years ago with our colleagues in the Public Dialogue Consortium, we began a dialogue project in the South San Francisco Bay area in Cupertino, a progressive suburban city that has undergone tremendous change in the past 30 years. We began our work there with a series of focus groups to see what the citizens were concerned about and how they related to their community. We first asked participants to tell us what Cupertino was like when they moved there. Then we asked what challenges they face, and finally, we asked them to tell us what changes they would like to see. That was an informative set of questions—stories from the past, present concerns, and imagined futures.

These initial focus groups were a first step in having residents create positive futures. Since then, we have sponsored many events in Cupertino, and every time we ask participants to have conversations that have the potential of making a constructive future for the community. Conflict opens that opportunity. Many conflicts are past oriented, but when we start talking about the future, there is a chance that the entire conversation will change.

We once mediated a difficult divorce. The mediation got off to a rocky start because the couple could not stop blaming one another for things that had happened in the past. In desperation, we suggested a ground rule: *You cannot talk about anything that happened in the past; you can talk only about the future.* Surprisingly, the couple accepted the suggestion, and the mediation took a constructive turn. The couple began to talk about expectations they had for one another's behavior, how they would handle time-sharing with their son, and the steps they would take to finalize the divorce in as constructive a way as possible.

Sometimes, participants construct a positive future by defining issues, creating options, deliberating, and forming agreements. We are always open to, and even invite, this kind of work. As systemic practitioners, however, we view "settlement" as one possible future among many. The clients must create their own future, and our job is to act in ways that help to bring this about.

▪ The Communication Perspective

We can thank our colleague Barnett Pearce for naming the perspective we have been describing here. In his book *Communication and the Human Condition,* Pearce introduces the term *the communication perspective.*

Normally, we think of communication as a process that is distinct and identifiable, a certain kind of thing. We walk, eat, sleep, and communicate; and these are different activities. But Pearce uses the term *communication* in a new way. For him, communication is a way of looking, a perspective from which any human experience might be viewed. Whenever you are looking at how social worlds are made, you are taking a communication perspective. So the meanings of walking, eating, and sleeping are constructed through communication.

When we look at how conflicts are made in communication, we are taking a communication perspective. When we look at how conflict intervention is part of an ongoing conversation that contributes to the making of a social world, we are taking a communication perspective.

Let's take a closer look now at the implications of this perspective.

Communication Is More Than a Tool

Many mediation trainers teach communication as a tool. They teach that mediators help disputants "communicate with" one another, and they provide practice in certain "communication skills," like active listening, reframing, reflecting, and so forth. We think all of these things are important, but we also see everything that happens in a conflict or an intervention as communication, because it is all part of the ongoing conversation that contributes to the making of a social world.

Communication is more than a tool. It constitutes the very environment in which all human action takes place. We always understand our experience in terms of the symbols and meanings we have attached to them over the course of our lives. When we communicate, we are constructing our realities, and those very realities in turn shape the kind of communication we do. This makes a circle, and sometimes it is a vicious circle.

Barnett Pearce and Stephen Littlejohn observed the vicious circle of conflict in many strident public conflicts such as abortion, religion, and the environment. In their book *Moral Conflict: When Social Worlds Collide,* they called these intractable public disputes *moral conflicts* because they involve a clash between deeply held moralities. The parties take one another's statements as proof that the other side is made up of idiots, a sentiment that hardens each party even more, so they continue to accelerate the conflict, proving even more to the other party that they are morally bereft. These types of conflict are not restricted to the public realm, of course. You have probably observed many private cases in which the parties make a certain socially constructed reality that they cannot get out of. Indeed, it would be an unusual reader (and author) who had not been caught up in this kind of dispute in his or her own life on more than one occasion.

Of course, parties to a dispute need not get stuck in an unbroken circle of negativity. One of the most important contributions an intervention agent can make is to introduce new resources to the system and suggest new forms of communication that might lead to a more humane result for the parties involved. Often after a facilitated meeting, participants are amazed that others did not behave as they expected them to, that they had shared values they were not aware of, that certain parties to the dispute changed their minds, that the participants were actually decent to one another, or that the outcome was something quite unexpected. New communication practices can lead to new understandings and a revised sense of what is going on.

Dan Daggett, an activist for collaborative decision making, tells the story of a group called 6-6. It began in 1989 when Daggett and other environmentalists were campaigning in Arizona to repeal a law permitting ranchers to shoot cougars and bears. The battle had become stalemated. In an unusual move, someone suggested that the two sides actually meet and talk. And they did! The meeting was arranged; a skilled facilitator was brought in, and 12 people showed up—6 environmentalists and 6 ranchers. The meeting began, not by discussing mountain lions and bears, but by listing what each participant wanted for the land. To their amazement, they found that the two groups wanted many of the same things. They made an agreement not to talk about their differences, but to stick with common interests and explore ways that they could all get what they wanted. The 6-6 has grown to far more than 12 people, and they no longer meet in living rooms. Instead, they form collaborative ranching teams that meet on the land, look at the situation there, and make management decisions on how to proceed. In his book *Beyond the Rangeland Conflict: Toward a West That Works,* Daggett tells the story of 10 ranches and how collaborative decision making has worked.

The communication perspective has several implications for the practice of conflict intervention. First, it helps us see that mediation and facilitation are particular types of conversation in which participants can produce certain kinds of relationships and outcomes. We see ourselves as active participants in these conversations, and from the moment of first contact with the clients, we enter and affect their system. This means that we are never neutral. We try to be impartial, but we can never be neutral.

So we have to take every intervention very seriously, for what we do and say will have consequences in the social world that is made. The outcome of a conversation is never determined singly by any one participant but jointly by all. Mediators and facilitators have an opportunity to invite change, but they cannot determine the course and outcome of the session by themselves.

People's understanding of their experience is reflected in their stories. Mediation and facilitation are processes in which stories that are important to the clients can get told and heard. Mediators do not act to "find" or "discover" the "facts" as they "really are," but act to expand awareness and possibility by exploring stories. Sometimes a "story of agreement" is constructed, and the participants draft a contract to settle their disagreements. Sometimes not.

In conflict situations, people tend to tell negative stories, and these must be heard, but constructive movement requires positive stories that reflect the strengths of the clients' system. In our work, we try to elicit positive stories and provide opportunities to explore new patterns of interaction that will help participants "get unstuck" and move forward in a constructive and healthy way. Mediation and facilitation, then, can become conversations of creative imagination in which new futures are made.

Thinking Systemically

As the title reflects, this book is about systemic practice. What does it mean to be a "systemic practitioner"? The communication perspective itself is systemic because it draws our attention to how things relate to one another and to the patterns of interaction in the system. The communication perspective focuses too on the ways that interaction both affects and is affected by something bigger, a kind of world, reality, environment, or context in which conflicts are understood and acted on.

We are consistently surprised, though we should not be, that disputants do not initially share a systemic view. Probably because most of them are from individualistic cultures, they are taught that conflict is a simple clash of interests or values between two parties. They don't think much about how the larger context can determine what they see when things "clash," or how their own ways of responding to one another contribute to that larger context.

One of our challenges, then, is to ask the kinds of questions that help participants see that they are not in this alone, that the ways they behave toward one another do matter, and that new patterns can lead to new realities. At the same time, however, we have consistently found this goal to be a challenge. Those little vicious circles within the system can sometimes be extremely hard to break. Systems can be amazingly durable. They have feedback loops that reinforce the same patterns over and over. When you think systemically, you look for these patterns, but you also try to provide opportunities for the participants themselves to see their own patterns and invent better ones.

The preceding paragraph may imply that intervention agents analyze the system and put together a program for achieving change. Very simple: Look and act. Yet the communication perspective reveals the inadequacy of this approach. Whenever you look, especially in an active way, you become part of the system. You interact with the system, you affect it, and it affects you. So being a systemic practitioner means more than looking for and intervening in systemic patterns; it means joining the system in some kind of fundamental way.

A simple mediation illustrates this fact very well. Two people are having a conflict about something important in their lives. They go back and forth in a pattern, and their interaction makes a system. Then someone else comes into the room and joins this conversation, a mediator. The mediator listens and talks, asks questions and gets answers, summarizes, and reflects. The clients respond to the mediator's intervention, widening the system to three people.

A group facilitator does the same thing. By entering a group, structuring a process, leading things along, the system is widened and changed. This is also the case with organizational consultants and those who intervene in community processes. In every case, the intervention agent becomes part of the system in some way. That is the very point in systemic practice. You engage the system and thereby raise the potential for change. We hope the change will be positive in some way, but the system will always determine its own course. Systemic practitioners ask questions and suggest processes that enable the system to find a course that can lead to a positive future. The systemic practitioner may not know what that new course will be but will join with the other participants to see where they can take it.

Almost everyone these days does homage to systems. People recognize that the whole is more than the sum of its parts and that what happens to people is determined by patterns of interaction that are bigger than any one person. But beyond lip service, much conflict management practice is not really very systems oriented.

Here's a typical consultation procedure: Enter the system. Assess. Diagnose the problem. Create a solution. Implement the solution. Evaluate. Get paid. Exit.

This is not a systemic approach. It imagines that the consultant is outside the system, makes objective observations about it, does something to the system, achieves a result, and leaves. This is a very linear idea that is antithetical to how systems actually work. It is also the kind of approach that gives consultants a bad name. So what's the alternative? A systemic practice is based on several principles.

Any version of what is happening is only one version. Rather than look for what is really going on, we listen for the stories, how they differ, and how they connect. For us, assessment is not diagnosis but story gathering. The stories we hear are the data with which we work, the material for systemic change. We want participants to hear one another's stories, to make the connections, to talk about the stories they would rather have, and to begin to "live" different stories from those that are troubling them.

Change results from interacting, not prescribing. As intervention agents, our interactions with the client are critical. What we say and ask and how we respond to what other participants say and ask will lead to an examination and possibly a restructuring of the ways things are done. This sensibility leads to the possibility of trial and error, like working through a thicket to make a path to a clearing on the other side.

Durable change is made by participants in conversation. Involvement is the key here. Participants in the system need to be involved with one another, and as intervention agents, we can provide processes that help them become involved in new ways. In our practice we say that "people support what they create," and our interventions are designed to bring people together in ways that can lead to creativity *on their part.*

Every intervention is a turn in an ongoing conversation. Whatever we do with others comes from something that happened before and leads to something that will happen in the future. Our interventions respond to previous acts, and the system will respond to our interventions. This is a very fluid process. It often looks a lot like trial and error. We listen to what the system has to say, put something out there, listen for the response, and adjust. In traditional consultation, assessment comes before an intervention, and evaluation comes afterward. For us, assessment and evaluation are ongoing and happen at every stage. We can listen and observe in many ways, sometimes using focus groups, sometimes with survey forms, sometimes through interviews, and sometimes just by noting our experiences as we go. When we say that we work "organically," this is what we mean.

The boundaries of the system are fluid. Systems are always part of other systems, and you have to decide on what level to enter and then where to move from there. Systems are like networks of interacting parts, webs of influence where ripples can fan out in a number of interesting directions. Anyone who has spent 30 minutes on the Internet has a feel for how this works. Finding the best place to start working with a system is sometimes difficult. As at cocktail parties, where several conversations are going on at once, we look for openings and start there. In our own work, we sometimes make openings by, for example, creating "projects" such as an advertised training or a community dialogue. Other times, we are invited in, as is the case when we get a phone call from someone who wants help.

Once you are working in a system, the principle of fluid boundaries should be kept in mind. For example, a divorce mediation may involve two people, a husband and wife. This dyad is a system, but it is part of many other systems that may be much more important, including the whole family, a community of friends, social service providers, and so forth. Sometimes in an intervention, we widen the scope and bring in more players. Sometimes we narrow the scope and work with fewer players. Sometimes we have participants talk about what is going on in the larger system, and sometimes we narrow the context to more specific things. By this process, the participants themselves begin to develop a bigger system consciousness. An interesting question we sometimes ask in a meeting is, "Who is not here today and what would they be saying if they were here?" The important point here is that as system practitioners, we must always shift our consciousness and keep various systems in mind as we work. In our practice, we call this *scoping out* and *scoping in.*

The system controls itself cybernetically through feedback loops. We don't intend to launch into a dissertation on control systems. But systemic practitioners need to be conscious of the fact that system patterns reproduce themselves by responding to feedback. The vicious circles of conflict that we wrote about above illustrate this. When things get too far off balance, the system has a way of reining them back in. This is why you see the same patterns over and over. It is the system's way of keeping balance, even when those very patterns are damaging or hurtful in some way. But systems also have an amazing ability to change. This happens through feedback too, as the system develops new ways to respond to outcomes. Systemic interventions are designed to invite the system to look at its feedback loops and think creatively about new ways to respond.

System influences can flow in any direction. You cannot control how influence will ripple out in a system. As a systemic practitioner, you become part of the system, if only for a time. Sometimes it is just a 2-hour mediation, sometimes it is a longer corporate contract, and sometimes it is a multiyear community project. We assume that by interacting with the system, the system will change. Sometimes we forget that we will change too. We rarely do a job from which we do not learn new ideas, develop new insights, or think of different ways of approaching the situation. Occasionally, we are even challenged to examine our own philosophy of conflict itself.

So these are a few of the system principles we use in our work. But how do these points translate into action? In many ways, of course. Here are some of the most important guidelines we like to use in our conflict intervention work:

1. *Work with patterns of interaction.* Don't be too concerned about what any one person says or does, who is right and who is wrong, or what the "facts" truly are. Instead, look at how people respond to one another, how

they behave toward one another, what they say to one another, and how their stories relate to one another.

2. *Work collaboratively.* Invite participants to work with you in designing the intervention. Avoid the tendency of telling the group what they should do. Try to work with the whole group as much as you can. Keep checking to make sure that what is being done seems to be on the right track, and adjust if you need to.

3. *Work creatively.* Avoid cookie-cutter models, trainings, and inter- ventions. Avoid the tendency to "hit and run" by presenting a package deal before going to the airport. Be creative in thinking of interesting new ways of working.

4. *Work toward constructive futures.* Keep asking participants to think ahead, to move forward, to look at "ends in view," and think about the system they would like to make.

5. *Never plan too far in advance.* Like any good conversation, take it a turn at a time. Listen, respond, and listen again. See where the path takes you.

6. *Work with the system as it is, not where you think it should be.* Later, we'll talk about learning the "grammar" of the system, which means simply the categories they use, how they talk, and what they think they are doing. Enter into this grammar and then challenge it.

7. *Shift your goals as needed.* What you think you are doing in an inter- vention may not be what you end up doing. See what is going on and set your goals as you work.

One of the most exciting jobs we have done recently was helping to facili- tate a series of youth summits in Waco, Texas. A delegation from Waco attended the President's conference on The Future of America in April 1997 and returned home charged to put together the first local summit in the nation. In just a few weeks, they raised thousands of dollars and organized a spectac- ular event that attracted 1,200 kids from central Texas. With colleagues in the Public Dialogue Consortium, we trained adult and teenage facilitators and worked with them in running Dream Catcher workshops. One of our col- leagues became a member of the event-planning committee, which consisted of a group of teens and an adult mentor, to ensure that our training and facili- tation designs would be an organic part of the overall event.

The various "parts" of the system included the planning committee, the trainers, the facilitators, and the participants. The planning committee was made up of teenagers, and they planned an event that they themselves partic- ipated in. The facilitators were members of the community, and many of them were youth and also participants at the summit. So we as trainers became a part of the system in interaction with all the other sectors.

We gave two trainings before summit number one, and although the first one was effective, we were not satisfied. We consulted with participants and planners and made adjustments for the second training to occur the following day. That training went beautifully, and we all had a wonderful time.

At the end of the Dream Catcher workshops at the first summit, each participant took a piece of scrolled "dream paper" from a basket at the center of the table. On this form, they wrote one dream they had for their communities and dropped it into a Dream Catcher basket by the door as they left. Many of these dreams were compelling and poignant, but we'll tell that story another time.

At the end of the first summit, we did not know exactly what would come next. There was a commitment to have some sort of follow-up event, to build on the kids' dreams in some way, and to move from dreams to action. Within a short time, action committees were formed to translate the ideas generated at the summit conference into concrete action. In addition, a second summit was proposed for community members around Waco. Our group once again helped by continuing the training we had provided before, designing break-out sessions for participants, and helping to facilitate the event.

We wanted to use the output from the previous summit as input for the current one, and we wanted to provide feedback to the action groups that had been formed at the end of the first summit. Again, we worked with the planning committee and representatives from the earlier conference in making plans. We kept checking at every juncture.

We planned what we called Dream Maker sessions, in which participants would carefully examine their personal and community assets for making a better community. We started these sessions by giving every participant one of the dreams created by the kids at Summit 1. We asked them to read the dream and pass it to the person next to them, read another dream, and keep passing. Then we had each person keep one of the dreams they felt they could "connect with," and work with that dream in a series of guided activities. At the end of Summit 2, we asked each participant to fill out a promise, one thing they would do to help make this child's dream come true. We plastered the walls with these promises, and it became apparent as the participants walked into the final plenary session that something very good had happened there. Those promises did not stay on the wall, of course, but were given to the action committees as feedback to help with their work in the communities. This does not end the process; we were able to use the momentum of the first two events to have additional community trainings and begin the process of capacity building to continue the work well into the future.

The Waco summits have been very special to us. They illustrate what it means to work systemically, to become part of the system, to enter the conversation, to assess and evaluate as you go, to scope in and scope out, to work with patterns of interaction, to pay attention to feedback loops, to intervene in creative ways, and to make a conversation that works.

▪ Toward an Ethic of Conflict Management

Many readers will be interested in the ethics of our work. Indeed, most discussions of mediation and conflict resolution include some discussion of ethics. Taking a communication perspective, however, makes it difficult to isolate ethical principles from the whole of everything we do. With an eye toward constructing better futures, building respectful relationships, encouraging collaborative problem solving, guarding the dignity of individuals, and developing the capacity of communities, we must view every action as an ethical choice. Rather than generating a list of rules, systemic social constructionism leads us to think in terms of basic principles that guide intervention decisions. Here are some of the most important:

- Act in a way that encourages collaborative, respectful relationships.
- Act in a way that empowers individuals, groups, and communities to find positive resources for humane, constructive change.
- Act in a way that enables groups to design appropriate systems and processes for managing difference.
- Act in a way that elicits and employs positive sources of power for the good of the system as a whole.
- Act in a way that builds community and systemic consciousness on the part of participants.
- Act in a way that helps groups to co-construct positive futures.
- Act in a way that empowers individuals, groups, and communities to make clear, conscious, well-considered decisions about their own futures.

In many ways, this book itself constitutes an ethic of conflict management. We hope that the whole of our practice is a manifestation of the ethical frame summarized here.

▪ Resources You Can Use

Daggett, D. (1995). *Beyond the rangeland conflict: Toward a west that works.* Flagstaff, AZ: The Grand Canyon Trust.

Fisher, R., & Ury, W. (1991). *Getting to yes: Negotiating agreement without giving in.* New York: Penguin.

Lakoff, G., & Johnson, M. (1980). *Metaphors we live by.* Chicago: University of Chicago Press.

Pearce, W. B. (1989). *Communication and the human condition.* Carbondale: Southern Illinois University Press.

Pearce, W. B., & Littlejohn, S. W. (1997). *Moral conflict: When social worlds collide.* Thousand Oaks, CA: Sage.

Program on Negotiation, Harvard Law School, 513 Pound Hall, Cambridge, MA 02138. www.pon.harvard.edu

Public Conversations Project, 46 Kondazian Street, Watertown, MA 02172. www.publicconversations.org

Public Dialogue Consortium, 504 Luna Blvd. NW, Albuquerque, NM 87102. www.publicdialogue.org

2

Dialogue

We once helped found an organization called the PDC. When we first organized this group, "PDC" designated the "Public *Dispute* Consortium." We were proud of this name, but were quickly disabused when we met Don Brown. Don is the City Manager of Cupertino, California, and we had approached the city to see if we might sponsor some citizen groups there to explore community issues. Don has since become a real ally, but his first reaction was not supportive. "*Dispute* sounds so negative," he said. "Why would the city want to do that?" This comment gave us pause, and within a few days we had changed our name to the Public *Dialogue* Consortium.

The term *dialogue* is much in favor these days. It seems to capture a feeling of good communication that appeals to many people. Although the word is commonly used, and sometimes abused, *dialogue* actually has a revered history. In their book *The Human Dialogue*, Matson and Montagu call it "the newest and oldest" theoretical development in communication. The term had special meaning among religious existentialists like Paul Tillich, Karl Jaspers, and Martin Buber, who taught that existence itself is communication, that life is dialogue.

▪ What Is Dialogue?

In literature and drama, a monologue occurs when one character speaks alone, and dialogue occurs when characters speak with one another. Sometimes in a play, a character will step aside and use a monologue to "talk to

25

himself" or address the audience. Even when other characters are present, they are not listening or responding.

In real life, our communication often takes on the qualities of a monologue, even when others are listening. At these moments, we seem most concerned about *what we are saying* rather than *what we are hearing others say.* Dialogue is a different kind of communication that honors relationships above individual perspectives, positions, and interests.

Dialogue Honors Relationships

There is an ancient Sufi saying, "You think that one and one are two, but you are forgetting the 'and.'" In a more contemporary idiom, the "whole is more than the sum of its parts." Dialogue is a yours-mine-and-ours activity, seeking to clarify what is important to each person and why. It aims to help each person understand the perspectives and experiences of others, but it does more. It calls attention to what communicators are making together. What are some of the features of a relationship that will come out in a good dialogue?

Dialogue makes it possible to explore the rules we are using to communicate with one another. We don't normally think of communication as a game, but it is. When we are interacting with others, what we say and do is very much governed by rules. A common rule is to defend yourself when under verbal attack, but you could make a conscious decision to use another rule and respond in a very different way. In dialogue, we suspend old rules of communication and try out new ones. This is why mediators and facilitators often begin with the "ground rules," and participants in dialogue can and do improve their patterns of communication in other sophisticated ways.

Dialogue makes it possible to explore our contexts of meaning. We always talk and listen from a particular frame of reference. These frames, or contexts, change from time to time, and different communicators often understand things differently because they have different frames of reference. We are not normally conscious of the frame of reference we are employing, and rarely do we examine it or share it with others. In dialogue, we have an opportunity to clarify our contexts and to see what would happen if we change them. We also have the opportunity to create new contexts of communication together.

In a recent mediation we had involving a young couple who had broken up a short time ago, a set of rings became an issue. The young man had given his girlfriend his mother's rings and wanted them back. She would not give them up. At first the discussion occurred entirely in the context of the monetary value of the rings. Wondering if a change of context might lead to a more constructive conversation, we asked each party to talk about the man's mother and how the rings symbolized their respective relationship with her. The tone of the discussion changed considerably as the disputants began to reveal their affection for this woman.

Dialogue makes it possible to explore our differences. In ordinary debates we are usually quite aware of certain differences, but we do not normally explore them in much detail. In dialogue, we can actually spend time coming to understand the basis for our differences. The couple in the mediation discussed above had a serious disagreement about the rings, and in mediation they were able to explore just what the rings meant to each of them. The man wanted the rings back because he felt rejected by his former girlfriend, and she wanted to keep them because they were the last vestige of a relationship that was once very good. Dialogue is an opportunity to learn significant new things, and that's exactly what happened in this mediation. Each party learned why the rings were important to the other.

Dialogue makes it possible to explore common ground. Where differences exist on one level, we may find much in common on another. Generally, one of two things will happen when we talk about important issues. The first is that we notice a conflict, express it, maybe debate it, and try to win the other person's support. The second tendency is to find an area of agreement and keep reinforcing it, like "preaching to the choir." But in dialogue, we can acknowledge our differences and then look for areas of common ground. We explore both—difference and similarity. For example, on one level we may disagree about the school voucher system. We could dwell on that, and maybe we should. At the same time, however, we may discover that we have a strong shared concern, the quality of education. That's a kind of common ground, and we can talk about that too. This is exactly what happened in the mediation on the rings. Although the couple differed on the issue of who should own the rings, they found that they both valued the relationship in which the rings were given, and both had loving feelings for the man's mother.

Risk and Safety in Dialogue

Dialogue can feel risky because it requires new, unfamiliar forms of communication. As conflict management specialists, we often invite people into dialogue, but they sometimes do not accept the invitation. We tell them that our job is to help make a safe environment, but they do not always feel safe. As the third party, it's easy for us to think, "What's so hard about this? Just give it a try," but in reality, people often feel they have much to lose by engaging in dialogue.

They may feel uncomfortable using forms of communication they are not accustomed to. They know intuitively how to fight, be defensive, clam up, blame, and persuade. They may not be very practiced at really good listening, and they have rarely put themselves in a strictly listening role, especially when they disagree with what is being said. A nurse in a healthcare facility steadfastly refused to be part of a dialogue group with coworkers because she did not want to talk to "people like that."

In dialogue, people risk change. If they experienced dialogue, they may change their opinion; they may question the way they used to do things; they may become sympathetic to a someone they formerly despised; they may learn uncomfortable new things; they may find out that people agree with them less than they thought; they may experience new feelings; and they may go away stewing about something that never bothered them before. Shifting from a "we-they" orientation to an "us" orientation can be pretty scary. Every mediator can tell stories about cases that fell apart right at the point where movement was starting to begin.

In dialogue people risk discovery. They may find out things about themselves they had not been conscious of before. They may have to face facts formerly glossed over. They may have to make uncomfortable acknowledgments. They may be moved to tears. We will always recall vividly a mediation between two coworkers. One of them was experiencing some personal problems that led him to react defensively at times. His partner was open to hearing about this and listened carefully, which encouraged him to talk more and more about the challenges he was facing at home. He was able to discover just how painful his life had become, and the tears flowed from both parties. These particular individuals were willing to have a dialogue, but it was not easy.

In dialogue people risk disclosure. We sometimes tell those with whom we work that mediations and facilitated meetings provide an opportunity for people to "say and hear what needs to be said and heard." In this kind of setting, where everyone is listening, we must decide what we want them to hear. As facilitators, we sometimes ask disputants, "What is at the heart of the matter for you?" and they need to figure this out. Self-disclosure is difficult in our society. We tend to hold back. In conflict situations many of us are more inclined to talk about the faults of others than share our own struggles. Sometimes we just don't want others to know, and we fear loss of esteem and respect, and we fear what others might do with new information they have about us.

To show what dialogue is like, we often have trainees engage in small dialogue groups in facilitation workshops. Even in these training exercises, we are constantly reminded of the power of self-disclosure in a safe environment. Participants often tell stories of very private aspects of their lives, and we rarely have a "mock" dialogue group without tears.

So dialogue feels risky. This is why one of the most important jobs of the mediator or facilitator is to help the group establish a safe environment. If all the risks are there and the environment does not feel safe, dialogue will not occur. We can do many things to help establish safety. Here are some of the most important:

Think consciously about time and place. The time should be right and the place should feel as comfortable as possible. We have seen many good dialogues in public, but often the situation calls for privacy. One of the worst things you can do is have a "dialogue ambush," in which one or more of the parties is taken by surprise by someone who wants to discuss an issue right then and there. Surprise is not an ally to safety. We have a friend who discourages surprise parties because she thinks many people aren't ready for them. She says that the guests and planners are delighted, but while putting on a good face, the "target" may be privately upset and dismayed.

We do not mean to imply here that people should never have spontaneous dialogue. If both people are ready, it can be the very best thing to do. We advocate this practice in our Team Mediation System, which you will learn more about in Chapter 4, but in this case the participants have a prior agreement to bring up conflict as it arises. If you have an agreement that it is okay to work through a conflict when and where it comes up, then you will be well prepared to do so, but even then you should be able to negotiate another time and place for the discussion if necessary.

Provide a structure that feels safe. People often fear that a serious discussion might get out of hand. It could blow up. It could turn into a shouting match. It could get emotional and defensive. And it could leave people worse off than if they had never talked about the issue. This is why good dialogue often requires structure. We might allow a certain amount of time. We might use a particular procedure. We might have guidelines or provide process tools. We might even use a standard set of questions for everyone. In other words, people can feel safer if they know the "game" will be played by "rules," and that someone is there to enforce them.

Solicit agreements on the discussion ground rules. Safety can be built by allowing everyone a voice in establishing the rules or guidelines to be used. Many facilitators will not proceed until everyone buys into the process and the guidelines, until everyone's concerns about process are met. Good facilitators will revisit these agreements from time to time in order to clarify, change, or reinforce them. Sometimes agreements are sought before the meeting. A set of possible agreements is sent out, and participants are asked to sign on. If anyone is reluctant, his concerns are heard, and the agreement may be modified as a result. Other times, guidelines are presented and discussed at the meeting. Sometimes this takes just a moment, and sometimes it takes considerable energy. We once facilitated a group of coworkers who spent the entire first day discussing the ground rules. Of course, they worked a lot out in the process of doing that, and we are convinced that the highly productive second day would not have been possible without taking the time to reach agreement on procedure the first day.

Promote good facework. Face refers to one's feeling of being honored and respected, and every culture has its ways of making people feel worthy. Unfortunately, in conflict situations we often attack the face of others, doing whatever we can to demean or dishonor them. Some mediations turn into a "degradation ceremony," in which one party uses the mediation as a forum for belittling the other. Probably nothing feels less safe than personal attack, and one of the reasons people avoid conflict is their fear of losing face. Ground rules, guidelines, and agreements are one way of promoting good facework. Another is to talk about good communication practice and model it. Strong communicators can do a lot to change the tone of a conversation by absorbing personal attack and responding calmly and constructively.

There is a tendency to think of facework as just "being nice," and this certainly is a way of expressing honor. But good dialogue should never be reduced to niceties. In fact, being too nice is a way of avoiding dialogue. Dialogue is often frank, clear, and compelling. How can you be honest and clear and still honor the face of others? Most of the practices we discuss in this chapter aim to do just this. For example, you can show respect simply by listening carefully, acknowledging, and taking seriously what someone says. Stating an objection in a way that invites others to disagree with you is another form of high respect. Maybe the best facework is just good listening. Not necessarily agreeing, but listening.

Respond to willingness and felt need. We think that good dialogue will happen only when the participants are ready, when they feel the need to try a new form of communication and are willing to give it a go. We aim for the spirit of dialogue in every mediation we have, but the disputants are often not ready to do it. That's OK. We certainly proceed with the mediation and help them try to achieve whatever positive result they are able and willing to accomplish. Other times they are tired of fighting and ready to do something else. We are repeatedly amazed at the high quality of communication that people can achieve when they are ready and willing to do so. We have heard many times, "I just don't want to keep going on like this. I want to move forward." When participants feel this way, you have a very good chance of changing debate to dialogue.

Find a shared level of comfort. Each dialogue is different. Some are very emotional and deep; others are more analytical and issue-oriented. Some are highly structured, and others are more informal. Sometimes the participants want a facilitator, and sometimes they prefer to do it alone. Some people feel safer in a formal, structured environment; others want a more dressdown place. Sometimes it works best in the natural environment, and other times people prefer to sit in an office somewhere. The factors of safety are not universal, so one challenge for anyone interested in dialogue is to find a shared level of comfort. What conditions are necessary for everyone involved to feel as comfortable as possible?

Leave an out. If people feel that they are being pressured to talk on a deeper level than comfortable, they will not feel safe. If they think they must share private things they would rather not discuss, they will leave, either physically or mentally. We handle this challenge in a variety of ways. One is to employ a "pass" rule. In other words, everyone can pass on any question without having to explain his or her reasons. Another is to avoid unsafe probing. Good probing questions are useful, but you have to be careful not to push too far. Another way to help build a safe environment is to allow each person to choose for himself what to say and how to say it, within agreed-upon ground rules. If someone feels free to say, "I'm sorry, but I really don't want to get into that," then you know that a safe environment is being built.

Use a facilitator. You can have a good dialogue without a facilitator. People often do. Husbands and wives may sit down and talk through an important family issue. Friends have a heart-to-heart talk at a moment of difficulty. Coworkers go to lunch to hash something out. When there is a need and the people are ready, they can have a constructive conversation that we would characterize as dialogue.

On tough issues where safety is especially important, a third party can help create a protected environment. Sometimes just the mere presence of a third party can make people feel safer. People think that the conversation will be more civil if someone else is there. One time recently we were hanging out with a couple of friends who suddenly and unexpected began an argument. It got pretty heated, and we didn't know whether to stay or go, but decided to stick it out. We felt pretty awkward being there, but both of them told us later that they were glad we stayed. A third party can also help create a sense of safety by providing structure, process, and tools for good dialogue.

Maintain impartiality. Our practice of mediation and facilitation demands impartiality. There are many reasons not to take sides, make judgments, assert content suggestions, or show preference. One of the most important of these reasons is that being partial can make participants feel unsafe. We once comediated with an apprentice in a barking-dog case. In an attempt to be friendly, she immediately announced that she had several dogs herself and knew that they certainly could be a challenge. Naturally, we were aghast at this comment. It was innocent and well motivated, but either party might have heard it as sympathetic to the other.

▪ Dialogue as a Constructive Conversation

Clearly, dialogue is a form of constructive conversation, but what does this mean? What makes a conversation constructive? We have learned some important answers to this question from the Public Conversations Project (PCP).

The PCP was founded in 1990 by family therapist Laura Chasin and her colleagues in Cambridge, Massachusetts. Established to promote good communication on difficult public issues, this group has developed a variety of ways of working with dialogue. They are perhaps best known for their dialogue groups on abortion in the early 1990s. Later, they began to sponsor dialogue workshops on various issues, and today they are leaders in the country in using these techniques for intractable public issues. In the following section, we would like to share some of the things we have learned from the PCP.

Treating People Like People

What an odd expression. Don't we always treat people like people? Actually, we sometimes treat others like objects, especially in conflict situations. We want to affect them, move them, use them. We "operate on" others by giving our point of view, telling them how it is, showing them the error of their ways, and directing what they should do. We tend to think of good communication as clear and persuasive talk.

The theologian Martin Buber in his book *I and Thou* called this practice an *I-It* relationship. The essence of dialogue, in contrast, is the *I-Thou* relationship, characterized by authenticity, inclusion, confirmation, and presentness. When you are genuinely curious and interested in people who have experiences different from your own, you stand at the threshold of dialogue.

When we are ego-involved in an issue, when we are faced with tough differences, and when we have very good reasons for believing and doing what we do, it becomes hard to move from the *I-It* to the *I-Thou*. As conflicts become more "public," in the sense that we have stakes beyond the personal, this movement is even harder. Public debates tend to be so positional and impersonal that treating other people as people becomes very difficult indeed. In these situations, we tend to camp up, solidify, polarize, and depersonalize. This is exactly the challenge that the PCP faced: how to put a personal face on what has become a depersonalized conflict.

The issue of abortion was classic in this regard. People's positions on this issue are intensely personal, but their public representations are predictable and polarized. Laura Chasin wondered what would happen if you put pro-life and pro-choice advocates in a private and safe environment and asked them to talk about this issue in a new way. Her first surprise was that when invited, people actually came. They too were tired of the old *I-It* communication in which they had been engaged. The second surprise was that when they met, some 20 groups in all, these individuals, who held fierce personal feelings on this topic, were actually able to listen well to one another's life experiences and good reasons for their views. Given a safe environment, encouragement, time, and structure, they were easily able to have an *I-Thou* conversation.

Taking Time to Explore

One of the simplest, but most important, elements of the PCP dialogue groups is that they provided time for participants to explore their differences and shared concerns. These sessions were usually about 3 hours in length. With only 6 to 8 participants in each group, 3 hours gave them time to get to know one another as persons and to talk fully about their respective experiences, ideas, concerns, and doubts. They could take time not only to share their experiences and perspectives, but to interact as well.

These sessions always began with a meal, and during dinner the participants were not allowed to reveal which side of the issue they were on. They were encouraged to get to know one another as persons first before identifying themselves with one side of the issue or the other. After the meal, the group would adjourn to the dialogue room, where they would sit in a comfortable setting and explore the issue for at least 2 hours. Contrast this with the customary practice of producing sound bites for public consumption.

Our mediation students often return from their observations frustrated that the pace of mediation seems so slow. As observers, the slow "back and forth" of the session drives them nuts. It had seemed so simple, they report. Why didn't the mediator just force them to compromise and get out of there?

By the end of the course, a thorough exploration of what mediation means, and participation in several role plays, the same students come to view time differently. They see that more time is often better than less, that if participants realize no one is going anywhere, they often relax and listen in ways they would not ordinarily do.

In the traditional "public hearings" format, many people line up to take their allotted three minutes to make a speech. The session may go on for hours, but ironically there is no time to really talk the issue through. The result is a string of demanding presentations delivered to a council or board. The worst of these we ever saw was a "town meeting" (quotation marks mandatory here) that went from 7 p.m. to 4 a.m. the following morning. The tiny town hall filled up early, and people were lined up for blocks to take their turn at telling the council what idiots they were. We must admire the poor council members for their endurance. If we ever needed an operational definition of *I-It* communication, we would need only to show a videotape of this event.

We facilitate many public meetings, but we insist on doing it differently. Given 2, 3, or more hours available for a public meeting, how can a productive process be created? Many ways are outlined in this chapter and later in the book.

Taking Turns at Listening

We normally think of a conversation as an event in which people take turns talking. How would conversations change if we thought of them as taking turns at listening? In many ways, that's just what dialogue is. Of course, you cannot focus on listening without also allowing people to say what's on their mind. The difference, we think, is that dialogue privileges listening and makes it a centerpiece of the conversation.

One way to promote good listening is to remove the pressure to respond. In a back-and-forth conversation, most people are thinking about what they want to say even before the speaker is finished. In its most obvious form, this practice comes out as an interruption. The "listener" is so sure about what he wants to say that he cannot even let the speaker finish. You know the frustration of being interrupted in the middle of a story or a line of reasoning. You want to scream, "Wait a minute! I'm not done." Everybody is guilty of interrupting from time to time, but when you become conscious of the value of good dialogue, you become especially impatient with this habit. The real frustration here is that the other communicator did not seem interested in hearing you out. We know a teacher who makes this point by having a rule that students cannot raise their hands until the student who is talking is finished.

You can help participants listen more effectively by providing a certain structure to the dialogue. For example, you can establish the order of talk. In the dialogue circles of the PCP, everyone takes a turn talking about what is important to him, and other group members are not allowed to respond, but only listen. In mediations, we ask participants not to interrupt, to allow the other person plenty of time to say what is on his or her mind, and to take notes about points they may wish to address later.

Another technique for promoting good listening is a "talking stick" like those used in certain Native American Council meetings. The speaker holds the stick. No one interrupts the person with the stick. When finished, he hands it over to someone else. When the stick leaves your hands, you agree to be in a listening role.

Another way to promote good listening is to control the kind of response that people can make. You are not permitted to respond in any old way, but you must listen for certain kinds of things that will structure what you can say in response. When we teach listening, we often use a "summarization exercise." You may have done this yourself in trainings. After selecting a controversial topic, the group begins a discussion, but all must follow one rule. Before they can share their opinions, they must summarize what the previous speaker said accurately, completely, and without judgment. Once the previous speaker has "approved" of the summary, the new speaker is free to state her opinion.

Another way to help participants concentrate on listening is to limit their responses to "questions of true curiosity." They are asked to listen for things they would like to know more about. Then in responding, they ask questions designed not to make a point, but to elicit more detail so that they can learn more about what others are saying. The PCP uses this technique effectively. After everyone has had a chance to share his or her experiences and views on a subject, others may ask anyone else a question of curiosity. These questions must be addressed to specific others, must be limited to things that person actually said, cannot be rhetorical, and must be motivated from a sincere desire to know more.

We have been describing some fairly rigid ways of helping people concentrate on listening. We are aware that some of these techniques can seem unnatural and stiff, but when we use them, especially with difficult and contentious topics, people often appreciate the fact that they are not just turned loose to "argue it out." Of course, we do realize that good dialogue often requires a smoother, back-and-forth, "popcorn" style of discussion, allowing people to speak whenever they are ready. As long as people are willing to listen well, to try to understand others before criticizing them, and to respond respectfully, good dialogue can be achieved.

Back in the 1960s, there was a "listening movement," in which people were supposedly taught how to listen better. Good listening was defined as paying attention, listening for information, and being able to recall what you had heard. We do not mean to minimize the importance of attention and information, but good listening is much more than this. Here are some of the things that good communicators listen for:

- *Lived experience.* What life experiences is the speaker sharing? What was it like to be involved in the things he has been through?

- *Stories told.* In addition to giving information and opinion, most speakers also tell stories. They relate events and happenings, pieces of history. Their stories have characters and plot lines and morals. What do these stories tell you about the perspective of the speaker?

- *Story connections.* Especially in groups, stories connect with other stories. One person's story begins where another person's leaves off. One person's character shows up in another person's story. Plot lines merge and branch off from one another. The different stories that people tell will not necessarily be consistent, but they will connect. What can you learn by listening for these story connections?

- *Values.* What is important to the speaker? What is not important? What things are rejected? A speaker may relate an opinion or attitude, but what is the underlying value?

- *Contexts.* What is the frame of reference of the speaker? What is the window she is looking out of when she sees the world? What frame gives meaning to her statements? Does she speak from the perspective of self, relationship with others, culture, or universal moral law?

- *Punctuation.* This term refers to the way we organize what we see, where we put our commas, periods, question marks, and exclamation points. When you listen, you can listen for how others organize their experience.

- *Rules.* What do certain things mean to this person? How does he understand various words and actions?

- *Differences and levels of difference.* As you listen to others talk, what true differences emerge? When and under what circumstances are these differences important, and when are these not important? What happens to these differences from one situation or occasion to another?

* *Common ground and levels of common ground.* What do various speakers have in common? Where do they agree? What common ground do they have in the face of disagreement? When and under what circumstances does this common ground occur? If you shift to another context, what happens to the common ground?

Asking Questions

Asking good questions is frequently overlooked as a skill involved in the art of listening, but it is crucial because it tunes you in to what the person is saying and expands what you learn. People ask questions all the time, of course. Many people are skilled at asking rhetorical questions that make a point, interrogative questions designed to uncover hidden information, and critical questions asked to point out flaws in the other person's argument. Although these kinds of questions have their place, they are not very productive in a dialogue because they threaten face and shut people down.

In our practice, we have come to believe that dialogic questioning is an art that needs to be cultured. A training exercise we like starts by dividing the class into pairs and asking students to share something important from their lives with their partners. When in the listening role, the student can respond only by asking questions of true curiosity, questions designed to learn more about the other person's experience. Students are asked not to respond in any other way, not to agree, disagree, commiserate, argue, or tell the other person that something like that happened to them too. They can only ask questions, and the questions must be open, nonjudgmental, and designed to learn more.

When we debrief this exercise, we explain to the class that this is an exercise in "abnormal" discourse. In other words, we do not usually respond only with curious questions, and it would probably be very strange if we did. The point, we say, is that questions constitute an important, but underplayed, part in conversations. Some students report that they found the exercise difficult, if not impossible. Other students tell us that asking good questions opened up the conversation, led to new learning, and invited elaboration and even more sharing. Students also confirm what we have found in our practice—that good questions help us understand, appreciate, and respect others' experiences. They also have a developmental effect on speakers. They open up avenues of thought; they stimulate creativity; they bring important connections and relationships to mind; they show that one's comments are being taken seriously and that listeners respect one enough to want to know more.

One of the most useful process tools we have taught in recent years is *story questioning*. Story questioning is designed to elicit more and more detail about stories. Our colleague Kevin Barge, a communication professor at Baylor University, created a simple story-questioning checklist, an effective tool to help trainees and participants think of good questions. It is also an aid for good listening, because it shows some of the things you can be listening for.

Of course, we cannot always expect participants to ask good, well-timed questions, so mediators and facilitators often take this role. In fact, we use questions as one of our most important interventions. Facilitators can use story questions as a way to help participants share more of their experience and bring out details that may help others understand various points of view. Two other types of questions can be helpful as well.

Systemic questions are designed to help participants talk about relationships. They are a way of helping the group shift from an individualistic context to a more collective, systemic one. These questions ask group members to think about and reflect on connections and make comparisons. Systemic questions can help build a sense that one is part of a larger system and is constructing a social reality through its interaction. Systemic questions call attention to the ways in which actions elicit other actions and how statements and behaviors are connected to other statements and behaviors. Such questions help participants see how their thoughts, actions, and statements are not isolated, but connected to what others think, do, and say.

These questions also tune people into the time dimension. They focus attention on the flow of events from one thing to another and the connection of events over time. We might ask, "How was it different then?" or "What changed when Betty was moved out of the work group?" In this process, people will begin to talk about how things have changed, and they can begin to imagine patterns of change that might happen in the future.

We recently mediated a dispute between a department head and physician in a hospital. As with most mediations, this began with each party telling us the horrible things they couldn't stand about the other party, the things the other one had done that offended or hurt them in some way. After a round of a few story questions, we began to ask systemic questions designed to widen the circle and shift the conversation to connections within the larger system. We asked who else was involved and how they

Table 2.1   Story Question Checklist

When questioning, we explore stories about SITUATIONS, at a particular TIME, occurring in a specific PLACE, involving people WHO ARE THERE, about what they do together, and their HOPES FOR THE FUTURE.

SITUATIONS
Explore what the situation means to the person.
> *As a teen, how do you make sense of the situation?*

Ask about the relationships among people.
> *How would you describe your relationship with Bob?*

Ask about the relationship among groups of people.
> *You have said that the families must work very closely with the directors of the youth outreach program. How would you describe their relationship?*

TIME
Ask about the history of situation.
> *What has brought you to this point?*

Explore why this issue has become important at this time.
> *You said that this issue has only become important during the past five months. Why do you think this has become an important issue now?*

Ask when certain people noticed this issue.
> *This issue has gotten the attention of a number of people. Who was the first to notice this issue? Who was the last?*

PLACE
Explore where people talk about this issue.
> *You have said that many people in the community are talking about the need to have additional recreational services. Where are people talking about this issue?*

WHO'S THERE
Focus on who is presently involved with the situation.
> *You've said that several people have been involved in conversations about drug resistance programs. Who specifically has been involved?*

Ask people who else needs to be involved with the situation.
> *You identified several people who have been involved with these conversations regarding recreational facilities for kids. Who else needs to be involved with these conversations? Who else needs to be invited to participate in these talks?*

Encourage parties to speak from personal experience.
> *You've talked about how other people would like to see how city government works. Tim, I'm curious about what your personal hopes are for how the city government will work in the future.*

Table 2.1 (Continued)

Explore other people's perspectives on the situation.
How do you think youth in the Waco area would perceive this situation?

WHAT THEY DO TOGETHER
Explore the time line (keep time alive).
I would appreciate it if you would talk about the situation.

When did it begin? What happened first? When X happened, what happened next?
Focus on behaviors.
Jake, you said that you felt mistreated by this group. How did they show their disrespect to you?

HOPES FOR THE FUTURE
Invite a search for shared concerns and futures.
People who disagree often have the same basic concerns. I want to take a few minutes to explore this possibility here. Could you each take a minute or two to talk about what you think your shared concerns might be?

Move past the problem.
You talked about how much you appreciated the efforts by those people involved with the youth theater program. And those people have said they also felt they were appreciated then. I'm wondering what would need to change for that former level of appreciation to return. If it did return, what would be different for you both?

Ask questions about the positive.
What attracted you to getting involved with the Neighborhood Association? I'm curious about what you really loved about the Neighborhood Association then.

Focus on the future.
It would be very helpful, I think, if each of you could talk for a few minutes about the kind of crime prevention program you would like to see developed here.

---

were involved. We asked how people acted and responded when others did certain things. We asked them to reflect on their own behavioral responses to the actions of the other and how the other person reacted to their reactions.

While story questions ask people to provide more detail about their own experience, perspective, or point of view, systemic questions require that disputants get out of their own heads and think about what their comments elicit in others and what others' comments elicit in them. For example, you can ask participants to reflect on what it might be like for others to be listening to what they have to say. We sometimes ask, "What have you been trying to say today that John is having a hard time hearing?" We can reverse this, of course, by asking participants to reflect on their own role as listeners: "What has John been trying to say that you are having a hard time hearing? What makes it hard for you to hear this?"

Often we use systemic questions to help participants imagine new patterns of communication. These questions sound something like this: "What would need to change for your meetings to become more productive?" "If your meetings became more productive, how would things be different?" "You have said that your meetings always turn into a shouting match. If you didn't shout at one another so much, what would the discussion be like?"

You can also use systemic questions to help clients connect feelings and opinions with overt actions or behaviors. So we might ask something like, "You have said that George is constantly disgruntled. How does he show this?" "Mary, you have told us that Betty makes you very angry. Does she usually know when you are angry, and how could she tell?" "You have said that you worry a lot about the fact that Don opposes everything you are trying to do. How can you tell when he is being oppositional?" Such questions can also ask participants to share their own reactions and responses. In a typical intervention, we might ask, "What most surprised you about Terri's story?" Or, "What is most challenging to you in this situation?"

Systemic questions can be a powerful way to (a) shift the dialogue from statements of what people want and need to a conversation about how they are relating to one another and to (b) explore new patterns of interaction that might work better for them. Another type of question that can be very helpful in this regard is the appreciative question.

Appreciative questions, or "appreciative inquiry" as David Cooperrider introduced the term, is designed to plumb the positive resources in the system on which participants can rely for constructive change. Appreciative questions can change the context of the discussion from negative, destructive talk to positive, constructive dialogue.

We recently heard a woman on a popular talk radio program describe the hatred she felt for the doctor who had misdiagnosed a problem she was having in her pregnancy. She explained that she gave birth prematurely because of the physician's mistake. The host, a psychologist, asked her if her baby survived. "Yes, he is a healthy and happy 1-year-old today," the caller said. "How did you get through the medical emergency?" the psychologist asked. "I realized something wasn't right," she said. She then told about how when she went to the hospital, the doctors found out immediately what was wrong and treated her effectively. When she delivered prematurely, the hospital staff did a wonderful job of taking care of her and the baby. "So," the psychologist said, "Many wonderful things happened as a result of this situation? As a good mother, you knew something was wrong and sought help; the doctors took good care of you, and today you have a wonderful baby."

In essence, appreciative questions ask people to reflect on the positive. After hearing from a group of coworkers about how horrible their workplace meetings were, we asked each of the disputants to tell us about meetings they have had with others in the past that were excellent. We asked them to describe these meetings in some detail and to tell why they were good meetings. As they were talking, we began to make a list on a flip chart of these qualities of good meetings. We then asked them to talk about whether and how they might be able to incorporate some of these things into their own meetings.

We once worked with an extremely acrimonious group. The situation called for mediation, but there was no basis of respect on which any mediation could have succeeded. Therefore, we decided to begin with a dialogue group designed to help these folks begin exploring more positive interactions, using a format very similar to that created by the PCP. We had the participants take turns responding to each of three questions in a highly structured, safe, and facilitated environment. The first question was, "Tell about a time in your career that was very positive for you, that energized you, that led to a positive result, or that had special meaning." After everyone had a chance to tell his or her story of this positive event, we asked each to address the next question: "Tell about one thing that could change in this work environment that would make your job easier." The final question was, "Share one thing you all could do together to make it easier to integrate a diversity of personal and professional styles."

The idea behind this session was to begin changing the conversation from negative to positive, to have the employees hear something different from one another, something constructive. The result was remarkable in several ways. These employees began to hear about experiences they had not heard before. They came to see new possibilities for their own interactions, and they began to build a basis of respect.

When people are very negative, we like to explore what we have come to call "the positive shadow." Behind every complaint lies a positive image of what might be. People tend to talk about the complaint rather than the positive vision, but a well-timed appreciative question can shift the context of the discussion. When someone is complaining about the horrible work environment, we might ask the person to share his or her idea of what a really good work environment would be like. When people tell us that they were insulted, we might ask them to tell us how they would like to be treated. When they say that they are not listened to, we ask them to tell us about a time when they felt listened to. We like to think that there is always "wisdom in the whining." When people are being very negative, they are really telling you something quite positive. You have to listen carefully and bring it to the surface with a good, well-timed appreciative question.

Appreciative questioning identifies the positive energy driving a negative situation. On the surface, things may look like a terrible fray, but even the most vicious fights are driven by positive energy. People are fighting for some positive reason, and you can refocus the discussion from the negative fight to the positive energy by saying something like, "I'm amazed at the concern you are all showing in this dispute. Could you tell me more about why this is so important to you?" Or, "I'm struck by the passion you all have for this subject. Could you each take a turn and talk a little about why your hopes on this issue are so important to you?"

Our colleague Elsbeth McAdam in London tells of work she once did with skinheads in Sweden, having been hired to do therapy with this violent group. In this work, she took three appreciative avenues. First, she asked them to talk about what they gained from kicking people around. It gave them a thrill, they said. Next, she asked them how violence benefited them. People paid attention to them, they claimed. Then she asked them to talk about times in their lives when they got a thrill by means other than violence and times when people paid attention to them without violence. She then explored with them how they might get what they wanted, thrill and attention, without hurting anyone.

Speaking Dialogically

So far we have concentrated on listening and asking good questions. We started there because of the importance of these elements to good dialogue. But dialogue also includes sharing, talking, presenting, and telling. The way people talk in a dialogue is different from the way they talk on other occasions. Here are a few of the qualities of speech in a dialogue:

- *We may speak to be understood, rather than to prevail or win.*
- *We may speak mostly for ourselves, and not try to represent others.*

- *We may concentrate on our own perspective rather than analyzing or criticizing the behavior of others.*
- *We may show how our beliefs are grounded in our unique experience rather than arguing in favor of them.*
- *We may talk in respectful, face-saving ways rather than threatening or attacking.*
- *We may recognize many points of view rather than polarizing just two.*
- *We may express our doubts and uncertainties rather than show blind adherence.*
- *We may explore ideas in new ways rather than speaking "the party line."*
- *We may explore complexity rather than oversimplifying.*

In other words, dialogue is personal, exploratory, open, and unpredictable. This is not to suggest that participants should never claim a point of view or advocate an action or a position. Dialogue is distinguished not by the positions that people take, but by how they express the positions they take.

The PCP has turned this form of communication into a high art. They have done this in some groups by having each participant take time to address a series of questions on a hot topic. They will first ask participants to talk about the experiences they have had that have led them to the position they hold. The important part of this question is *experience*. People are encouraged to tell stories from their lives that show why they believe as they do. Only after everyone has had a chance to talk about his life experiences does he turn to the second question: What is at the heart of the matter for you? Here each person addresses the most important thing about his position. Notice that no one has been deterred from advocating a point of view, but points of view have been explored in a new way.

By the time the group has explored these two questions, it is usually ready for the third, more difficult one: What are your doubts, uncertainties, and gray areas? Almost everyone has such uncertainties, but these are rarely expressed in polarized settings. In a dialogue, they can be, but only after a certain amount of trust has been built. The PCP has found that even on the most contentious topics, this method really works. If a safe environment is achieved, participants can and do change the nature of their interaction on a certain subject.

Dialogue does not deter people from expressing their opinions, but it does ask them to ground their comments in personal experience. This changes the meaning of the term *why*. Usually, when people ask why we believe something, we give them a set of standard arguments. But in dialogue, the term *why* can mean, "What in your experience leads you to this position?" This refocuses the discussion from traditional argument to storytelling. It humanizes an otherwise depersonalized process. This is the way of many traditional societies, of course. Although we Westerners are usually inclined to defend our opinions "scientifically" by evidence and reasoning, other cultures often support their views with stories and other experiential forms. There is nothing wrong with standard forms of argument, but dialogue opens up other possibilities as well, as we ourselves have discovered when having dialogue about topics important to us, from breastfeeding to gun control to homeschooling.

Our friend Ann Skinner-Jones, an art therapist, does dialogue with art. She asks participants to create pictures or other artworks that express something important to them on the group's topic. They show their work, talk about it, and ask questions. One could do the same thing with skits, songs, and other forms of communication.

Being Profoundly Open

In his remarkable book *In Over Our Heads: The Mental Demands of Modern Life,* Robert Kegan (1994) explores many ways that human beings manage differences. Small children learn to recognize differences and to distinguish the self from others. Later, children learn about persuasion and winning. At a higher level, people can come to accept and embrace differences, but the world in which we now live requires even more than this. Contemporary life requires that people find the truth in many points of view, even opposing ones.

Our friend Anne Kass, the Chief Justice of the Family Court in Albuquerque, says that both the husband and wife in divorce cases are usually right most of the time. The mother wants to create a stable home for the children by having them live with her, and she is right. The father wants to establish a loving relationship with and a positive influence on his children by having them live with him, and he is right. Both are right. Much of the time, we must *live in the tension* between opposing truths. Dialogue is a process in which this can happen.

Kegan tells disputants to "value the relationship, miserable though it might feel, as an opportunity to live out your own multiplicity; and thus, focus on ways to let the conflictual relationship transform the parties rather than on the parties resolving the conflict." He calls this "a kind of 'conflict resolution' in which the Palestinian discovers her own Israeli-ness, the rich man discovers his poverty, the woman discovers the man inside her" (pp. 320-321).

In a forum we once sponsored, an African-American woman, a professor and campus leader of affirmative action and multiculturalism, shared the stage with a white male mathematics professor, an opponent to these developments. Using an interview technique, we asked them to share their personal experiences, reflect on the interaction between them, and comment on the position of the other side.

Several things about this event struck us. These two speakers had been engaged in a highly visible and vocal dispute, yet until this day, they had never met one another. The campus conflict on this issue consisted of a clash of claims, arguments, and attributions, yet when we took the time to talk with each of these advocates personally, they shared stories from their lives, talked about their fears and hopes, and truly listened to one another. The public dispute had become depersonalized, yet when given a chance, these two showed their humanity. In the final few minutes of the event, we asked each of them to reflect on what had happened. We smiled as we heard one of them say, "What we need is to take a long car ride together and really get to know one another."

Both of these parties maintained their positions throughout the discussion. They stood their ground, and yet we believe they changed. As our friends Kim Pearce and Barnett Pearce remind us, in dialogue, we must *live in the tension between standing our ground and being profoundly open*. We express our opinions, feelings, values, ideas, and interests clearly, but we listen openly to those of others.

In the discussions on abortion sponsored by the PCP—some 20 in all— participants rarely, if ever, changed their positions on this issue. But they almost universally reported that they were different as a result of the dialogue. How is this possible? What can change when you have a true dialogue with people different from yourself?

- *We may learn more about our own experience and why we believe as we do.*
- *We may understand the position and experience of others better than we did before.*
- *We may discover important differences among people who take the same side on the issue.*
- *We may discover shared concerns and common ground among those with whom we disagree.*
- *We may come to respect our adversaries.*

- *We may come to realize that the issue is far more complex than we thought.*
- *We may become a little better able to live with ambiguity and fuzziness.*
- *We may learn new ways to frame the issue.*
- *We may discover new ways to talk productively about the issue.*
- *We may discover that old animosities and hostilities are reduced.*
- *We may find ways of working together despite our differences.*

So it is entirely possible to stand your ground and still be profoundly open. We like to think of this outcome as *harvesting the wisdom in disagreement.* At the end of most of our dialogues, we have a harvesting session, in which we ask participants to step back and reflect on what they learned from the conversation, or where this journey took them. We often get the feeling that the harvesting is as important as the planting and nourishing that occurred throughout the discussion.

▪ Outcomes of Dialogue in Conflict Management

Dialogue is only one way to manage conflict. Adversarial methods such as litigation and arbitration are common. Many mediators and settlement facilitators avoid dialogue, meeting with disputants privately to broker an agreement between them. These methods are designed to *resolve* conflict, not to promote positive communication. But if we bring parties together in the spirit of dialogue, many good things can happen. They can discover what lies at the heart of the matter; they can build respect; and they can defuse polarization.

Discovering the Heart of the Matter

As we mentioned earlier, after the participants in the abortion dialogues had a chance to talk about their lives, the facilitator would always ask something like this: "Now we would like to hear a little more about your particular beliefs and perspectives about the issues surrounding abortion. What is at the heart of the matter for you?" Here, participants would need to reflect on what really mattered to them, what was most important. When mediations start to get bogged down with claims, counterclaims, details, and confusion, we often interrupt with the same question: *What is really at the heart of the matter for you? What is most important here?* Of course, there are many ways to have participants think about this question, and if they do so, they may clarify the center of their concerns.

In a dialogue—whether it is carried out in a mediation; a small, private group; or a public forum—we hope participants will come to learn about their central values, moral principles, and interests. We hope they will express these clearly, and acknowledge those of others. Bush and Folger in *The Promise of Mediation* call this the dual process of empowerment and recognition—the empowerment to know what is important to you and the recognition of what is important to others. Oddly enough, the heart of the matter is frequently lost in traditional modes of conflict resolution.

Building Respect

Another positive outcome of dialogue is creating a basis of respect on which settlement and future working relations can be built. Respect is rarely an outcome of traditional conflict resolution. Disrespect, hostility, and even hatred are common. The collateral damage of our customary ways of expressing conflict can be substantial. Yet dialogue can lead to a different outcome:

I respect you because you listened to me and took me seriously.

I respect you because I can see that you have good reasons and life experiences that lead you to your position, even though it is different from mine.

I respect you because you are making your way through a difficult life with the resources available to you.

I respect you because of your commitment and passion, even though I have different commitments and am passionate about different things.

I respect you because of the positive resources you have developed to manage complexity, even though I don't always do things the same way you do.

I respect you because you are willing to explore hard issues with me in a dialogue and are open to the possibility of collaborating.

Defusing Polarization

For the most part, we experience the world as bipolar. We tend to classify things as A and not-A, this and that, or ours and not-ours. Yet a moment's reflection reveals the world to be far more complex than this. In dialogue, participants can discover that the issues they are discussing are in fact multivalued, as many positions and distinctions can be made. One of the most frustrating things about politics in the United States is that the election process more or less prevents people from seeing beyond the two-party system. Politicians themselves know that the divisions are not clear, and yet the system forces them to play the game as if they were.

The tendency to polarize is especially acute when conflict gets emotional and when we play out our roles in "public." The abortion controversy is depicted publicly as pro-life versus pro-choice, yet participants in the abortion dialogues discovered that pro-lifers have significant differences among them, as do pro-choicers.

Also, the divisions that seem so important to us at a certain point in time may evaporate when we talk on a new level. We may discover shared concerns we did not know about before. Despite deep moral differences, a pro-life advocate and a pro-choice advocate may share a strong concern for children in society. Although they disagree about how unplanned pregnancy should be handled, they agree that all children should be loved, honored, and nurtured. Changing the discussion from abortion to goals for children turns the kaleidoscope into a new pattern.

Building a Context for Collaboration

The literature on conflict resolution is full of material on collaboration, which has been called integrative problem solving, interest-based bargaining, win-win solutions, principled negotiation, or the Harvard Model. Anyone who has even the slightest exposure to alternative dispute resolution is familiar with the values of collaboration, yet it is often very hard to achieve. It requires a lot of seed work and cultivation, and dialogue offers a way to build a base of collaboration.

All of the kinds of learning and listening we have discussed so far in this chapter can help build collaboration. It can help identify issues, values, and interests. It can reveal positive resources and building blocks for collaboration. It can open creative thinking. And it can create a multivalued system for constructing solutions. We do not always have a dialogue primarily to solve a problem or settle a dispute, but it can serve as a stepping-stone toward this end.

▪ Using Dialogue Creatively

There are many ways to have good dialogue. Although most share the features outlined in this chapter, one dialogue may look very different from another. We try to promote dialogue in each of the settings in which we work—interpersonal, organizational, and public. In the following chapters, we explore what dialogue looks like in mediations, in work groups, in organizational systems, and in communities. We show how dialogue becomes multilogue, as the conversation moves from small groups to large sectors of society.

In Chapter 3, we share some of our tools for facilitating dialogue in private disputes, helping people talk so others will listen and listen so others will talk. In Chapter 4, we write about dialogue in work groups and how the spirit of dialogue can be infused into the ordinary workplace. Then in Chapter 5, we look at large organizations and the challenge of promoting dialogue in large systems, such as government, corporations, schools, and communities. Later, in Chapter 6, we explore a type of large-scale intervention using the gaming metaphor to encourage multilogue between stakeholder groups. And finally in Chapter 7, we focus on how to have dialogue on difficult public issues.

▪ Resources You Can Use

Arnett, R. C., & Arneson, P. (1999). *Dialogic civility in a cynical age.* Albany: State University of New York Press.

Buber, M. (1958). *I and thou.* New York: Scribner.

Bush, R. A. B., & Folger, J. P. (1994). *The promise of mediation: Responding to conflict through empowerment and recognition.* San Francisco: Jossey-Bass.

Cooperrider, D., & Srivastva, S. (Eds.). (1990). *Appreciative management in leadership: The power of positive thought and action.* San Francisco: Jossey-Bass.

Kegan, R. (1994). *In over our heads: The mental demands of modern life.* Cambridge, MA: Harvard University Press.

Matson, F. W., & Montagu, A. (1967). *The human dialogue: Perspectives on communication.* New York: Free Press.

Pearce, W. B., & Pearce, K. A. (1999). Combining passions and abilities: Toward dialogic virtuosity. *Southern Communication Journal, 65,* 161-175.

Public Conversations Project, 46 Kondazian Street, Watertown, MA 02172. www.publicconversations.org

Public Dialogue Consortium, 504 Luna Blvd. NW, Albuquerque, NM 87102. www.publicdialogue.org

PART II

Conflict in Small Systems

3

····

Mediating Private Disputes

In 1984, we were at the University of Massachusetts studying the conflict surrounding the Moral Majority, which was a big news story at the time. This got us interested in large disputes on public issues. While we were busy working on this project—viewing videos, sifting through piles of newsletters, photocopying clippings, and interviewing participants—we received an unexpected call from the community mediation center in Amherst. They wanted us to observe some cases and provide feedback. We thought this would be interesting, so we agreed.

We proceeded to reserve the observation room, write up a protocol, put a research team together, and begin to schedule mediations. Over the course of several months, we viewed quite a few mediations and became increasingly interested in the pitfalls and prospects of this form of conflict resolution. As we sat on tall stools behind a mirror hearing disputants tell their stories, we became aware that what we were seeing was not unlike large societal conflicts in which the "disputants" are huge organizations and factions struggling to prevail. That was a watershed moment for us, as we realized that the conflict processes in which we were gaining increasing interest show up on a variety of levels, from private to public.

It was during this time that we began to think systemically about conflict and how people manage differences. Today, our communication perspective provides a set of principles that guides all of our work, in private, semiprivate, and public situations. Of course, mediation is not limited to private interpersonal disputes such as those we observed at the University of Massachusetts. Often, large-stakeholder groups are involved, and in later chapters we share some techniques for mediating these "bigger" conflicts. Still, mediation is especially well suited to the management of interpersonal conflict.

Although we saw important similarities between the conflicts we observed in our mediation research and those in our public-issues studies, we noticed significant differences also. The Moral Majority dispute was played out mostly in the media. High-profile individuals representing huge sectors of society spoke out in a national debate. Occasionally, the adversaries would meet one another briefly on a stage and quickly take seats at opposite sides to debate in front of an emotional crowd. With one or two noted exceptions, however, opponents did not know one another and did not spend any time in direct interaction in a private setting.

The mediations we saw, in contrast, involved persons representing themselves on matters of personal importance in a setting in which they could take time to explore the issue in some depth. In these mediations, as in scores of cases we have mediated since, the parties had a personal face. They often have an ongoing relationship as well. Although we sometimes mediate "one-shot" cases between people who will never see one another again, we are most challenged (and gratified) by cases in which the parties learn to communicate better and maintain an ongoing relationship that works.

▪ Entering the System: Communication Goals

You can usually spot a novice mediator right off. Having just completed 40 hours of basic mediation training, this person will follow a predictable style and series of stages to "get the agreement." If the mediator is talented, however, he or she will soon loosen up.

With experience, you begin to realize that every case is different. We have done cases that settled in 15 minutes because the parties just needed the opportunity to sit down together and quickly write up what they wanted to do. In contrast, we once facilitated a workplace meeting in which the entire first day was taken up arguing over ground rules. With experience, you come to realize that the goals of mediation depend upon what is happening between the disputants. You may begin assuming one set of goals will be necessary and quickly shift as your attention is directed elsewhere.

When we do mediation demonstrations for our trainees, we like to use cases that illustrate the full range of goals that one might set as a mediator.

One of our favorites is a workplace dispute between the owner of a small advertising company and the art supervisor. This dispute is fascinating because it can involve any number of relationship and work issues. We like to see what will happen when we invite various people to take the roles of the disputants in different training sessions. We never tire of this case because it always plays out differently.

We set the scene: The owner and supervisor have not been getting along. The supervisor is privately angry because the owner recently "stole" one of his creative ideas for an orange juice campaign. Sometimes this issue gets worked pretty hard, and sometimes it barely comes up. The owner is trying to build the business and feels unappreciated by employees. The supervisor thinks that the company's success depends on the work of the designers and feels that the owner does not appreciate their contribution and in fact tries to micromanage it. Again, it is interesting to see how these issues evolve in the different versions of this case.

What we as mediators do in this case depends upon the pattern of interaction between the disputants. Often the disputants grapple for a while trying to express what they want and need. Here, we ask questions that help clarify their positions and empower them to be clear with one another. Almost always we go through a period in this mediation during which hard feelings come out. Respect seems to decline between the two, and their relationship seems to be eroding. If this happens, we will frame their comments in ways that help the other party see their good reasons and how they might legitimately feel the way they do.

One of the neat things about workplace conflicts such as this is that there are always absent parties. There is a larger system of interactions among employees that should be taken into consideration. At some point in this mediation, we often find it necessary to try to build this kind of social consciousness, and we do this by "scoping out," or asking questions about, how the business works, who works there, how they do things, and how they relate to one another. If this intervention is successful, the disputants become more conscious of the whole system and begin to realize that their conflict is taking place in a bigger context that will need to be considered.

Sometimes in this demonstration, the parties get stuck and keep going around in circles. They repeat their statements over and over, and they don't seem to have a clue about how to move forward. This gives us a chance to demonstrate other techniques that invite the owner and supervisor to look ahead and begin to imagine different futures.

─────── Relational Mediation ───────　　　─────── Settlement Mediation ───────

COMMUNICATION GOALS

Empowerment	Recognition and Respect	Social Consciousness	Moving Forward	Issue Definition	Deliberation	Decision
"I have my good reasons."	"I see you have your good reasons too."	"We have made this conflict together, and we will determine its outcome together."	"We will need new patterns to get unstuck."	"These are the issues that divide us."	"All of the options have pros and cons."	"Now we choose."

Figure 3.1. Communication Goals in Mediation

Then, of course, there is the job of helping parties discover where they disagree, generate options, deliberate and, if things go well, make some decisions about what they should do.

After we do this case, we find it helpful to talk to our trainees about seven goals that might come into play. We give them a copy of what we now call our "goals chart" and talk about how you would identify the need for each goal and what you might do to accomplish it. The goals chart is presented in Figure 3.1. Notice that the goals are grouped into two types—relationship goals and settlement goals. The goals on the left address patterns in which the relationship between the parties needs attention, and those on the right concentrate more on substantive issues, solutions, and agreements.

The goals are arranged on our chart from left to right, suggesting a kind of logical progression from one goal to the next. It would be a rare conflict that presented itself in exactly this way. Hardly any dispute involves all seven goals, and they rarely occur in this order. Sometimes you spend all of the time on just one or two goals. Sometimes you zoom along from one goal to another, skipping quickly to the end. Sometimes you go backward, from settlement-oriented goals to more relationally oriented ones.

Although these goals have obvious application in mediation, they are also useful in virtually every other kind of intervention. As a third party in any system, you can use the chart as a device for looking at patterns and making decisions about how to act into the system at that point.

▪ Thinking Relationally About Mediation

Traditionally, mediation has been viewed as a process of settling disputes. As a case in point, the district court in our city has a settlement week, in which mediators donate their time "for the public good" to clear as many lawsuits off the calendar as possible and make life easier for everyone associated with the court, not to mention the parties and their attorneys. Compared to the battering that most disputants experience in litigation, settling via mediation can be a very good thing.

It is no wonder, then, that most mediation and mediation training is settlement oriented. Mediation skills are geared toward resolving the conflict, and the effectiveness of mediation is evaluated in terms of the settlement rate. Mediators often feel a certain amount of pride if they settle a case and a certain amount of failure if they do not. Yet we hold a different view.

Our friend Susan Barnes-Anderson, the director of our local Metropolitan Court Mediation Program, recently shared an interesting tidbit with us. She told us that in the previous month, they had the highest agreement rate in the history of the program—82%. The curious thing about this is that she had been advising mediators not to push for agreements. She had in fact observed that mediators were slowing down, providing more time for parties to gather information and think through the situation, and not getting upset if parties did not reach an agreement. And the agreement rate went up.

We do not want to be guilty of faulty causal reasoning here, but this anecdote adds to our growing suspicion of the strong settlement orientation of traditional mediation. We do not object to a settlement focus in mediations; indeed, it has real virtues. But mediators sometimes become so focused on agreements that they become oblivious to the downside.

If you concentrate solely on pressuring parties to settle, you may miss opportunities to help them work on useful communication skills to manage their own disputes, maintain a working relationship for the future, and evaluate clearly for themselves what the outcome of the mediation should be. Mediator pressure to settle removes responsibility from the parties to make their own decisions about what an appropriate outcome might be.

We once observed a family mediation in which the parents were having trouble with their teenage son. It was a typical adolescent situation, with lots of testing, power struggles, and emotional flare-ups. We have experienced similar conflicts with our own teens, as have most of our friends. In this case, the mediators pushed hard for an agreement. They had the family members make lists of what they wanted. They goaded the son to come up with demands and proposals, even though he could not be clear on what he wanted or could offer. We watched in agony, as the mediators squeezed an agreement out of this family. The result was screwy, including provisions such as (a) we will be nice to one another, (b) we will not fight, and (c) we will work out our differences. As soon as they got home, the mother proudly attached the agreement to the refrigerator with magnets, but we learned from a follow-up call that it did not last a week. We came to call this "the case in which an agreement was not a solution."

In some ways, the term *resolution* better fits mediation than does *settlement* or *agreement,* if we define resolution broadly. Our friend Jeff Grant reminds us that for some people, resolution can mean simply being heard, feeling safe or secure, or just getting a good night's sleep. For others it may be a full-blown settlement agreement, and that's OK too. For these reasons, we use the definition of mediation in Kathy Domenici's book *Mediation:*

Empowerment in Conflict Management: "a process where parties are encouraged to see and make clear, deliberate choices, while acknowledging the perspective of the other. In this process, mutually acceptable agreement is one possible outcome" (p. 28).

The publication of Robert Baruch Bush and Joseph Folger's book *The Promise of Mediation* in 1994 probably did more than anything else to raise consciousness in the mediation community of the limits of the settlement model of mediation. In this controversial work, they argue that overemphasis on settlement detracts from empowering parties to establish their own process and outcome and to recognize the perspectives, ideas, and interests of other parties. We agree with their conclusion that mediation should be primarily a relational intervention.

Bush and Folger called the kind of mediation that concentrates on relationships the *transformative* model and the type that focuses on settlement the *satisfaction* model. For us, the terms *relational* and *settlement* work as well. Lately, a new term *settlement facilitation,* as opposed to *mediation,* is being used increasingly to designate the kind of intervention in which parties are pressured to come to agreement. We like distinction between the two forms of third-party intervention, each of which has virtues and drawbacks.

In our mind, it is entirely possible to do good settlement work and also be very relational in approach, but it takes a certain perspective and skill. We are eager to help parties write agreements, if that is the outcome that emerges in their conversation, but our first hope is always that both parties feel that the mediation worked for them, that they learned significant new things from the conversation, that they felt empowered to make clear decisions, and that they came to recognize others' perspectives with respect. When that happens, whether an agreement was written or not, we feel very good about the session.

A settlement facilitator would probably make the point that their clients have no ongoing relationship and that there is little if any hope that good communication can ever be achieved between them. Certainly in large-stakes litigation cases, this is probably true. The settlement facilitator would say that it is a waste of time and a diversion to think about building positive relationships. That would be hard to disagree with if we limited our view of relationship to the current situation. Taking a broader view, we want to know if the parties might learn that collaboration is possible, that constructive forms of communication can lead to positive outcomes, and that people can think of better ways to settle disputes than through lawsuits. In other words, mediation has implications for society beyond settling the immediate dispute. If the parties learn new ways to relate to others in the process of mediation, then a larger social end is being achieved.

▪ Mediation as Collaborative Communication

Since the 1970s, conflict management theorists have promoted the values of collaboration as a form of conflict resolution. Collaboration, or the win-win solution, became especially popular among practitioners after the Harvard Program on Negotiation, mentioned in Chapter 1, got off the ground. We still have our students read Fisher and Ury's classic *Getting to Yes,* and we use principled negotiation in our practice as well. But this is not where we begin or end our thinking about collaboration.

For us, collaboration is an ideal against which we always measure our work. When conflict management processes are at their best, parties collaborate from start to finish, and the process as well as the outcome is constructed jointly. In the deepest sense of the term, this means that parties work together to establish what they want from mediation and how they want to accomplish it. We have done mediations in which the parties just want a chance to tell their stories and have these recognized by the other party. We have also done mediations in which parties are mostly interested in testing the possibility of agreement to help them make a decision about whether to go on to court or not. Often, of course, parties are not sure what they want, or they disagree about what they want to accomplish, and the mediation becomes a process to help them clarify and negotiate the best course of action for both.

It often happens that the parties in mediation want very different things from the process, and we work with the parties to make it possible for them to achieve their respective goals. We try not to prejudge what those goals might be. One party might want to get a financial settlement, and the other party just wants to have the conflict over so he can move on with his life. As mediators, we will reality-test respective goals thoroughly to make sure that each party clearly understands and accepts these possible outcomes, but ultimately it is the parties themselves who must be responsible for deciding what they want. If both parties ultimately work to make it possible for each to achieve his or her goals, they are collaborating toward that end.

As mediators, then, our role is to open a space for the parties to negotiate their own outcomes. This means a great deal more than unlocking the door and putting tablets and pens on the table. We open a space for collaboration from the first contact with the client, and we keep it open in a variety of ways throughout the mediation. In this chapter, we present a number of techniques—ways of keeping the space open for collaboration.

A collaborative space includes many things. It is a space in which people can say what needs to be said and hear what needs to be heard. It is a space in which the parties can work out and clarify what they want. It is a space in which disputants are free to change their minds. It is an experimental space, in which parties can play with ideas and suggest new approaches. It is a creative space, in which ideas can be generated. It is an exploratory space, in which ideas can be tested, elaborated on, modified, and extended. It is also a space in which new and different processes and forms of communication can be tried.

For all these reasons, a collaborative space must also be a safe environment. As we pointed out in the previous chapter, however, what is safe for one person may be threatening to another. So the parties must also collaborate to create the kind of environment in which everyone feels sufficiently safe to proceed constructively. We tell our students that a mediation session is rarely just one mediation. It can involve several mediations going on at once. We might be mediating the rules. We might mediate the process. We might mediate desired outcomes. And, of course, we might mediate an agreement. A "meta" mediation that is always going on involves how to construct a safe environment.

In the previous chapter, we outlined a number of ways to help establish safety. These include:

- *Think consciously about time and place.*
- *Provide a structure that feels safe.*
- *Solicit agreements on how the discussion should be done.*
- *Promote good facework.*
- *Respond to willingness and felt need.*
- *Find a shared level of comfort.*
- *Leave an out.*
- *Maintain impartiality.*

We try to keep these points in mind throughout any mediation.

Introducing Mediation

We think that the opening of a mediation session, the way it is presented to the clients, is a vital first step toward beginning the collaboration process. Because we take a relational approach in our mediations, our introductions sound somewhat different from the standard opening taught in basic mediation training. Here are some guidelines we use:

We keep our introductions general and open. Our introductions are not very prescriptive. We keep our introductions quite simple and brief. We usually say that mediation is an informal process for the parties to discuss their "situation." We don't call it a *problem, dispute,* or *conflict* because we want the parties to define it in their own way. We tell them that mediation is an opportunity to work through the issues that have brought them here. We describe ourselves as impartial facilitators who will help them have a constructive conversation. We try to give them an idea of what to expect. We usually say that we will ask lots of questions, and we encourage them to listen well to one another. Although we are cautious about caucuses, we tell them that private sessions are possible.

We do not overemphasize ground rules in the beginning. Many mediators begin with a list of ground rules, but our preference is to keep the rules somewhat open at the beginning. We normally prefer to see how things go first and let the disputants themselves indicate what they want and need. We might simply ask the disputants to use normal standards of politeness. If we have reason to believe that safety requires strict rules from the beginning, we might suggest a few, though we are more likely to invite the disputants themselves to negotiate their own rules. If things get out of hand later, we can always take a pause to suggest additional rules at that point.

We present agreement only as one possible outcome. We always mention the possibility of agreement, but we never push it. We may show the disputants the agreement form and say that it is there if they choose to use it. We also say that we can help them write up the agreement if they get to that point.

We tell the parties we want the mediation to work for them. We tell disputants that mediation is their process, and they should collaborate to use the time for beneficial outcomes. We never suggest what those outcomes might be.

We are explicit about our desire to help make a safe environment. We tell parties quite clearly that this is our job. We invite them to keep us informed about their comfort level and to work with one another to keep things safe.

We try to establish a relaxed environment. We work nonverbally to give a relaxed feeling. We always try to be friendly, to connect with the parties, and to be responsive and inviting in our demeanor. We greet the parties warmly and thank them for coming. We prefer to set up the chairs around the table in a circular fashion and allow the disputants themselves to determine how they want to orient themselves.

We ask the parties if they have special needs or requests. We ask them quite directly if there is anything they need to make the mediation work well. We ask them if they have any requests about the process itself that would make it easier for them.

We ask the parties to keep us informed about how the process is going throughout the mediation. We tell our disputants that because mediation is a collaborative conversation, they should let us know of things that are making them uncomfortable or making it difficult for them to proceed. We encourage the parties to make process suggestions at any time, and we tell them to feel free to request a private meeting with us if they wish.

We ask the parties how they would like to begin. Often the mediator establishes the order of things in advance. Some mediators want to have the disputants take strict turns. Some want to allow the party with least power to begin, a judgment we would rather not make. Some begin with the person who brought the complaint. Our clear preference is for the disputants themselves to decide how to proceed. Sometimes, a general discussion begins without a lot of formal turn taking, and that can feel quite comfortable in many cases. Other times, they prefer for one party to begin with a formal statement followed by a statement from the other side. Often, the disputants start off somewhat formally and later move to a more informal back-and-forth discussion.

Caucuses

Caucuses, or private meetings with the parties, are common in mediation. Most settlement facilitations are entirely caucus based. In these cases, the mediator typically meets with the parties in a brief joint session at the beginning, separates them, and then conducts a kind of shuttle diplomacy. We know an attorney who recently traveled 500 miles to represent a client in mediation and ended up sitting all day in a small room waiting for the mediator, who finally made a 10-minute appearance. This is probably an exceptional case, but it does illustrate what caucus-based mediation can be like.

Heavy use of caucuses makes sense when the sole goal of mediation is settlement and the primary process is negotiation. But caucus-based mediation has many hazards, especially for a relationally oriented mediator. Here are just a few:

- Because caucuses are confidential, a disputant may tell you something that is impossible to check with the other party.
- Parties will see caucuses as an opportunity to win you over to their side rather than negotiate in good faith.
- You collude with the parties in keeping secrets, which leads to suspicion and erodes trust.
- The parties do not have a chance to hear, acknowledge, and recognize the perspectives and stories of the other.
- The parties do not have a chance to work on building a relationship or developing new communication patterns with one another.
- Patterns of polarization and separation are reinforced.

For these reasons, we prefer to downplay the use of caucuses. We would rather work openly in an environment in which the parties can deal directly with one another. Still, caucuses do have their place, and we use them occasionally. It sometimes happens that one or both parties simply do not feel safe in the presence of the other. They believe they will be intimidated, threatened, or "out powered" in some way. So when a party asks for a private meeting, we honor that. Of course, if we meet with one side privately, we will meet with the other privately as well. Sometimes, too, we may sense that private meetings are necessary to give the parties a chance to explore and express their interests, goals, and ideas more safely without the other party present. If that happens, we will suggest a caucus but check to make sure that everyone is OK with it. When might we feel that collaboration and safety would be well served by moving to caucus?

- The parties become stuck—unable to move forward—and seem unresponsive to mediator interventions.
- We sense that a party is afraid to talk about something.
- Emotions are so high that the parties need a break from one another.
- A party seems withdrawn, confused, discouraged, or unable to speak clearly or listen well.
- The session has gotten out of control.

Almost never in our practice do we find it necessary to stay in the caucus mode, and we will always return to joint sessions as soon as it feels appropriate to do so.

A special case of the caucus should be mentioned at this point. We sometimes use a premediation caucus with the parties, especially if we learned during the intake process that one or both have special concerns about the process. Here a caucus can actually serve as a tool of collaboration by allowing parties to explore their special needs, suggest ground rules, or alert the mediator to particular things that might make the mediation feel safer to them. We use this technique rarely, but it can be helpful in special cases.

Mediation: Hard or Soft

We recently ran into a colleague on the street and stopped to talk for a few minutes. We were surprised when he mentioned that he thought our respective styles were different. He characterized his own style as *hard* and ours as *soft*. He really did not mean to be judgmental, only to describe a difference.

The hard-soft metaphor is often used to make a distinction among conflict-resolution practitioners. The word *hard* seems to mean formal and results oriented; and *soft* means informal, subjective, and not particularly concerned about results. We think this is an unfortunate metaphor for a variety of reasons. First, it implies that you have to be one or the other, and we believe that it is entirely possible to work toward settlement and be relationally oriented at the same time. Second, it implies that relational mediation is formless and without a clear procedure, whereas this kind of mediation actually requires a great deal of skill, relies on sophisticated techniques, and often demands adherence to process. Further, the distinction between results-oriented and non-results-oriented mediation seems false to us. Although settlement facilitation (the "hard" side of mediation) measures its effectiveness in terms of clear, well-articulated agreements, this is only one kind of success. Relational mediation also has outcomes that are often more important than an agreement. Just because you cannot fold those results into an envelope does not mean that they are "soft." Often these less tangible results are absolutely essential for other "harder" outcomes to occur.

We believe that settlement facilitation is an honorable practice and serves a vital function in society. For us, however, building relationships and providing enduring process tools are even more important, and they are essential in systemic practice.

▪ Thinking Systemically About Mediation

In your training, you may have been taught that an early step in mediation is the "information-gathering" stage, the time when the disputants tell their versions of what happened. Here the mediator is supposed to ask questions to clarify the situation and learn the facts—which are agreed upon and which are disputed. This is seen as a period to learn what the parties' positions are and possibly to uncover their interests. However, we prefer to cast this stage somewhat differently.

Rather than "information gathering," we prefer to think of this stage as "story telling." Although our disputants sometimes produce documents and evidence to try to prove their version of the facts as if they were in a court of law, what we are really working with in any mediation are stories, the participants' depictions of events. These stories have characters, plots, episodes, dialogue, and all of the elements of a good narrative. We get good "information" from these stories, but from a systemic view, the stories themselves are the raw materials that can be worked. Although it is instructive and convenient to teach mediation as a series of "stages," every mediator knows that this oversimplifies the process. Indeed, we work with stories from beginning to end. What you really end up with is a pile of stories on the table, and good mediation means knowing how to work creatively with these.

Working With Stories

We once mediated a case between a homeless man and a social services agency. As the mediation proceeded, the parties told us story after story from the past. The homeless man told about his illness, discomfort, and inability to get medical attention. The agency representative told about efforts to locate the man, take him to the hospital, and the man's abusive treatment of social workers and medical personnel. This storytelling went on for some time, back and forth. New stories were added, and previous stories were elaborated on and sometimes changed. Some stories were disputed. Some stories were shared by both parties. Some stories had a more or less positive ending, and some were quite sad.

This exchange illustrates the first kind of story that we often encounter in mediations—*stories of the past*. When these stories are told and heard, they give the participants a chance to see history through the eyes of the other. They give parties the opportunity to express and work through what happened and to discover the heart of the matter for each of them. When mediators ask good questions, the participants add detail to the stories and learn more about what seemed most important, what mattered the most, and how they perceived events.

Another kind of story we hear in mediations is *stories of the present*. Here we get various versions of what is going on in mediation. Why are we here, and what is this all about? How do we want to use this time? What do we hope will happen, and what do we hope will not? In the social service case, the agency repeatedly told of its desire to hear from the man what he wanted and how it could serve him better. The agency also said how much it wanted him to hear its frustrations in providing him service and the aggravating limitations placed on the agency because of budget declines. The homeless man was less clear on how to use mediation. In this case, we encountered a common problem—one party was able to tell a coherent story of the present, but the other could not.

A third type of story, maybe the most important of all, is the *story of the future*. Here the parties begin to imagine the future. People tell what they want, and they share how they might get there. In the case above, the homeless man was not very good at telling stories of the present, but he was very good at telling stories of the future. He was crystal clear about the kind of relationship he wanted and the kind of services he believed he deserved.

These stories provide information about how the participants define their system, how they view their relationship, what patterns of interaction they have experienced, who else is involved, and what might be done. As mediators, we always listen for story connections—what characters the stories have in common, what plot lines are shared, how one story extends another. We look for how stories of the past, present, and future connect with one another. We point these connections out and ask questions about them. We look for positive resources in the stories that can be used as building blocks for collaboration.

The social worker in the above mediation told a passionate story of how he used to drive around and look for his homeless client on the street, check on him, take him to the doctor, and follow up by seeing how well he was doing. He continued this story by expressing his sadness at not being able to do that any longer. The villain in this story was the state, which had recently cut the funds necessary to provide this kind of case-management work. The homeless man told the story of feeling abandoned and losing services that were his legal right. His villain was the social worker, who never showed up anymore. These two stories connected in some very interesting ways. Each had the same characters and events, but the motives and villains were different. Each was a story of the past that contained seeds for stories of the future. The challenge in connecting these stories, it seemed to us, was to find in the social worker's concern and past behavior a way to build a future story that fulfilled the other man's vision.

Stories, then, are the material we work with in mediations. We ask questions about them; we connect them, and we reframe them. When these stories are explored, certain metastories begin to emerge, and these larger stories tell us how the participants define and characterize their system. These metastories are extremely important because they suggest points at which we as mediators might enter the conversation and how. Initially in most mediations, metastories tend to be negative, but every negative story has a positive counterpart. The negative metastories show us where to enter the system, and the positive ones provide clues as to where the system might move.

Some Common Metastories of Mediation

The Negative Story of Confusion and the Positive Story of Empowerment

It often happens in mediation that the first rounds of stories are somewhat confused and contradictory. Sometimes disputants are not clear about what story they want to tell or how to tell it. They really don't have a clear grasp of what they want or how to say what they want. They may tell short, cryptic stories that don't make sense, or they may tell long, rambling ones with no clear point. In mediation, people can think the story through more carefully, try different versions, decide what elements really matter and, in the end, make a coherent statement that represents their sense of past, present, and future. When this happens, the negative story of confusion is transformed into a positive story of empowerment.

The Negative Story of Disrespect and the
Positive Story of Recognition

There is a common pattern seen in mediations. One side tells his story. The other side tells hers. The first side angrily repeats his story, and the second then repeats her version. This process goes back and forth. Eventually, the mediation will stall, the participants will get frustrated, and the hope of positive results will fade. At some point, however, a new pattern can emerge, and this is a pattern of acknowledgment—the realization and reflection from the parties that the other person's story has integrity. They may not share the story, but they begin to see how and why the other person holds to it. In its highest form, the parties hear one another's stories well and acknowledge one another's good reasons for believing as they do. Here a negative story of disrespect is transformed into a positive story of recognition.

The Negative Story of Blame and the
Positive Story of Respect

Perhaps the most common pattern we see in the first stages of mediation is blaming. Disputants say in so many different ways, "If it weren't for you . . ." And sometimes that pattern remains throughout the mediation. We sometimes even get to the point of signing agreements, and the blame still remains. More often, however, this pattern changes during the course of the mediation. If the parties are willing to listen to one another and collaborate in achieving a positive outcome, positive regard begins to grow. You don't have to agree with someone to respect him or her. Respect happens when we understand and acknowledge another person's perspective and come to realize that his position is reasonable within his experience. We are always gratified to see a story of blame be transformed into one of respect.

The Negative Story of Competition and the
Positive Story of Cooperation

Another extremely common pattern in mediation is the competitive stance. We have an acquaintance whose neighbor filed a complaint against him for his barking dog. This case was referred to mediation, and the parties agreed to go. Knowing of our background in mediation, our friend came to us to get some tips on "how to win." We still laugh about that today, and in retrospect he now laughs with us. Many people enter mediation because they believe it will give them a forum in which to make compelling arguments to win the other side over to their point of view. They think that if they can state their case clearly, the other side will see the error of its ways. Disputants are actually surprised when this doesn't happen. No matter how well they state their case, the other side doesn't see it. Not only that, but the other side has the gall to try to persuade them too. After a few rounds of "persuasive" speeches, the disputants come to the realization that this pattern is not going to work. Some just give up and leave at that point, but we can usually get them to stay long enough to see other possibilities. When disputants shift from trying to win to trying to work out a solution, when they start negotiating in good faith, we see the transformation from competition to cooperation.

The Negative Story of "Being Stuck" and the Positive Story of "Moving Forward"

Even after those with whom we work develop a degree of respect for and cooperation with each other, they often find themselves in a repetitive pattern they don't know how to transcend. They get stuck. Because their individual interests are still important, they cannot figure out a way to get beyond restating what they want. They may wish to change this pattern, but they don't know how. On several occasions, we have heard disputants actually say, "I really want to get this over with. Can't we just do something?" We like to hear this statement in mediation because it signals to us that the parties are ready to change the pattern in some substantial way. They want to transform the story of being stuck to a story of moving forward.

The Negative Story of Disorganization and the Positive Story of Order

Effective conflict-intervention professionals are not afraid of complexity. By itself, complexity may be a positive story rather than a negative one. It becomes negative when the parties are confused because they are not able to bring any kind of organization or analysis to the complexity. Mediators can really help with this kind of problem, and a host of traditional mediation techniques can help the parties transform their stories of disorganization to stories of order.

The Negative Story of Indecision and the Positive Story of Commitment

One of the most interesting and frustrating moments in a mediation occurs when the issues are defined and the options are laid out, and the parties just cannot agree. They cannot commit or decide. Too many mediations fall apart at this point. One of the biggest challenges of collaboration involves transforming the story of indecision to one of commitment.

The Negative Story of Rage and the Positive Story of Passion

Mediations vary in the level of emotion displayed. Some cases are rather placid, and others are quite volatile. Dealing with emotion is often an important consideration. We like to think of emotions as story elements. They are both part of the story and part of the style of telling. For us, emotions are not just emotions, but they must be looked at in terms of how they fit into the narrative of the mediation.

The conventional wisdom of mediation says that disputants simply need to get their emotions out, and mediators are advised to allow a period of venting so that the parties can settle down and get rational. This sometimes works, but the metaphor of "venting" can be problematic. It imagines that feelings are all bottled up and need to be released to lower the pressure. Often, however, "venting" does not calm the parties down. Sometimes, it just works them up. Rather than venting, expressing strong emotion can be more like stoking. We also believe that vociferous expression of feeling by one party is sometimes very threatening and unsafe to the other. In these cases it is more like aggression than venting. So when emotions are running high, we must make a judgment about what to do. We might feel that the parties should vent, or we might feel that something else would be better.

Emotion is both common and expected in serious conflict situations. The expression of emotion per se should never be taken as a negative. The determining factors are how emotion is expressed, what it represents, and what it makes between the parties. We have seen many cases in which strong emotion is the force that leads to collaboration in the end. We have also seen many cases in which strong emotion erects a barrier that is never overcome.

If handled inappropriately, strong emotion can become rage. If handled well, it becomes a passion that says, "I care enough to be here and work this through."

Working in Mediation: The Construction Triangle

We tell our students that mediation is an art, and we truly believe that it is. The canvas is the disputants' system, the medium is the collective stories told, and the tools are the many techniques that mediators employ. From the first moment to the last, we make artistic judgments about how to work within the system, what stories to connect, and how to connect them. This is why formula mediations don't work. Formulas do not allow the mediator to see what is going on, decide what to try to accomplish, and make judgments about the best thing to do at each moment.

Using the construction metaphor explained in Chapter 1, we like to think of mediation as a process of building. In particular, we think of ourselves as working in concert with disputants to build three things—(1) empowerment and recognition, (2) community consciousness, and (3) commitment. As in any system, the parts are not independent but work as a whole. For this reason, we have come to display the three parts of the mediation construction as a triangle (see Figure 3.2). As we work, we think about connections among these three.

We usually find that we go back and forth between these three kinds of work, and we may work on two or three simultaneously. Just when we think we are moving toward commitment, old issues of empowerment and recognition come up, and we go back and revisit these. After we define the issues and set a problem-solving agenda, we discover that the parties have lost the larger system view, so we go back to help rebuild a sense of community. Now let's take a closer look.

▪ Building Empowerment and Recognition

Empowerment and *recognition* were made popular as twin concepts by Bush and Folger in *The Promise of Mediation*. These are two fundamental goals of mediation in the relational tradition—to empower parties to understand and express clearly what they want and need and to enable parties to acknowledge the positions, interests, and values of others.

One of the most poignant cases we have ever mediated involved two women who had been close friends. One owned a business, and the other had

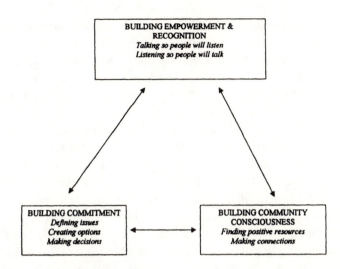

Figure 3.2. The Construction Triangle

been her employee. But things went bad. The owner found herself in the position of having to fire the employee, and the employee filed a discrimination case and sued the owner for damages. Still, despite the harsh feelings that resulted, the two were willing to try mediation. The initial stories went something like this:

The owner told us that her former employee's performance had declined and that she was unwilling to do assigned tasks. The employee had completely dropped the ball in following up with a client, causing the company to lose the account. She said that the supervisor had talked with the employee but could not seem to get her to change her behavior. She said that she did not want to fire the employee, but felt that she had no choice.

The employee said that she had had problems with the client that had gotten so bad that she was unwilling to work with the person anymore. She sought support from her supervisor, who was unwilling to provide it. She said that in every other way, she had been a responsible employee and was shocked when she got fired.

As is almost always the case, the initial stories in this case were somewhat vague and undeveloped. We sensed that each of these women had important things that needed to be said and heard, and we began to probe gently. We asked the former employee to tell us more about the situation with the client. She slowly began to open up and told about severe sexual

harassment experienced in this client's workplace. She was so uncomfortable working with this client that she just could not continue to do so. She
also told us that she had been embarrassed by this situation and had been
unable to talk about it. She said that she did not want to bring up this ugly
thing and rock the boat at work, so she presented the problem in somewhat
general terms to her supervisor. The supervisor just kept pressuring her to
go back to the client and "work things out."

The owner listened to this story. She expressed surprise, saying that she
did not know about the harassment. She asked her former friend why she had
not told her about it and said that she would certainly have protected her
from it if she had only known. She learned that the employee wanted this job
very much, needed the income, and did not know how to be specific about
what was going on without hurting her employment situation.

During the course of the mediation, the parties learned many new things
from one another, not least of which was how much they had valued the
friendship they once had possessed. At one point, one of them took a fancy
pen out of a shopping bag and put it on the table. Both parties grew teary
when this gift that the owner had once given her friend was revealed. After
some emotional exchanges, the parties began to get to work and talk about
the specifics of an agreement, and the mediation ended successfully.

This case was especially satisfying to us because the parties displayed
both empowerment and recognition. They were able to tell their stories
clearly and well. They came to a point at which they were able to talk about
what was important to them and to recognize the feelings and concerns of
the other. The mediation provided a place where they could do this in a way
that had not been possible before.

Years ago, we taught workshops for parents on *how to talk so children
will listen* and *how to listen so children will talk.* This is what we hope to
achieve today in mediation, not just with children and parents but with all of
the people with whom we work.

Helping People Talk So Others Will Listen

One of the problems with the settlement model of mediation is that parties are not always given an opportunity to "tell their story." Sometimes, in
fact, storytelling is discouraged because it distracts the parties from concentrating on the provisions of an agreement. Our colleague Mark Bennett, here
in New Mexico, tells of a lawsuit resulting from the death of a young man in
a skiing accident. In mediation, the parties—attorneys for the ski company
and the parents of the victim—became stalemated on the amount of the set-

tlement. At this point the mediator decided to get the parents directly involved and asked them to talk candidly, not about the money but about what this case meant to them. They told about their son and said no amount of money could bring him back. They revealed that money was not the real issue here. As they talked, the representatives of the ski company could hear that the parents just wanted the life of their child and his tragic death acknowledged. They wanted some kind of outcome that would honor their son. After this, the mediation took an entirely different turn, and the parties collaborated on setting up a fund for ski safety in the name of the young man.

Mediators use several techniques to empower people to talk openly and clearly about their concerns and hopes. In general, these boil down to three things:

1. Invite the parties to talk.
2. Show that you are taking them seriously.
3. Acknowledge their perspective.

We realize that these three principles may seem simple, even simplistic, but they are not always easy to achieve and require some experience to do well.

How do you invite parties to talk? This certainly includes providing the time and space to do so. If you immediately separate your parties, you provide no invitation to talk in a way that the other side will hear. But time and space are not enough. You have to make the environment feel safe enough for people to open up.

In addition to making things feel safe, we also want to show that we are serious about having the parties talk about what is important to them. Bush and Folger make a distinction between *macrofocusing* and *microfocusing*. When a mediator macrofocuses, he or she is concentrating on the "big picture," or the mediator's overall plan. When microfocusing, the mediator is concentrating just on where the parties themselves are going with their statements. Although we try to keep an eye on the big picture, Bush and Folger have convinced us that the most important topic of the moment is what the speaker is saying, and that's where our concentration should be. We think that macrofocusing discourages the disputants from telling their stories, and microfocusing encourages them to do so.

We once comediated a landlord-tenant case with an apprentice mediator. It was a tough case. The "landlord" was an apartment manager who was working at the behest of an owner who put him under a lot of pressure to collect rents and evict anyone who had a history of late or nonpayments. The manager did not particularly like this role, but his job required it. The tenant had gotten behind in rent payments. We listened as she told her story:

Her "old man" was in prison and she had become solely responsible for supporting her three children on pieced-together part-time jobs. She was desperate and wept as she told us that she did not know where her family's next meal would come from, and now on top of everything else, she was facing eviction. At this moment, we glanced over at the apprentice, who was doing some figuring on a calculator. She looked up and announced: "I see that you two are only $123 apart." That response—a gross example of macrofocusing—does not do much to invite the parties to tell what is important to them.

This comment showed that the mediator either was not listening or did not care about what the tenant was saying. We think it is important for mediators to show that they are taking people's statements seriously. This does not mean that we show sympathy or agreement; it means that we show that we want to hear the statement and that we treat the statement with respect. And we show the same respect to all the parties. Many basic mediation techniques help here. Repeating content, reflecting feelings, and summarizing show that you are listening and taking comments seriously. One of the keys to empowerment, then, is feeling heard.

These techniques are all forms of acknowledgment. When we acknowledge, we say verbally and nonverbally *that* we heard and *what* we heard. In ordinary communication, people have a hard time separating acknowledgment from support or agreement. We normally acknowledge others by showing sympathy toward their points of view. This gets hard in conflict situations when the natural "comeback" is to argue or disagree. In mediation, however, we can model a third form, and that is acknowledgment without either agreeing or disagreeing.

Most basic mediation trainings cover the topic of power balancing. The idea here is that the mediator has some responsibility for balancing the power. At first glance, this would appear to be an important step in helping parties with less power express what they want and need. Yet we are uncomfortable with the concept of power balancing, and we do not think of our work in these terms. The problem is that the mediator, who is really an outsider, cannot know what sources of power parties might have available to them. It might look as though a man is out-powering a woman by dominating the conversation, but the woman may have a great deal of power in her silence. It may look as though a well-to-do businessperson has more power than a blue-collar customer, but the customer may have connections and buying power that give him or her a great deal of power. It may look as though a parent has more power than a teen, but anyone who has raised teenagers might disagree.

Though the term is overused, we still prefer *empowerment* to describe what we do when we help people talk so others will listen. Rather than judge who has the power, we want to empower both parties to do and say what needs to be done and said, to identify the problem in their own terms, to establish what a successful outcome would mean for them, and to create ideas for achieving that outcome.

Helping People Listen So Others Will Talk

One of the problems with the notion of power balancing is that it puts too much responsibility on the mediator. In fact, the parties themselves bear much responsibility for empowering one another. Saying clearly what you want and need is only one side of the equation. The other half involves hearing well what others have to say. One of the greatest moments in mediation occurs when the parties start talking constructively with one another and ignoring the mediator. Sometimes the best intervention is no intervention. You can unwittingly dampen constructive conversation by enforcing a rigid pattern of sequential speechmaking in which each party takes turns talking at the mediator.

In the previous chapter, we wrote that good dialogue consists of living in the tension between standing your ground and being profoundly open to the other. A good mediation conversation is like this. Both sides talk openly about their needs, both listen and acknowledge each other's needs, and they together move to a new place where cooperative action can start. In this progression, we see the two-dimensional process of empowerment and recognition. In our practice, we rely on four principles for building recognition:

1. Model good listening and recognition.
2. Help the parties microfocus.
3. Acknowledge recognition when you see it.
4. Frame statements so they can be taken seriously.

When we are listening intently, restating, reflecting, and summarizing, we not only signal to the speaker that we are interested in what he or she has to say, but show the other party what this kind of listening and recognition is like. Sometimes parties are ready to "see" this modeling, and sometimes they are not. One of the values of mediation is that the presence of a third party, especially in a listening role, can bring a degree of civility to the conversation. When clients smile and express genuine appreciation at the end of a session, we like to think there is a subtext that reads something like, "Thanks for showing us how to get through this."

If mediators micro- and macrofocus, so do disputants. The macro-focusing of the disputants takes a somewhat different form, however. For them the "big picture" is their individual goals and a plan for how to prevail. One reason it is hard for disputants to listen to one another is that their attention is focused on how to get what they want—they are thinking about the best argument, response, or answer. When mediators repeat, reflect, and summarize, they not only help the speaker clarify his or her own needs, but help the other party focus on what the speaker thinks is important.

There's a lot going on in a mediation. It can be difficult at times for the mediator to get everything, let alone the disputants, who have their own emotional agendas. Sometimes being in a mediation is like listening to a radio that is set between stations—a lot of static and two or three signals buzzing together. The mediator can turn the dial slightly to bring in one station at a time. Taking time to work through one person's points, helping to organize these, repeating what seems to be most important, and reflecting feelings help everybody tune in.

Of course, many disputants can and do recognize the interests of the other party. They usually don't stand on the chair and wave a checkered flag, but they will, often subtly, show that they recognize the difficulties, concerns, ideas, and values of the other person. A good mediator will watch very carefully for these signs of recognition and acknowledge them. Because they sometimes go by so quickly, signs of recognition can be missed.

A standard tool of mediators is to help parties frame what has been said in ways that might lead to recognition of one another's contributions. As mediators, we frequently reframe statements, and there are numerous ways in which to do so:

We can reframe from negative to positive: *You have said that the dog's barking keeps you awake. I see that you would like more peace and quiet in the neighborhood.*

We can reframe from past to future: *You are angry that he did not show up for your meeting last week. As I understand it then, things will move more smoothly if he attends future meetings.*

We can reframe from hostile to neutral or positive: *You feel that you were not told the truth and you would like to work in an environment in which honesty is valued.*

We can reframe from individual interests to community interests: *You have asked for a door to be put on your office. You seem to feel that the group could work more efficiently if everyone had a bit more privacy.*

We can reframe from complaint to vision: *You said that Tommy hasn't been home for dinner in 2 weeks. You would really like to have more time for the family to be together, wouldn't you?*

We can reframe from criticism to request: *You said that Maude was pretty vague in her evaluation of your work. It sounds as if you want her to be more specific in the future.*

In each case, reframing makes tough statements easier to hear and the perspectives of others easier to recognize. It can also help to move the conversation from one that is spiraling downward to one that begins to cycle up.

▪ Building Community Consciousness

The United States, in which we live, is mostly an individualistic society. Empowerment and recognition in private disputes reinforce this pattern because they focus on individuals' respective interests. Sometimes you can have a very successful mediation within the strict confines of individual interests. Indeed, principled negotiation is designed to do exactly this: Come up with a solution that meets everyone's individual interests.

For a variety of reasons, however, strict adherence to individual empowerment, recognition, and negotiation belies the full potential of mediation. For one thing, not all disputes can be cast accurately as a clash of individual interests. Often community interests are at stake. Sometimes the interests of third parties are at stake. Also, many cultures, even within this country, are more collectivist than individual in orientation.

For us, though, the most compelling reason to try to move beyond individual interests is that, although the parties do not always realize it, every dispute is part of a larger system of people, actions, settings, and influences. Further, the participants through their interaction construct the system itself. If they think about the problem in system terms, they can begin to see ways to reconstruct or redirect the system. This is why, as mediators, we often feel the need to help parties think in a larger, more inclusive frame, a process we call *building community consciousness.*

We use the term *community* here to mean some kind of collective group. It might be a region, town, neighborhood, organization, work team, family, or maybe just the two disputants together. Divorce mediation is a perfect example of the need to move from an individualistic to a system context. Any divorce can be seen as a clash of individual interests. The couple is fighting over who gets what property. They struggle with who gets child custody and visitation. They struggle over who should pay alimony and child support and how much. Although a divorce mediation can be conducted as individual negotiation, a moment's reflection leads to the inescapable conclusion that the husband and wife are part of an ongoing system that has a history and a future.

Our friend Anne Kass, a family court judge, sees many divorcing couples in and out of court. She reports that they tend to think divorce is a way of being able to escape having to deal with "the jerk," but that couldn't be further from the truth. In the vast majority of cases, the ex-spouses will be part of each other's lives for a long time. Anne suggests that divorcing couples redefine their relationship and treat it as a business, a very strong business that will work well into the future. When they do this, they have successfully built a community consciousness. She sees this as transforming a relationship rather than throwing it away.

When we work with disputants to develop community consciousness, we try to do three things. First, we attempt to raise awareness of the connections parties have with one another and other parties. Here we are interested in helping them see that their decisions are affected by and affect the interactions and lives of others. Second, we want them to think about how they can participate in reconstructing or redirecting the system so that it works better. Finally, we want the parties to look for the resources in the larger system that can help them move in a more positive direction. In essence, then, we are asking participants to think about how they influence the community and how the community can influence them.

Raising Awareness of Connections

It would be totally inappropriate for mediators to tell disputants how they are connected to some larger system. We cannot know, and any attempt to do so would be our story, not theirs. We can ask questions to help them identify their own connections. As we pointed out in Chapter 1, any system can be defined in numerous ways, and the parties should decide what system is most important to the events affecting their current situation. When they do this, they begin to broaden their stories to include other characters, larger events, and longer plot lines. Their stories reveal connections within the community.

When it seems right to move to the community level, we will begin asking *systemic questions,* which can help accomplish several things:

> They can ask people to characterize how other people behaved or reacted to an event: *How does your son react when your wife takes a long phone call?*
>
> They can ask participants how they reacted to the actions of others: *After your neighbor came over to talk to you about the fence, what did you do next?*
>
> They can ask people to compare the behavior of one person with that of others: *You said that the staff gets agitated when the boss does not get home from a business trip on time. Who gets most agitated?*
>
> They can ask for reflections on past change in the system: *How are things different since Sally got promoted?*
>
> They can ask for ideas about how the system might change in the future: *You said you wished the team acted like a well-oiled machine. What would need to change for them to act like a well-oiled machine?*
>
> They can ask how one event leads to or connects to another: *You have said that paychecks are often late. What are things like around the office when the paychecks do not arrive on time?*

Because they ask people to think differently about their disputes, systemic questions often sound odd and can be disruptive if they are not well phrased or if they are mistimed. These questions need to be asked "in the grammar of the participants." In other words, use their words and language as much as possible. Make these questions fit into the context of what is being discussed. When asking systemic questions, use the answers as a basis for new questions so that the respondent can think more deeply about community connections.

Constructing Community Through Appreciative Inquiry

Once people become aware of the community connections and start to think systemically, it is very easy for them to explore creative ideas for making a better system. This move in mediation has some distinct advantages. It creates the feeling that participants can make things better for themselves. They come to realize that a better community can only be made cooperatively. They look for positive resources in the system to help them redesign it, and they imagine possible futures. Participants can get unstuck and think of new patterns of interaction that can move them forward in a positive direction.

When we work to help disputants move forward in this way, we usually mix systemic questions with appreciative ones. Appreciative questions have several qualities, as outlined in Chapter 2:

- *These questions ask participants to tell about positive experiences.*
- *They help parties explore the positive shadow behind concerns and complaints.*
- *They ask about the positive energy driving a negative situation.*
- *They encourage parties to imagine positive futures.*

Like systemic questions, appreciative questions should be asked in a conversational and natural way, in a language with which the parties can identify. As much as possible, they should adapt to what the parties are talking about in the moment. They can also be used during a pause to redirect the discussion.

We are always looking for openings for good appreciative questions. For example, if a disputant is complaining about a problem, we might ask him to tell us what he would prefer. Let's say that one of the parties in a workplace dispute is complaining that the other person is constantly eating in the office. We could ask her to tell us why that bothers her, but in an appreciative frame, we would prefer to ask, "What office behaviors do you think contribute most to a comfortable environment for everyone?"

If one of the parties is telling about a problem or complaint, we might ask him for a positive example to help set the stage: "You said that your office is always frantic and behind schedule. Have you ever worked in a really good environment? How was that different?" We also look for opportunities for the parties to be prospective: "What would need to change for your office to feel less frenetic?"

When things seem to be stuck in a mediation, we often ask the following question: "If this mediation works really well for you—let's say you are driving home and feel really good about what just happened—what would need to happen here today to make you feel that way?"

Systemic and appreciative questions can be combined in interesting ways to help participants see possibilities and positive connections in the system. For example, if someone is complaining about a problem, we might ask, "Who is doing the most to help and how are they helping?" Or, "If you were to put together a group to help solve this problem, who would be involved and why?" If a disputant comes up with an idea for change, we might ask, "What would be the first step you would take and who would you talk to first about it?" We might even ask, "If your idea were adopted, who would appreciate it the most, and how would they show their appreciation?"

You can see that we are painting a picture of an ideal mediation. The parties started without being able to articulate their needs or hear the interests of the other side. They got to the point in which each was empowered to define his or her needs and goals and to understand and respect those of the other. They then began to realize how the situation has been created by their interactions with one another and other parties. They are starting to think more broadly about the system, how things are connected, and how it might be improved, and they are ready to begin making some decisions about the future. At this point another cluster of goals comes into play—building commitment.

▪ Building Commitment

If sufficient groundwork has been laid with empowerment and recognition and community consciousness, eliciting commitment will probably be fairly easy. In some cases, the groundwork is already laid—there is understanding, respect, and a desire to collaborate. When this happens, the parties are ready to get to work drafting a set of action plans. In a circular fashion, too, mutual commitments further build empowerment/recognition and community consciousness.

For the most part, building commitment is a process of helping the parties define their issues, see their options, and have a critical discussion of the pros and cons of possible actions. This is really a decision-making process that involves three subgoals—issue framing and deliberation.

Issue Framing

Issue framing is a process of identifying the questions that the disputants need to work out, listing these, prioritizing them, and generating solution options. With a simple mediation, there may be only one issue—how to divide an inheritance, let's say. In more complex mediations, there may be several. For example, in a workplace mediation, the parties may need to talk about workload distribution, use of space, schedules, and office layout. Once all are in agreement about their issues, they should decide what order they wish to use. There are several criteria for *agenda setting* covered in any basic training, and we will not list them here. The most important thing is that the parties themselves collaborate in setting their own issues agenda.

The parties then take an issue and brainstorm various options. These are pared down and clustered into a small number of approaches. For example, let's say that a divorcing couple must decide what to do with their home. Perhaps they have three approaches—sell the house and divide the proceeds, have the wife and children live in the house, or rent the house and delay a decision what to do with it.

To get to a realistic set of options, it is often helpful to make quick judgments about several ideas that have been listed. We like to use a system called YNI, which stands for "yes," "no," and "interesting." We once did a multiparty workplace mediation for a large federal agency. After the group agreed upon their issues, they brainstormed possible solutions. We listed these down the left side of a flip chart page. We then went down the list again and had the parties make judgments about each idea—*yes, we like it; no, we do not;* and *this is interesting.* We then threw out the no's and went more carefully down the *interesting* list. We had some very fruitful discussion of why certain ideas were interesting, which helped the group clarify their values. Often at this point, a final set of solutions emerges from the discussion and an agreement can be written.

Often, however, there are still different opinions or confusion about the best course of action. When this is the case, we encourage a more careful deliberation about the options.

Deliberation

Deliberation is a careful consideration of choices. If we get to this, we like to suggest that our parties talk about each option one by one. They should discuss why they like it or do not like it, what advantages and disadvantages would accrue from it, and what tradeoffs they would or would not be willing to make. In deliberation, you may find ways to combine ideas or invent new ones.

Sometimes, the parties will come to consensus after deliberating on the options. Other times, further discussion is necessary. One interesting approach is to use *scenario deliberation,* in which the parties create alternative stories of the future without being specific about how they might achieve these futures. They deliberate on the merits and drawbacks of each scenario, pull out those aspects of the story they wish to incorporate in a consensual future and then discuss how to get there.

In basic mediation training, you learn that one of the most important aspects of the agreement process is *reality testing,* looking hard at what is acceptable and doable and what is not. If deliberation is done well, reality testing is embedded in it. The parties have a pretty good idea of what will work and what will not by the time they go through careful analysis of their issues, option generation, and deliberation.

In this chapter we have described a process in which a solid relational base is constructed and a systemic problem-solving process is employed. In real life, mediations are rarely this tidy. The respect and understanding necessary for collaborative problem solving cannot always be built. Often it is built momentarily, and we discover that relationship issues need to be revisited throughout the session, even during issue framing and deliberation.

We would like to end this chapter where we began—with the need to work relationally, collaboratively, and systemically. We have presented some techniques that can be helpful, but in the end, we must adapt our interventions to what is happening relationally, collaboratively, and systemically. Let the disputants decide where they want to go and work with them to help them get there.

▪ Resources You Can Use

Bush, R. A. B., & Folger, J. P. (1994). *The promise of mediation: Responding to conflict through empowerment and recognition.* San Francisco: Jossey-Bass.

Domenici, K. (1996). *Mediation: Empowerment in conflict management.* Prospect Heights, IL: Waveland.

Fisher, R., & Ury, W. (1991). *Getting to yes: Negotiating agreement without giving in.* New York: Penguin.

Folger, J. P., & Jones, T. S. (Eds.). (1994). *New directions in mediation: Communication research and perspectives.* Thousand Oaks, CA: Sage.

Kolb, D. M. (1994). *When talk works: Profiles of mediators.* San Francisco: Jossey-Bass.

McKinney, B. C., Kinzey, W. D., & Fuller, R. M. (1995). *Mediator communication competencies: Interpersonal communication and alternative dispute resolution.* Edina, MN: Burgess.

Moore, C. W. (1996). *The mediation process: Practical strategies for resolving conflict.* San Francisco: Jossey-Bass.

Pearce, W. B., & Littlejohn, S. W. (1997). *Moral conflict: When social worlds collide.* Thousand Oaks, CA: Sage.

Shailor, J. G. (1994). *Empowerment in dispute mediation: A critical analysis of communication.* Westport, CT: Praeger.

Slaikeu, K. A. (1996). *When push comes to shove: A practical guide to mediating disputes.* San Francisco: Jossey-Bass.

Working With Groups and Teams

During our years as teachers in colleges and universities, we often assigned group projects to our students, bringing forth both sighs of relief and groans of disappointment. Many students were relieved, knowing that a group project would give them an opportunity to combine a diversity of viewpoints, working styles, resources, and experiences, resulting in a potentially better project and better grade. Other students looked at this project with dread, imagining the tension associated with combining different personalities, different schedules, and differing motivations and the inevitable conflict that occurs in that situation.

In our practice, we work with many other groups, such as families, sports teams, self-directed work teams, staff groups, informal interest groups, church groups, taskforce groups, and our own project workgroups or task teams. We have experienced the satisfaction and the frustration of group communication and are committed to understanding the dynamics necessary for this communication to be effective. Whenever people work together, their successful interaction depends on the interpersonal skills that enable them to make decisions, manage conflict, share participation, and build a supportive atmosphere that helps them achieve their goals.

■ The Team Concept

We differentiate groups from teams by their functions and purposes. Gay Lumsden and Donald Lumsden in their book *Communicating in Groups and Teams: Sharing Leadership* (1993) define a group as "two or more persons who are interacting with one another in such a manner that each person influences and is influenced by each other person" (p. 13). Such a group of people gathered with us in the Santa Cruz Mountains in 1996. These folks were interested in resolving conflicts peacefully while thinking and working systemically. We worked together over the course of four days, modeling new ways of working and discussing our common and separate visions. This gathering is a perfect example of a group, but we would not call it a team. It was a loosely knit group of individuals who experienced a wonderful four days of mutual influence.

When does a group like the participants of our Santa Cruz conference become a team? The Lumsdens say that a team creates critical work processes and shares responsibility and participation in achieving their mutually defined goals. At the time of this writing, we are organizing a second meeting of the Santa Cruz group. This meeting will be designed to move the group to the level of a team. We will have a joint project on which we all work. We will plan it together, design the process and goals together, do the work, and debrief what happened. When this takes place, we will see that wonderful transformation from a loose group with a common interest to a tight team that accomplishes a task.

We recently contributed to a group's becoming a team in the Tri-City area in Washington State, when we designed and facilitated a three-day community conference and taught a concurrent facilitator training session. The conference was designed to explore possible collaboration in building a positive future in the three cities. The group was made up of citizens and agency leaders concerned with the future of their community. After three days, some of the participants coalesced into a team with a task of making 2000 the "Year of Our Children." This team has begun to create goals, along with a process and actions to achieve those goals.

In any system, it takes work to make "the whole more than the sum of its parts." How do you capture the potential of the whole? This question is being explored in many different arenas across the world. The emphasis on teams and teamwork is like a revolution, with an increasing number of organizations relying on teams to yield better ideas and productivity.

We have watched Total Quality Management (TQM) sweep the United States and other countries for the past thirty years. The basic concepts of TQM are mirrored in many projects and methods designed to promote full participatory involvement by employees and customers throughout all levels of an organization. The process is not always easy, however. For example, some TQM "quality circles" met with problems when the desire for teamwork was not genuine, the members were not trained, and teams were not adequately supported. On the other hand, there are multiple success stories of increased productivity—goals met *under budget* and *before deadlines.* In these cases, teams were able to create interdependencies that fostered commitment to the team's vision, goals, or objectives.

The increased use of teams has been the subject of countless books, articles, and discussions. As we have explored the dynamics of teams, and specifically, teams within systems, we see the powerful potential of teams to influence the workplace and the world. Teams can be effective when basic components exist, such as shared responsibility, respect for diversity, development of a cohesive identity, and consensus on mutually defined goals. Teamwork differs from individual effort because of the interconnected energy of its members that creates a system of actions. As a system, *the team works within a context of other groups, teams, and systems.*

Advanced Micro Devices (AMD) is a leader in the microprocessor industry. Like many of its competitors and partners, AMD uses natural work teams extensively. These teams are responsible for managing time, money, and other resources; recognizing and rewarding achievement; providing the initial charter and scope of the team's work; and making necessary changes. Team members share the responsibility for team functions, and the facilitator coordinates team efforts and communicates with the manager when appropriate. Not only must teams coordinate their own efforts, but they must relate constructively to the larger system too. For example, teams may overlap on shifts, and AMD has built-in processes for teams to manage their interface with other parts of the system. We devote most of this chapter to methods that can be effective in environments like that at AMD. In the next chapter, we present the AMD case in more detail.

▪ Mediation and Teams

As traditional vertical management models are replaced with horizontal ones in which leadership and management duties are shared, attention to conflict management processes becomes critical. More and more organizations are recognizing the need for mediation processes, and they are exploring a variety of methods for integrating mediation as a conflict management process. Typically, two general approaches are common—*external* and *internal.*

A large nonprofit organization in our community provides work and career opportunities for the physically and developmentally disabled. One of the key stress points in this organization arises from the need to manage diversity, which inevitably contributes to conflict situations. This organization uses an **external** approach and chooses to hire mediators from the outside. In external mediation programs, organizations contract with independent mediators or mediation organizations to provide services, usually on a case-by-case basis. These external methods of managing conflict within groups and teams can be effective, especially when conflicts are noticed and attended to early enough and given appropriate time and resources. We also have often seen that these approaches can be a "Band-Aid" that ignores larger systemic concerns. In these cases, one conflict may be resolved, but a new one erupts to take its place.

In contrast, many organizations use an **internal** mediation program. A model for this type of conflict management is the city of Albuquerque. As in many large organizations, the city consists of many departments (legal, planning, human resources, etc.) and occasionally creates smaller project teams or committees. The city's Alternative Dispute Resolution Office coordinates this program by training mediators and setting up mediations. When a dispute arises in one department, trained employee-mediators from another department are brought in to mediate the case. The city occasionally contracts with outside mediators, but this is becoming increasingly rare as its internal program has strengthened. Many schools also use internal mediation programs, in which students are trained to provide mediation services to other students, even to staff and faculty. An efficient use of resources, internal mediation also benefits students as they learn a new way to communicate in conflict situations.

In our work over the years, we have experienced the strengths and limitations of both the external and internal approaches. Although both models can be beneficial, we are becoming convinced that neither will be entirely successful unless groups and teams draw on the benefits of mediation very early—before bridges begin to blaze. Fortunately, a third approach makes early intervention more likely.

We call this third approach *systemic*. It infuses mediation skills and practices throughout the workplace and creates a culture in which differences are managed seamlessly. Systemic mediation involves a set of characteristics and skills that contribute to an effective work environment in which conflict can be managed constructively. Here, employees are encouraged to manage conflicts in their work environments as they arise at the lowest possible level. This model is appropriate in any organization in which employees are empowered to establish positive work relationships among themselves. For this reason it is especially suitable in team-based organizations. We call it the Team Mediation System.

The Team Mediation System (TMS)

We have been amazed as we experience the versatility and skills that mediators offer. We have helped people use these tools in many types of everyday situations. For example, when a colleague was trying to decide where to spend her vacation time, we used mediation skills to help her identify her interests, explore a variety of options, and reality test those options in consideration of her interests. Another set of friends, a couple, was struggling with the decision about whether to adopt a child, and through mediation, we helped the two move forward with the decision. We have used the same tools in numerous work situations, helping groups do strategic planning and problem solving. As we stated in Chapter 3, mediation is a kind of collaborative communication that is useful and effective in a variety of circumstances.

The same skills, then, can be useful in helping members of work teams manage their interaction. In the TMS, members are invited to use a "new way of speaking and listening" that helps them actively and creatively manage their own problems as they occur. The potential for such a system is that teams can head off problems before they even reach a conflict stage. When a conflict does happen, it is managed directly and skillfully. The TMS is really a constructive pattern of communication that builds healthy, functioning teamwork.

Consider what might happen, for example, if an outspoken team member complained openly about the frequency of team meetings. In the normal course of events, several kinds of reactions would be common. Some members would probably jump on the bandwagon. Others would likely become defensive. And some would just examine their fingernails hoping the point would be dropped. In the TMS, however, none of these kinds of reactions would be encouraged. Instead, something like this would happen: A colleague sitting across the table might say quite directly, "You seem to feel very strongly about minimizing time away from your project," whereupon the meeting critic might reply, "Yeah, I have so much to do and hate to see my time wasted at these meetings." The colleague might then ask "How can we conduct our team business without taking too much time away from work?" A productive conversation could then commence, exploring creative options for getting the team meeting work done. We actually witnessed this scene in a group we were observing. A team member simply acknowledged the critic's point and asked the team to discuss creative solutions—two simple mediation techniques. In the remainder of this chapter, we explore the TMS in greater detail.

▪ Creating an Environment for the Team Mediation System

Jokes are made about the "quick fix" gimmicks consultants bring into organizations. Employees often recall times when they left a training session shaking their heads, half in amusement and half in anger that they had wasted time away from the job. The problem with so many "systems" is that they are paste-in-place procedures not supported by the environment in any way. They are recipes void of nutrition, architecture with no sense of landscape. Organizational skills should both build and reflect a positive environment.

We stress the importance of building such an environment in any system that uses mediation. What does a constructive conflict-management environment include? We think there are five overlapping characteristics: a safe environment; collaborative communication; power management; process management; and positive facework. These five characteristics are illustrated in Figure 4.1.

Safe Environment

In a safe environment, the team is able to explore its differences productively and without threat. Teams thrive on similarity and difference. Similarity builds cohesiveness, and difference breeds creativity and perspective. The problem is that we too frequently see similarity as a resource and view difference as an obstacle. Our colleague Murray Anderson-Wallace, an organizational consultant in the United Kingdom, reminds us that by letting differences stand in view, systems can open up many channels for productive action. Exploring difference, however, often feels uncomfortable and unsafe. When team members do not feel safe, they may be hesitant to contribute, resort to disruptive behavior, withdraw, or quit.

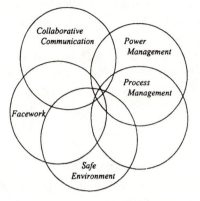

Figure 4.1. Characteristics of a Positive Environment

A safe environment requires management commitment to diversity and constructive conflict management. Management must be able and willing to help employees learn processes and skills for exploring multiple perspectives without threat. One reason our work with AMD was successful was that management held a vision of positive cultural change. An example of a message that came from management to teams using the TMS is, *"We support your movement toward greater responsibility, autonomy, and accountability. You can create a work environment that supports constructive conflict mediation."*

Another component of a safe environment is the valuing of confidentiality. The work environment needs to allow confidential conversations to occur, with a process to bring any appropriate concerns to management. Confidentiality is a difficult concession for many organizations. They are concerned that private conversations can lead to solidarity, where management-bashing employees gain strength. Another fear is that management will not get the information it needs about employees to keep the organization running smoothly. As team members and management negotiate this safe environment, these issues and many others can be taken care of with upfront "agreements." These discussions may include:

1. This is a system that does not seek to place blame, determine right or wrong, or punish or reward individuals.

2. The team will create its own decision-making methods and practices.
3. The team can make periodic "process checks" to evaluate the TMS and look toward improvements.
4. Leadership of the team can be decided by the members. This may be rotating leadership, project-specific leadership, or a designated leader.
5. Each participant agrees to make a good faith effort to continue communicating appropriately within the TMS. This may include respecting confidentiality of discussions.

If team members feel safe enough to air their concerns, an environment is created where members also feel free enough to generate creative options for the issues or problems they are facing. In Chapter 3 we outlined a number of principles for establishing a safe environment, all of which apply to good communication in teams.

Collaborative Communication

In a collaborative team environment, members have shared goals or priorities and rely on each other (and themselves) to achieve these together. Countless books and articles talk about collaboration and the power it yields. We read once that a gaggle of geese can fly higher than a single bird because the uplift of their many wings creates a synergetic force. Thomas A. Kayser quotes a *New York Times* article, "Although the Boston Celtics have won 16 championships, they have never had the league's leading scorer and never have paid a player based on his individual statistics. The Celtics understand that virtually every aspect of winning basketball requires close collaboration among all players." Like a basketball team, a workplace team must realize the importance of working together to manage conflict when it arises or even before.

A common fear in use of collaborative systems is that participants have to "give up" too much. They think that because they have to consider others' actions, their own actions will be minimized. In our experience, when groups shift to collaborative work environments, individuals don't end up losing power. They end up with a new power of sorts, a shared responsibility that calls for diligence and motivation. Team members need to realize the gain they get from the diversity of the team and commit to unleashing that potential in a communication system that gives them ultimate responsibility over their decisions and actions.

Michael J. Papa and Daniel J. Canary consider collaboration to be a feminist perspective that involves power in partnership and compassion rather than domination and aggression. This collaborative "power" is not a passive one, however. Conflict provides an opportunity for the team members to empower each other through a safe and creative discussion or even confrontation. The key here is the collaborative goal of achieving mutually satisfactory results (a goal of most mediations!). Utilizing collaboration shows concern for work goals (production) and for relational goals (people). By working together to achieve the production goals, team members can also maintain their relationship using the TMS skills.

Power Management

In teams where power is managed, team members are empowered to express what they need from others while also being sensitive to the variety of styles and ways in which team members express themselves. We have already mentioned that there can be power in partnership, power in collaboration. This is not the traditional view of power. Many organizations relish the fact that they can harness power through domination, loudness, lots of money and other resources, bullying tactics, and on and on. Many stories display the results of organizations that use this type of power.

A teacher friend of ours, Patti Gronewald, has mobilized a different kind of power—partnership power—in her classroom. A team of three teachers shares the load, and each contributes from her own wealth of experience and knowledge. The kids love coming to this classroom with its variety and depth. In contrast, another teacher at the same school insists on teaching from a position of traditional power. This person wants to control what the students learn and how it is presented. As you can imagine, the kids dread going to the classroom.

In the TMS, the focus is on empowering all participants instead of balancing the power that exists. Let's use the metaphor of a seesaw to illustrate this. When two children are riding on a seesaw, they adjust their weight to make the action flow smoothly. The equipment itself does not tell them anything; instead, the children have a feeling of imbalance and adjust their positions to accommodate for it. In a mediation, the mediator gives parties maximum opportunity to speak, listen, explore, and choose (gives them the seesaw), and it is up to the parties to adjust as they see fit. As we explored in Chapter 3, mediators are not in much of a position to judge how much weight or power each player has, but they can create an environment for empowerment to take place. In similar ways, the TMS allows power dynamics to be played out in a safe way, respecting each person's unique way of communicating and learning. No one makes decisions about who has more power. How can you judge who has more power anyway? Does higher status or more experience automatically mean more power than lower status or less experience? Does a louder person have more power than a quieter one?

We have already referred to the work of Bush and Folger, who identified the importance of empowerment in mediation practices. In conflict situations, team members may become fearful, disorganized, and unsure of what to do next. To empower them is to give them a more confident entry into the next steps and a sense of their own capacity to handle the situation. Remember our earlier example of the outspoken colleague who didn't want so many team meetings? He was asked, "Do you have any ideas how you could contribute maximally to your project and still help us deal with the important team issues that we discuss in team meetings?" This was an empowering response because it gave him the opportunity to consider his own contributions, gaining a clearer realization of what matters most to him and what options he can offer. Guided by the work of Bush and Folger, we see that team members can feel empowered when:

1. They clarify their priorities.
2. They see why these priorities are important to them (and to the team).
3. They become aware of the options available to them and their control over those options.
4. They increase their use of conflict management skills: listening, communicating, organizing, option generation, and option evaluation.
5. They make clear and deliberate decisions.
6. They assess the strengths and weaknesses of their own (and team) interests and make decisions in light of these assessments.

Individual team members can aim for communication environments that utilize empowering interactions. The resulting self-worth and security can induce team members to bring confident contributions to the team.

Process Management

In an environment that honors process management, teams address the "how" of their work as well as the "what." These teams will make several key decisions about what processes they will use to work through conflicts and even about how they will make decisions. When we get together with our colleagues from the Public Dialogue Consortium, we always experience the pleasure of process management. When we need to make a decision about next steps in a project or even about internal organizational issues, this group first spends a little time determining a process to make that decision. It is often tempting to jump right into the "work" side of the project and discuss all the implications. Almost always, someone will make the comment "Let's step back and discuss 'how' we should go about deciding." Once, when we needed to design an event, we spent 15 minutes discussing the process and decided:

1. Kathy and Jeff would meet and brainstorm the general features of the design and develop a couple of samples of possible interventions.
2. Jeff will fax these samples to Stephen, who will finalize the design and bring it to the next PDC meeting.
3. Stephen will present this design to the rest of the team.
4. The team will evaluate this design in terms of the objectives.
5. Stephen will facilitate this evaluation, recording questions and comments.
6. The team will commit to next steps after the evaluation.

We know that these process steps look laborious and time-consuming to many people, but we feel that a clear process allows our team to function effectively and do the work the way we do best. Plus, everyone feels ownership in what we do.

An important question to ask when considering process management is "How will these processes be directed?" Teams need to determine the type of leadership they are going to use. Teams usually need to establish both process and content leadership. This can be done by using the same person, different people, rotating leadership, or allowing leadership to emerge. When one person handles both the process and content leadership in a team, he needs to be clear which facet of the team he is attending to. These facets can often be confused, and the leader has to "take off the process hat and put on the content hat" on occasion (and vice versa).

A team member acting as a process leader can aim to clarify communication, prevent miscommunication, assist the team in managing conflict, and note the patterns of communication that exist or arise in the team. A deliberate conversation can then take place about *how* this team can manage the conflict or deal with the pattern of communication. T. A. Kayser gives a great definition of a facilitator that works well for TMS leadership. He sees a facilitator as a person who helps a group free itself from internal or external obstacles or difficulties so that it may efficiently and effectively pursue the achievement of desired outcomes. As a process leader, the facilitator guides the group along steps such as these:

1. Determine the goal or desired outcome of the session.
2. Note the direction that the group is actually heading. Is it toward the goal or desired outcome?
3. If it is not in the intended direction, the leader may intervene to offer redirection of the group toward its goal or desired outcome.

One organization in which we participated used a creative rotating facilitation for its work team. They had monthly project meetings and took turns facilitating the process. Each facilitator brought a technique from the process toolkit, introduced it at the beginning, used it in the meeting, and evaluated it in the end. This was done for one year, and the team accumulated 12 different facilitation tools to be used in the future internally or with clients. Five of these methods are described in Table 4.1.

Another method of process leadership is quite innovative and takes a real dedication to process management: emerging, or shared, leadership. Here, the team members would carry on their work processes with the confidence that they all share some responsibility for leadership. They use good communication skills and rely on each other to manage conflict as it occurs. Occasionally, a situation may arise in which one team member would offer to lead the discussion. Maybe this offer would not be made explicitly but would be more implicit, with the team member stepping in to assume leadership of the process at various points. In very trusting and committed teams, we have seen one member go up to the flip chart, uninvited, and begin facilitating the conversation. Once the TMS is underway in a team situation, we can imagine more emerging, or shared, leadership would be used.

As in mediation sessions, it is helpful for process managers in teams to consider team ground rules, guidelines, or common courtesy considerations. Chapter 3 offers a few of these considerations in the mediation introductions. Sometimes the guidelines may be task-specific: "Team members will use the color copier by appointment only," or "A brief outline of the day's activities will be left on the bulletin board by team members each day." Some of the guidelines may be process-specific, such as: "Each per-

Table 4.1 Sample Facilitation Methods

Multiple Perspectives Wheel—Put the team members' names around the edges of a circle of paper. Pin this "wheel" to a larger circle of cardboard. On the cardboard forming the outer circle, put a variety of perspectives on the issue to be discussed. Spin the wheel and see whose name ends up next to each perspective. That person will discuss the issue at hand using the perspective shown. Repeat the process as many times as is fruitful.

Decision Styles Agenda—Go through the agenda, discuss each item briefly, then make a team decision about whether to: DO IT; DELAY IT; DUMP IT; OR DELEGATE IT.

Garden Metaphors—Take a planning issue facing the group. Have each member think of one way the planning process is like a garden. Have the members present and discuss their garden metaphors. Then explore things the metaphors suggested that might help stimulate the creativity of the group in its planning effort.

Asset Brainstorming—For each of several team goals, brainstorm the various assets the team has to accomplish the goal. Then discuss the ways the team can mobilize these resources.

Reflection Process—After each committee report, the team members reflect on what they noticed and the connections they observed as they listened to the report. After the reflection period, the person who gave the report responds to the group's reflections.

---

son is allowed uninterrupted speaking time" or "We will discuss confidentiality considerations at the beginning of each team meeting." Process leaders can refer team members to these guidelines as needed.

A process leader also can benefit from setting a clear agenda before a meeting, a session, a project, or a time period. This agenda creates a set of assumptions for the team and allows team members to trust the process and focus on the work at hand. This is why we often like to refer to leadership as "process management." It should be called on at the beginning of each phase or project and revisited throughout the duration.

Facework

A team environment in which "face" is managed allows team members to maintain a feeling of dignity and self-worth. Team members often work in close proximity. Whether they are on an assembly line, in a research center, in a suite of cubicles, or even on a basketball court, team members work next to each other, sometimes close enough to be touching. In these situations, team members are very aware of their "face," or positive image. When mediation skills are used in teams, an effort is made to maintain an individual's face—not making a person feel embarrassed, noticeably uncomfortable, put on the spot, or defensive. Even more, good facework honors the contributions and diverse styles of team members. If we practice positive facework, we acknowledge that we are different but that each contributes something important to the team.

One time, we became members of a somewhat contentious university department. The faculty and staff got along OK, but they did not always see and respect one another's contributions. The tendency was to focus on a person's foibles, weaknesses, and failures rather than on his strengths, contributions, and successes. We began to take note of the latter, to compliment people on what they did well, to solicit help in areas of strength, and to acknowledge publicly the contributions of everyone. This is what we mean by positive facework.

Our colleague Leslie Fagre describes process managers or mediators as "face managers," emphasizing Fisher and Ury's components for effective negotiation described in *Getting to Yes*. Their popular advice, "Separate the people from the problem," helps team members save face. When a conflict arises in a team, the members can view the conflict as a problem for the team to solve or an issue to be managed. A face-saving environment does not allow the team to see the conflict as someone's fault or as a signal that someone needs to change.

We have seen group discussions in which whining seems to be escalating and dominating the conversation. A team member or team leader who is interested in saving face for the whining participants can make comments that don't single them out or comment directly on their disruptions. For example, "These points are very helpful, and I want to make sure we get back to them, but I think we need to get back to the agenda or we won't get through everything in time," or "It looks like many of us feel very strongly about this issue and have some definite concerns. What would be a helpful way for us to discuss them so everyone gets to talk?" Ideally, after these types of responses, defenses will not be raised and people can feel safe enough to make further contributions.

Leslie Fagre describes three types of face needs—autonomy, fellowship, and competence. *Autonomy face* is exhibited in people who want to project an image of a mature, responsible adult, in control of his or her own fate. These people want to be seen as self-sufficient, independent, and reliable. This face is threatened when people feel that they are being constrained or imposed on by others. Team members can use a variety of techniques to protect one another's autonomy face:

- They can practice nonjudgmental listening. At least at first, listeners need not impose their own personal values, suggestions, interpretations, or judgments.
- They can use *active listening,* in which they give each participant their complete attention and show that they want to understand and take a team member's comments seriously.
- They can *restate* what they heard to check their own understanding and correct any miscommunication.
- They can ask *open-ended questions* to allow the participants more choice in deciding how much or what kind of information to share.
- They can use *reality testing* to explore the feasibility of options without showing judgment or disbelief. Participants are allowed the opportunity to change their mind if they need to.

A second type of face that can be threatened in team situations is *fellowship face.* People want to feel a part of the group. If they are besieged by feelings of jealousy, betrayal, fear, mistrust, or anger, they find it difficult to contribute in productive ways to the team's work. Team members can address these feelings by practices such as:

- *Commending* colleagues on the progress they have made *together.* A member might comment on how hard the parties worked in discussing a difficult issue, how they showed a cooperative spirit in the last discussion, and how far they have gone together exploring the issues.
- *Inviting* other team members to participate. A party who feels of lower status may not believe he or she has much to contribute. Team members can remedy this situation.
- *Modeling* cooperative behavior.

Competence face can be threatened when the role with which a person identifies is jeopardized. An employer wants to be viewed by employees as a good boss. A landlord wants to be seen by the tenant as fair. A service provider wants a customer to think he or she is providing a quality service at a decent price. In each of these relationships, the parties' competence face is significant. Team members can address competence face in a variety of ways:

- They can acknowledge one another's ability to solve disagreements collaboratively rather than competitively.
- They can meet privately to vent their feelings out of the public eye.
- They can reframe statements to neutralize attacks or accusations that may slip out, especially regarding professional role capabilities.

We see these face needs as universal human needs that arise often in interpersonal relationships. The skills that mediators use can be applied in team situations to constructively maintain face needs and keep the process flowing smoothly. Appropriate energy can then be used to manage any conflict that arises.

▪ Putting the Team Mediation System to Work

As we have mentioned already, we are intrigued with the many applications of mediation skills, principles, and methods in other arenas in life. Whether it is interpersonal decision making, large-group strategic planning, or workplace team conflict management, the language of mediation has proved to be valuable and powerful. We developed the TMS specifically for self-directed teams that work together throughout a project or as permanent knowledge-based natural work teams. Since we have implemented this process in work teams, we have used the TMS in a variety of other venues. We are using this TMS concept in our work with a national laboratory that is concerned with its communication with the public. We led the laboratory team through a process using TMS skills to "keep the conversation going." We have used a TMS focus internally, as we do our work on projects, with clients, and with each other. We have offered TMS skills to facilitators who are leading large groups of people through exercises to build community or envision a future.

We call the skill set associated with the Team Mediation System *LARC*, which stands for Listen, Acknowledge, Respond, Commit. The general idea is that when team members are talking about an important issue, maybe one that is a potential source of conflict, they *listen* well to understand one another, *acknowledge* one another's perspectives, *respond* clearly with their own point of view, and *commit* to a course of action.

Although we discuss LARC in a linear way, it is not a linear process. These are simultaneous skills that are used to enrich discussion and construct an environment that possesses each of the five overlapping characteristics we addressed in the previous pages. Figure 4.2 illustrates the LARC model.

We once noticed a disturbing bumper sticker on a car that read "Conversation is like competition, and the loser is the listener." This sad statement emphasizes a set of assumptions we often notice in communication situations. Speakers are privileged, and listeners are the passive ones, the unim-

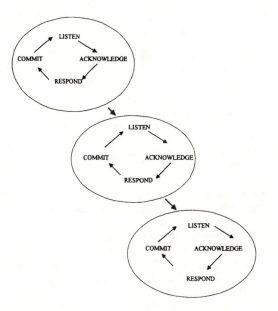

Figure 4.2. LARC Model

portant ones. Karen Foss and Sonja Foss challenge this assumption that significant communication is produced by the speaker by reminding us that "communication is a process jointly constructed by the interactants that does not necessarily have a clear beginning and ending." We often invite people to "interact in the system," a process that carries weighted responsibilities for speakers and listeners. Notice in the LARC skills outlined in Table 4.2 the assumption of shared responsibility for communication.

Listening

Why do people have the conception that listening is a passive process? Is it because it is done so quietly, with sound waves hitting the eardrum? Or is it because we are lazy, thinking that we can relax when we listen? We know that this misconception is the cause of many interpersonal and workplace conflicts. How many times have you heard, "He was not even listening to me?" or "She just doesn't understand," or "They did not even hear a word I said." These problems occur because we forget that listening is an active

Table 4.2 LARC Skills

Step 1: Listen
   DELAY judgment.
   ATTEND to as much of the message as possible.
   ASK questions to clarify.

     Step 2: Acknowledge
       RESTATE the content of what others say.
       REFLECT the feelings shown by others.
       IDENTIFY interests, goals, values, and needs.
       COMMEND positive contributions.
       REFRAME comments in constructive ways.
       SUMMARIZE what has been achieved.

       Step 3: Respond
          STATE your own interests, goals, values, and needs.
          DISCOVER mutual or differing interests, goals, and needs.
          FRAME issues and options.
          SUGGEST positive resources for change.
          DISCUSS team implications.

          Step 4: Commit
             DECIDE on an appropriate course of action.
             CREATE a positive environment for discussion.
             EXPLORE the problem further.
             SOLVE the problem collaboratively.
             MEDIATE through a third party.

---

process, where the work *begins* when the sound waves hit the ear drums. The listener has the responsibility to take the information that was heard, think about it, attempt to clarify any misunderstanding, assimilate it with previous information, and give some kind of feedback. In the TMS, we offer a listening step as a priority for team members working in conflict situations. As this system was implemented at AMD, team members were invited to pay attention to one another's statements. If those statements are attended to early, before they blow up to the stage "no one is listening to me" at which work processes might have to stop to deal with the resulting conflict, teams can conserve time, energy, and money. The starting point for good conflict management is to *listen for what others think, feel, and want—their reasons and experiences.* When we encounter a different opinion, try to do three things:

Delay judgment. Thomas Crum, in his book *The Magic of Conflict,* notices that people often see communication as a big scoreboard in the sky.

He sees that when one person speaks, the other person gets ready to refute the statement and get a point on the scoreboard each time the refutation hits home. Before judging, we should first try to comprehend the message. It is important not to be too quick to criticize what the other person is saying, *even in your head.* There will always be time to make judgments later, but in effective conflict management, the careful listener does not react quickly.

Attend to the whole meaning of the message. When we try to sense as much as we can of what the person is expressing, our understanding seems more complete. Remember the exercise where you state a sentence many times with a different emphasis each time? Each sentence has a different meaning, which would not be apparent if you just heard the words.

My boss never looks at me when I am speaking.
My **boss** never looks at me when I am speaking.
My boss **never** looks at me when I am speaking.
My boss never **looks** at me when I am speaking.
My boss never looks at **me** when I am speaking.
My boss never looks at me when **I** am speaking.
My boss never looks at me when I am **speaking.**

Listening to all aspects of the message means listening for the content of the message, the importance of what is said, the implications for others, the nonverbal aspects of the message, and the feelings behind the statement.

Ask questions to clarify. Who said listening has to be nonverbal—a quiet process? Since listening is active, we have the responsibility to attempt to clarify, through our questions and comments. We believe that people have good reasons for their own opinions and perspectives, within their own experience. Try to find out as much as you can about the other person's perspective by asking good, nonjudgmental questions.

For the person who says, "I just can't take any more time out for these staff meetings," we may ask, "How does it affect your work when you attend the staff meetings?"

For the person who says, "My boss never looks at me when I am speaking," we could ask, "What kind of situation are you usually in when this occurs?"

For the person who says, "I will not work that shift for you," we might ask, "What is it about my shift that makes you hesitant to take it?"

This type of careful listening is difficult, especially when ideas clash. We have been impressed with groups and teams that do take the time to work at listening. This up-front work prevents the defensiveness that arises in many conversations and can spread like wildflowers through the group.

Acknowledging

Instead of the quest for one more point in the "scoreboard in the sky," communicators have another choice. After they listen to a comment, a perspective, an opinion, or even a complaint from another person, they can indicate that they heard the comment and are attempting to understand it. Acknowledging what you heard signals a respect for the interaction and a desire to continue the conversation and move past the difficulties. We often use the exercise in our class of having a discussion with one rule—you must acknowledge the comment of the person who just spoke before you can give your own comment. Participants in this exercise often remark on the difficulty of remembering to acknowledge before responding quickly with a perspective of their own. Following are several productive ways to acknowledge.

Restate the content of what others say. If a workplace supervisor says, "I want to make sure everyone is at the weekly staff meetings," you could restate in these ways:

- So you want 100% attendance at the weekly meetings (restate main points).
- It sounds like you want to make sure the meetings are attended each week (restate important detail).
- Did I hear you right? You want to take responsibility for getting all staff at the meetings (restate information you might not quite understand).

We notice that restating often feels unnatural to people. To smooth out these statements, we suggest easing into the statement with these beginnings and endings.

Begin your restatements with:

- Let me see if I heard you correctly . . .
- You're saying . . .
- It sounds to me like you think . . .

- Let me make sure I understand you . . .
- Let me summarize what I've heard so far . . .

End your restatements with:

- Is that correct?
- Did I get that right?
- Do I understand what you're saying?
- Did I hear you correctly?

These acknowledgments help people to understand and to be understood, while modeling a quest for continuing the conversation with respect and interest.

Reflect the feelings shown by others. Besides restating the content of others' messages, it is important to attend to the emotional dimension of the communication. Imagine that your officemate is moving to another department and she states, "I am so upset to be moving so far away. I will miss all of you." The following reflections acknowledge this statement.

- You seem very sad to be leaving our department (reflect strong expressions of emotion).
- It sounds like you are especially upset at the thought of leaving all of us here in these cubicles (reflect feeling statements that may not be heard by other members of the group).
- You are very frustrated by this move (reflect feelings that come across through body language).

Reframe comments in a constructive way. In contrast to restating, in which we mirror the words fairly closely in our acknowledgment, reframing changes the conceptualization a bit to soften and neutralize hostile comments, encourage forward movement, and introduce creative possibilities. A worker says, "I am so frustrated with my secretary. She keeps forgetting to give me my messages." This comment could be reframed in the following ways.

- You would like to see all your messages (reframe from past to future).

- You are interested in keeping up with all your phone calls (reframe from negative to positive or neutral).
- So messages are not getting received (reframe from personal attack to problem definition)?

We know that reframing is tricky and takes careful thought to include in our communication. Be careful not to change the meaning of someone's comments so drastically that the person thinks you did not hear him right. The tone of voice is important, speaking in a way that allows the person to correct you if necessary: "Yeah, that's what I meant," or "No, that's not what I meant."

Summarize what has been said or achieved. Mediators often joke that when they are stuck in a particularly divisive mediation, they can rely on their old friend, summarization. When we want the group to see its progress, to identify shared concerns, to define issues, or to stay on track, we may say, "Let me summarize what I've heard so far. . . ." If important information has been shared, especially if two or three points, proposals, or ideas have emerged, the group can see its progress when someone summarizes those points. If a transition is needed or the conversation is out of focus, a summary can provide movement in the desired direction. We also find that if the conversation is tense, or thought time is needed, a summary gives a refreshing break. Natural breaking points are also good times to summarize, such as at the end of an agenda item, before or after a break, at the end of a meeting, or at the beginning of the next meeting.

Identify interests, goals, values, and needs. An important component of most mediations is a stage in which parties move toward constructive, creative problem solving. We acknowledge a person's interests, goals, values, and needs by identifying them. When a person makes a demand or suggestion, look for the following:

- what he or she hopes to gain
- what's important to the person
- what is wanted or needed
- how the team or group might benefit

When a person complains about something, look for

- needs not being met
- frustrated goals
- hidden ideas about how things might be improved

This acknowledgment may come naturally ("It looks like you are interested in this") or it might be a deliberate break ("I have an idea. Let's take a few minutes to talk about what is really most important to us in this matter. John, I hear you emphasizing more private time. Is that something you really want?"). If the participants are beginning to suggest ideas for settling the conflict or issue, it might be helpful for someone to identify the interests, values, goals, and needs for the group ("It sounds to me like we are all interested in better communication in our workplace. Some of us want better use of e-mail, and others of us are interested in more staff meetings. What do we hope to gain from this conversation?").

Commend positive contributions. The forms of acknowledgment we offer here are helpful in assuring others that you are listening, interested in understanding, and not immediately criticizing. We want people to feel confirmed for the efforts made, the process being used to communicate, and the actions undertaken in the interaction. After a difficult community meeting, in which divisive issues were discussed, one way to acknowledge this hard work is to commend in these ways:

- Commend hard work and progress—*"Wow, you really put a lot of effort into this meeting. Good job!"*
- Commend positive, respectful interaction—*"I appreciate the way you handled this delicate conversation with respect and attention."*
- Commend recognition of others—*"It sounds as if you have made an effort to see Bill's point of view. Thanks."*
- Commend forward movement—*"Hey, we are making progress. Your contributions were most helpful."*
- Commend shared concern and common ground—*"Even though we have different perspectives on the location of the bridge, it sounds as if we are both concerned with easing traffic congestion."*
- Commend agreement—*"It sounds as if we all agree that the city council should attend the next meeting."*

It takes careful attention to nonverbal communication to commend in a genuine and meaningful way. Deliberate eye contact signals that you have a point to make that you want the other to hear. Of course, it would sound silly to overload a conversation with such commendations or compliments, making others defensive in much the same way criticism would. Sometimes a brief acknowledgment can be the key that unlocks the passageway to a forward-moving conversation. Other times, the acknowledgement is passed by in favor of more pressing content statements. Either way, we encourage an acknowledgment step *before* responding with your own comments and viewpoints, keeping in mind that you can commend another person without agreeing with him.

Responding

In our trainings and classes, when we teach LARC skills, students are often relieved to get to the "respond" step. Here is where they are able to make a point, share views, and offer a perspective. Remember the scoreboard in the sky we mentioned earlier? This step is *not* the time to breathe a sigh of relief and say, "Now we can get our point on the scoreboard." This step is an appropriate response to what you have listened to and acknowledged. We will explore five productive ways to respond.

Let's return to the community meeting. The central planning committee has been working on a plan that may include a bridge's being built to connect two communities. The planning committee has just discussed the effect that the bridge will have on schools. People have voiced various comments that have been acknowledged appropriately. Although perspectives differ greatly on this topic, an atmosphere of respect still exists. The following responses may be appropriate:

1. *"I am concerned about overcrowding at the elementary school on the east side of the proposed bridge. My goal will be to assess the effect of a new bridge on the schools."* This response **states your own interests, goals, values, and needs.** A pragmatic response, it states objectively what the speaker wants.

2. *"I hear that the developer needs a decision on this proposal in the next month. I cannot see our making that decision until we get the traffic analysis from the city, which may take six weeks."* We realize in our conversations that all participants will not agree on the issues. We often respond in these situations by **discovering mutual or differing interests, goals, and needs.** This type of response serves as a springboard to the next problem-solving steps needed to manage the conflict.

3. *"We have three main issues that need resolution. We have to decide the bridge's effect on the schools, the traffic, and the proposed budget."* An organizing response like this one serves as another type of springboard, from which the group may decide to set an agenda for problem solving based on the identification of issues. This type of response *frames issues and options.*

4. *"Since many of the city council members have expressed interest in our discussions, let's get on the agenda for the next city council meeting."* One way to listen is to search for positive resources within the system. These may be people, actions, money, time, previous work, or other resources that might come in handy for the work at hand. These resources can be plumbed to help with the current effort. This appropriate response *suggests the positive resources for change.*

5. *"Noting our differing perspectives, I see that we can hit a snag if we meet with the neighbors too soon. Let's have one more committee meeting to iron out the remaining issues."* It is helpful to remind the group of the implications for the whole committee. We like to see our responses as *scoping in* (seeing the smaller system and its status) and *scoping out* (looking at the larger system and the interaction of systems). Moving from an individual response to a group response scopes out a level. Another level of scoping out may note, *"The neighbors are not organized enough to have this discussion with us. When they and the developers are prepared, we will indicate a desire to meet with them."*

These responses address team or group implications and are usually heard best by participants who themselves feel "listened to" and acknowledged. Our responses must be stated without any hidden agendas or criticisms. Nothing is so unprofessional as a response that includes a speaker's dislike of another's comment, *"Obviously, our neighbors on the east side do not care about overcrowding in schools. I think we should do a school assessment to note the effect of the bridge."* These types of comments are quite the showstoppers, bringing an otherwise productive conversation to a halt.

Committing

How often do we work on a conflict situation with a group or team and then walk away wondering, "What did we accomplish here?" We might have hashed out a subject, "talking it to death" (as some people declare), but often we do not know what our next steps could or will be for further attention to the subject. There are some inevitable advantages to hashing out a conflict. We might learn more about one another's perspective. We might learn more about our own perspective. We might spur on our group, bringing the realization that something must be done. We might even touch on some options that could possibly help us all manage the conflict more effectively. But if our group does not commit to a course of action, chances are that we may not revisit the issue again until it rears up in our face.

In the TMS, we utilize a skill that mediators often employ to bring some kind of closure to an issue, a conflict, or a stage in the mediation agenda. We offer a commitment step. This step occurs after some listening, acknowledging, and responding has occurred and is a *must* for these team conflict conversations. As we will explore here, there are several possible types of commitment. Although the word *commitment* may connote a decision for a major course of action, we use the term *commit* quite differently, asking that the team or group decide on some type of commitment, albeit small, every time they talk about the issue. Depending on the complexity of the issue, the importance of the issue, the number of people involved, and the resources available, these commitments might sound like the following.

We can decide on an appropriate course of action. This is the typical exchange where the team makes a decision and moves forward. Often it occurs quickly, such as, "The break is over, let's move the machine near the window." If there is time pressure, or the issue is minor, or if it affects some members of the team more than others, a quick decision might be appropriate. When you suggest a decision, these tips are helpful:

- Be open to the suggestions of others.
- Reality test the solution by discussing how this solution will work, who will do it, when will it get done, and where the resources will come from.
- Be tentative in the suggestion. We don't want to make others defensive.
- If the decision falls apart, be ready to revert to the LARC model: Listen, Acknowledge, Respond, and Commit.

We can create a constructive environment for discussion. This is a process commitment, building the right setting so all members feel safe and ready to work through the difficult issue at hand. This type of commitment often begins with a statement such as, "It looks to me like we need a separate meeting to discuss this topic. I suggest we meet in one week, at 8 a.m., with our whole team present. We can begin by setting an agenda and guidelines for discussion. Ideally, Jane can facilitate the meeting." Notice that this comment includes mention of the place, the time, the people; attention to agenda and communication guidelines; and discussion of roles. Mediators often spend time discussing process commitments at the beginning of and throughout the mediation. Teams and groups can personalize these process decisions and adopt their own guidelines for discussion. For example, one group holding a strategic planning meeting developed the following guidelines:

- The facilitator will be a process manager, guiding the process and not contributing to the content.
- The team will follow the LARC model. Time will be left at the end of the meeting for commitment discussion.
- Any items of contention will be set aside in a "bin" (flip chart page). A discussion will occur at the end of the meeting about a process for addressing these items.
- Goals for the meeting will be agreed on at the beginning. At any time during the meeting, someone can call a "process check," inquiring if the group is still on course toward the goals. If not, a process decision will be made.
- Discussion in the meeting will be confidential, unless otherwise specified.

We can explore the problem further. If time and resources permit, it is helpful to further discuss the issue, helping the team or group to better understand the problem and possible solutions. This type of commitment offers creative processes to spend more time and energy on the problem. You might hear someone say, "We have 30 minutes left in this meeting. Let's look specifically at the issue of the copy machine location, and then finish with the items in the bin."

The CVA model, developed by the Public Dialogue Consortium, has been a successful way for groups to explore a problem. This method guides the group in exploring the relationship between concerns, visions, and actions. The team can start at any of the three points and keep going around the triangle. For example, in the case of finding the right spot for the copy machine, the team might start by exploring concerns. These will be listed on paper or a flip chart. Concerns might include, "I want the copy machine in close proximity to the secretary's desk," "It would be very helpful to put the copy machine in the break room, so we all can use it," or "The copy machine needs to be out of the way, so it doesn't take up much room."

The next step in the CVA is to ask what things would be like if these concerns were met, looking for the visions. If the concerns stated previously were met, the copy machine would be placed where it was easily accessible to all staff and where it did not impede office traffic. The final third of the triangle is to ask what actions need to be taken to achieve this vision. Someone might offer to locate the machine in the break room corner for a month and then query everyone to its usefulness in that location. Someone else might offer to assist and to check with the secretary as to his opinion. The final commitments can be reality tested by again asking what concerns the team has about the course of action they have chosen, and if so, how has the vision changed. Moving around the triangle can continue until all are satisfied.

The team can use collaborative problem solving. The team can make a deliberate choice to work together to solve a conflict. Mediators often use this type of commitment and offer it in most basic mediation trainings. Look at these steps, imagining a team working through them together.

1. Define the problem as a team problem. Make sure everyone sees the problem the same way.
2. Discuss goals. What do various team members want, and what should the team as a whole achieve?
3. Brainstorm possible solutions. List solutions that will meet as many goals as possible.
4. Try to achieve consensus on what will make a good solution. Keep in mind that you are going to try to meet as many team members' goals as possible.
5. Narrow the choices to a few realistic options.
6. Deliberate on the pros and cons of each option, and discuss the tradeoffs you would be willing to make. Weigh each option against the goals and criteria.
7. Make a tentative decision.
8. Reality test the decision.
9. Discuss how to put the decision into action.

Teams may choose to mediate the conflict using a third party. In the TMS, we anticipate that teams will be committed enough to handle most of their conflicts and issues directly without the help of a third party. Occasionally, it will be necessary to call in the help of a neutral third party, trained in mediation techniques, to help the teams work through the conflict. This may be another member of the team who has a good grasp of the skills necessary to facilitate conflict discussions. In some cases where trust and neutrality are issues, the mediator may be brought in from another team.

In Chapter 3, we saw that a mediator can make the environment feel safe for discussions, building an atmosphere of understanding and respect. A mediator can also help the team build commitment and ownership of solutions they work out, further enhancing crucial team dynamics. Most important, the third party should facilitate the discussion between those involved without suggesting what they should do. The team members need to decide their own course of action. In the TMS, these are some considerations when deciding whether to bring in an outside person:

• First, since the team has had experience with the TMS, and, it is hoped, participated in a training for the necessary skills, it may be most appropriate for another team member to mediate the conflict. This can be done informally and on the spot, or the team may set up a scheduled mediation in the near future.

• If the whole team is caught up in the conflict, one team member may offer to act as a facilitator for a team meeting instead of bringing in an outside mediator. This is tricky, because the facilitator may be tempted to offer advice or suggestions. Sometimes, these internal facilitators temporarily "take off their facilitator hat" to contribute content and then return to process facilitation.

• A team should make arrangements to bring in an outside mediator when it is obvious that no other team members could take the mediator role or if the problem is very complicated or heated. If the team has already tried internal mediation, it may be time to call a mediator from outside.

• When teams feel that they need outside help, they should resist processes that polarize or build more defensiveness, such as litigation, some grievance panels, or investigations. These processes should be the absolutely last resort.

We have adapted the TMS to many venues. Because these skills are not limited to conflict situations, we sometimes call it the Team Communication System. Here, the same skills serve as guidelines for individuals to communicate in interpersonal workplace situations. We sometimes offer the system as a leadership model to help managers and others see the value of process leadership and the importance of sharing responsibility within and among groups and teams. As with all the other methods and processes discussed in this book, we always personalize tools so that they adapt to the people and groups using them.

▪ Resources You Can Use

Barker, J. R. (1999). *The discipline of teamwork: Participation and concertive control.* Thousand Oaks, CA: Sage.

Barker, J. R., & Domenici, K. L. (2000). Mediation practices for knowledge-based teams. In M. M. Beyerlein, D. A. Johnson, & S. T. Beyerlein (Eds.), *Advances in interdisciplinary studies of work teams* (Product development teams, Vol. 5). Stamford, CT: JAI.

Bush, R. A. B., & Folger, J. P. (1994). *The promise of mediation: Responding to conflict through empowerment and recognition.* San Francisco: Jossey-Bass.

Crum, T. F. (1987). *The magic of conflict.* New York: Simon & Schuster.

Domenici, K., & Littlejohn, S. W. (1998). *The team mediation system: Effective communication in teams* [Video]. (Available from Domenici Littlejohn, 504 Luna Blvd. NW, Albuquerque, NM 87102, 505-246-9890)

Fagre, L. (1995, February). *Recognizing disputants' face-needs in community mediation.* Paper presented at Western States Communication Association Conference, Portland, OR.

Fisher, R., & Ury, W. (1991). *Getting to yes: Negotiating agreement without giving in.* New York: Penguin.

Foss, S. K., & Foss, K. A. (1994). *Inviting transformation: Presentational speaking for a changing world.* Prospect Heights, IL: Waveland.

Kayser, T. A. (1994). *Building team power: How to unleash the collaborative genius of work teams.* New York: Irwin.

Lumsden, G., & Lumsden, D. (1993). *Communicating in groups and teams: Sharing leadership.* Belmont, CA: Wadsworth.

Papa, M. J., & Canary, D. J. (1995). *Conflict in organizations: A competence-based approach.* In A. M. Nicotera (Ed.), *Conflict and organizations: Communicative processes* (pp. 154-179). Albany: State University of New York Press.

Public Dialogue Consortium, 504 Luna Blvd. NW, Albuquerque, NM 87102. www.publicdialogue.org

PART III

Moving to
More Complex Systems

5
■ ■ ■ ■

Constructing Conflict
Management Systems

One of the authors has a "family meeting" twice a year with her husband and three teenagers to discuss issues that need to be addressed. Even though the teenagers grudgingly attend the meeting, everyone realizes the value of the decisions made. Throughout the rest of the year, when questions arise over differences of opinion, the family has a list of decisions taped to the refrigerator, the result of the family meeting.

The decisions are made by a process of discussion and reality testing. For example, one issue is parking. With four cars in the family and a few prime parking spots, arguments can arise. The family discussed preferences, parking problems, and arrival and departure times for school and work. An invitation was given, "What can be done to assure everyone of a place to park that works for their schedules and needs?" The responses were examined and then reality tested with other questions such as, "If Erik parks to the left of the driveway, will Pete be able to leave for work early the next morning?" A final decision is one that is satisfactory for everyone and is added to the list: *We will try to park the white van as far as possible in the rocks; Willie will park in the turnaround driveway; Erik will park in the left driveway; Pete will park in the right driveway; and Kathy will park at the front of the house.*

In another conflict that occurs in the rush of early-morning schooldays, the family can rely on the following decision: *On schooldays, Willie will drive Lucy to school on Monday and Friday at 7:10 a.m. The other days, Lucy will walk, or parents will give her a ride.* Even some small decisions that need to be recorded for future reference are listed: *Pete offers $20 to whoever sells the Chevette for $600.* Of course, this rosy description of a family meeting and resulting decisions has its snags and challenges. The decisions do not cover every issue that arises to disrupt family life, and some of the decisions outlast their usefulness. Someone may break the rules, and the list may not offer appropriate consequences for each situation.

These family meetings represent a conflict management system used to promote constructive communication and a smoother flow of day-to-day interactions. Though small in scale, it has all of the fundamentals of the conflict management systems found in large organizations. In the past ten years, we have seen an increase in the number of organizations that work proactively to construct a conflict management system for themselves. These large companies, small nonprofits, colleges and universities, and even working teams, committees, and offices see the need for a system to use as conflicts arise. The systemic practitioner views this work as important in ensuring that groups can work and live together functionally. This chapter will review some of the traditional work in conflict management system design and give some examples from our work. We will explore some basic principles of system construction and delve into the specific elements of constructing a system for managing conflict.

▪ Some Basic Approaches to System Design

The book *Workplace Dispute Resolution: Directions for the Twenty-First Century,* edited by Sandra Gleason (1997), offers a view of the emerging trends in workplace dispute resolution and methods of addressing conflict. In the introduction, Gleason discusses three general approaches for resolving disputes from the perspective of the employer-employee relationship (pp. 6-8). She calls these the *traditionalist, behavioralist,* and *principled* approaches.

In the *traditionalist approach,* used from the 1890s through the mid-1940s, conflict was seen as a destructive force, and the role of management was to eliminate it from the organization. Dispute management was a reactive method with adversarial mechanisms reflecting the hierarchical structure predominant at that time. People who created conflict did so because of their flawed personalities and bad tempers.

The *behavioral approach,* which was dominant from the 1950s through the 1980s, accepted conflict as natural in organizations. Managing that conflict occurred through strategies to prevent or reduce differences. These methods included employee training to change behaviors or attempts to change attitudes, thereby reducing the sources of difference.

Gleason says that the *principled approach* prevails today. Here, conflict is also seen as a natural part of organizational life but as necessary and to be encouraged in productive organizations. Heavily influenced by Fisher and Ury's book *Getting to Yes,* the principled approach gives more attention to interest-based problem solving, using negotiation and other alternative dispute resolution methods.

An important contribution to the growing literature of conflict management design using the principled approach is the book *Designing Conflict Management Systems: A Guide to Creating Productive and Healthy Organizations* by Cathy Constantino and Christina Sickles Merchant. We applaud this book as it supports our motto that "people support what they create." Constantino and Merchant see that people are likely to use a system of conflict management if they have had a hand in creating it. Constantino and Merchant rank such systems in importance with other organizational systems such as human resources, information management, and financial management. Following is a fairly typical method they describe for designing a system to manage conflict:

1. *Entry and Contracting.* With the assumption that this work is done by external consultants, the designer (consultant) begins where the organization is and engages in a process of learning as he or she proceeds. A *process* is designed, not a *product.*

2. *Organizational Assessment.* This is the *who, what,* and *why* of conflict management. The important questions include, "Who are the stakeholders?" "What are the types of conflicts?" "What dispute resolution processes are currently available?" The designer conducts interviews or focus groups to solicit feedback and develops a proposal to address the unmet needs of the organization. This strategy to revise the system in turn furthers the organization's mission.

3. *Design Architecture.* This is the *whether, when,* and *how* of conflict management system design. In this stage, the appropriate alternative dispute resolution (ADR) methods are determined, as well as when they should be used and how to use them.

4. *Training and Education.* Participants in the system need to know how to access the system, understand their options, and have confidence in the processes they choose.

5. *Evaluation.* The system clarifies its goals and measures progress toward those goals by evaluating methods that look at measures such as program effectiveness. These methods are created at the beginning of the design effort.

6. *Implementation*. Some testing through a pilot program is often offered, which may be a small, one-department program or a companywide pilot that precedes full implementation.

7. *Incentives and rewards*. Support for the system offers participants opportunities for recognition—a chance to achieve the mission or fulfill a personal vision—and it may affect economics or increase productivity.

8. *Resistance and Constraints*. Resistance is anticipated every step of the way. Any forces that constrain change are identified and prepared for.

We used an approach similar to this when we designed a system for managing conflict at the University of New Mexico in 1993. An ongoing assessment of conflict management options had been taking place at the University for a few years. Grievance services were available in human resources and through the Equal Opportunity Program. Students could take a problem to the dean of students, and a counseling office existed for staff. These programs were satisfactory for many problems but left a large gap in dealing with conflict situations.

The proposal we designed began in the Communication Department. Beginning with the creation of a basic mediation class, in which students would be trained to mediate disputes among students, staff, and faculty, the program expanded. A Mediation Clinic was established, and several guidelines were created:

1. The dispute resolution option offered by the University of New Mexico Mediation Clinic is one that facilitates communication effectiveness without aiming to place blame or find guilt.

2. Participation in the mediation process is a voluntary one and does not preclude the use of any other dispute resolution offices at the University of New Mexico.

3. The mediator is a neutral third party who facilitates a process of dispute resolution, issue clarification, and option generation. The role of a mediator is to assist the client in reaching a mutually acceptable resolution plan.

4. The mediator is neither a judge nor an arbitrator; the decision-making power rests with the parties.

Bill Warters, an expert on dispute system design in school settings, provided materials that were immensely helpful in creating the Mediation Clinic. Warters has since compiled a vast amount of research and information concerning campus mediation centers and the design of dispute resolution systems in higher education. Warters ran Campus Mediation Workshops at Syracuse University in 1991 and set up a Campus Mediation Center. The center provides disputants with two neutral comediators from a pool of trained volunteers. The comediators facilitate a problem-solving process between the parties. The Syracuse center was organized with a board of directors, a board of advisors, a faculty supervisor, interns, and volunteer mediators. It handles conflicts from residence halls, security, student activities, housing, teacher assistant and faculty problems, landlord and student struggles, and legal and student government issues.

▪ A Systems Approach to Design

Ironically, it is hard to describe system design systemically. Attempts to describe the elements, processes, or stages often seem linear, as you may have noticed in the outline of Constantino and Merchant's eight steps. Such descriptions oversimplify the complexity of this kind of work. One way to capture the complex nature of design work is to address several principles that permeate system design work.

System Principles

The principle of interdependence: Systems consist of a network of relationships among interacting parts. Look for the connections among things and the ways in which parts of a system react to each other. For example, employees or even departments often get trapped into negative patterns of action and reaction toward one another. The tendency is to concentrate on individual or departmental behavior rather than to scope out to the pattern of interaction among parties. When designing a system, we want to look at how those patterns might be improved. For example, we might train employees in how to negotiate with one another directly at the lowest possible level, or we might develop a regular liaison function between departments to handle a back-and-forth flow of constant negotiation.

The principle of connection: Systems connect to one another and are always part of other systems. Just as one part of a system is connected to other parts, one system is always connected to other systems. Never treat any one system as isolated. When designing conflict management systems, look for ways to build on positive connections among systems and create new positive connections. We often hear, for example, that "the left hand does not know what the right hand is doing," that resources in one part of an organization are not available to solve problems in other parts of the organization. This kind of problem means that system designers must look at the big picture and develop processes to connect systems with one another in productive ways. For example, we might make use of resources in the learning and development environment to provide ongoing skills for conflict management in production environments.

The principle of control: Systems develop self-guiding feedback loops. It is amazing and ironic that the most well-intentioned solutions reproduce the very problems they are designed to overcome. Often conflict resolution systems will actually breed more conflict. Designed systems must be self-reinforcing rather than self-defeating. Management intervention is an example of one kind of system that may actually make conflict. An alternative that has worked well for many organizations is confidential peer mediation. In some organizations, this approach may be better because it brings employees into collaborative rather than competitive relationships.

The principle of balance: Systems tend to resist deviation and maintain a steady course. If you push against the force of a system, it will tend to push back. Attempts to change a system from the outside are often resisted, as the system tends to bounce back to where it was. On the other hand, if you work within the energy of a system, going with it and directing it, you will be capitalizing on the positive energy that is already there. For example, if employees are engaged in power struggles with one another, look at power as a positive resource. What kinds of power are being invoked, and how can those sources of power be used in a constructive way to get a good conflict management design in place?

The principle of adaptation: Systems must change in order to survive in a dynamic environment. One of the paradoxes of open systems is that in order to survive, they must maintain stability, but stability in a dynamic environment requires change. Systems manage the tension between stability and change in many ways, and it is important for system designers to find the points at which stability and change intersect. You will find at some moments in organizations that employees are threatened by change and tend to act out to sabotage it. One answer to this is to find the points of frustration and develop processes that can overcome these. For example, if there were a logjam of grievances, you could find ways to resolve conflicts before the grievance stage and prevent conflicts from spinning out of control.

The principle of redundancy: Systems have many pathways for accomplishing goals. When one pathway is blocked, others open up. For example, if employees are frustrated that formal channels are not handling their complaints, they will find informal ways to act out their frustrations. A system designer, therefore, may want to build in a number of attractive, effective options for conflict management. Recognize that redundancy will happen and work with, not against, this principle.

Establishing a Systemic Mediation System: The Case of Advanced Micro Devices

Typically, organizations will create one of three types of dispute resolution systems. The first is *external,* bringing in mediators from outside the organization, sometimes even on retainers, to provide mediation services. The second common type is *internal,* in which an office or function of dispute resolution is established within the organization to intervene in disputes. The third form, which is really quite rare, is *systemic.* Here the organization attempts to infuse constructive dispute resolution capacity throughout the organization. Although we know of very good external and internal systems, we believe that the virtues of systemic mediation warrant serious attention.

We had the opportunity to help establish a systemic mediation program at the Austin Fabrication Plant of Advanced Micro Devices (AMD). AMD is a multinational microprocessor company that uses a team-based organizational structure with two types of teams. Project teams are brought together to solve a problem, make work-process improvements, or accomplish a specific task. Natural Work Group teams are individuals who work together every day, have frequent communication with one another, share goals and objectives, and coordinate their efforts. Our colleague Garry McDaniel, from AMD's Corporate Leadership Design Center, noted that this team-based structure consistently showed improvement in most areas except that of conflict management. In employee surveys, goal-setting meetings, and interviews, McDaniel found that employees wished they could get past frequent conflicts that hindered their productivity and simply made life miserable.

Knowing that our intervention was a turn in the ongoing "conversation" at AMD, we decided as systemic practitioners to work organically within their system. Realizing that many versions of "what is going on" occur naturally in complex organizations such as this, we entered the system by listening to stories from different parts of the system. We had conversations with management. We had focus groups with varying levels of employees. We met with intact teams and sometimes with cross-team combinations. In each of these meetings, we asked for stories of their interactions with each other. We asked for stories of successful team experiences and stories of challenging times, when conflict occurred.

We learned about their team structure and how each team has a facilitator, or guide, who coaches the team in using team methods, problem-solving tools, and continuous improvement tools. Frequently swamped with job tasks, this facilitator too often had to add another hat to an already demanding number of roles. The teams also had a team sponsor, the manager who is responsible for authorizing use of time, money, and other resources. This sponsor is responsible for rewarding and recognizing achievement. We found that since this person was not a member of the day-to-day work of the team, he or she was often hard to reach and difficult to update on team challenges. We even got to spend time with a team in the ultraclean "Fab" where the microchips were being built and tested. We saw the added challenge of having to work in clumsy "bunny suits," which allowed little nonverbal communication. You had to look carefully through the mask to get even a glimpse of eye contact.

We knew that change results from interacting, not prescribing, and we saw these interactions as critical to our understanding of the patterns of their communication and our ability to cocreate a system that could work for them, as they had invited us to do. We summarized our observations and presented them at a meeting of a design team made up of people from various levels of the company. This group gathered for a 2-day training, at which we offered some of the skills and methods helpful in conflict management. In the training, they were encouraged to personalize the information and construct a system that could work in their unique team-based environment.

AMD did make some interesting adaptations to our LARC model explained in Chapter 4. LARC became CLARC:

1. **Confront** each other about real or potential conflicts.
2. **Listen** to understand concerns, emotions, and needs, not just the stated position.

3. **Acknowledge** to the other party's satisfaction that you heard their position.
4. **Respond** appropriately with your concerns, issues, or perceptions.
5. **Commit** to an action plan to avoid future conflicts or problems.

A process was begun where the teams were supported and encouraged to manage their own conflicts internally. Each team and its sponsor attended an 8-hour workshop to study the CLARC skills and the requirements in the following paragraph for autonomous team conflict management. The aim was to achieve collaborative communication, process management, power management, and a safe environment where they did not feel their "face" threatened.

Management's support of this internal team conflict management system was evidenced by occasional trainings, meetings, and consultations to assess the effect and success of the system. AMD saw that sometimes, despite the best team efforts, conflicts still would threaten the health or unity of their teams. In the past, teams would defer to a higher authority such as a manager. In the new system, teams might choose third-party mediation when the issue was extremely emotionally charged, if no progress was being made with their internal efforts, or when every member of the team needed to be involved. When mediation was deemed necessary, teams were encouraged to follow a continuum of choices:

1. *Ask another team member who is not affected by the issue to mediate.*
2. *Find a mediator from another team.*
3. *Bring in an external mediator from another department or from outside the company.*

In sum, we approached our work at AMD as an "opening" that could lead to the development of a system that fit their culture and mission. We did not offer a "cookie cutter" program but collaborated with them on a process where they could build ownership and commitment to the final product. We learned much from AMD and what they now call their "Conflict Mediation Process."

▪ Revisiting the Five Characteristics of Constructive Conflict Management

At various points in this book, we have noted the five characteristics of communication that we try to accomplish in our work as systemic practitioners. When constructing systems to manage conflict, these characteristics are topmost in our minds. Let's return to them one last time and explore their impact on system design.

Collaboration

We work *with* people to construct systems, not *for* them. Any discussion of collaboration must include the following story, which is one of the roots of our motto, "people support what they create." A social psychologist, Kurt Lewin, came to the United States from Germany in the 1930s interested in the power of small groups to change people's behavior. Severe meat rationing was in place during the war, and the government wanted the public to use less desirable cuts of meat (liver, brain, tongue, etc.). As part of this effort, Lewin set up what is now a classic experiment. An audience of women heard a dietician describe the nutritional value of these cuts of meat, giving demonstrations, recipes, and a lecture. Then, half the women went home while the other half discussed what they had heard in small groups. At the end of the discussion, these women were asked to make a public commitment. Six months later, researchers asked the women who had heard the lecture about their use of these cuts of beef. Those who had participated in the discussion and had made the public commitment were much more likely to have bought and served these cuts of meat than those who had only heard the lecture. Participation leads to commitment.

When applied to conflict system design, this principle suggests that we should take advantage of internal collaborative design teams, employ cross-functional work teams, and check carefully with participants every step of the way—all these steps can lead to important ownership of the system and its results.

Power Management

A conflict management system that offers opportunities for participants to "see themselves" and "see the other" (remember empowerment and recognition from Chapter 3) includes commitments to fairness and freedom from reprisal. The system needs to be backed by all levels of management, and management should hold itself accountable for some level of the program effectiveness. Participants should feel that they can speak, listen, and be heard when meeting with a peer or with a manager. Differing communication and decision-making styles are respected in processes where power is managed effectively.

We were fortunate to work with an excellent group of individuals from the management leadership team at the Albuquerque Hyatt Regency Hotel. This team consisted of the top executive from each department, such as human resources, catering, sales, etc. The general manager, Mike Casey, impressed us by promoting processes and decisions in which he shared power with his employees at all levels. He would ask in the weekly staff meetings, "What can I do to support you?" Mike builds trust and balances power by his commitment to be flexible and responsive to changing situations, his efforts to jointly develop clear goals and approaches, and his attempts to establish communication that supports real-time problem solving. Mary Cooley, the human resources director for Hyatt, energized the employees with a working vision they could all contribute to and strive for. Consequently, the Hyatt turnover rate was wonderfully low during Mary's tenure.

A variety of options are available to help participants make clear, effective choices about how to manage their conflicts. Many systems use conciliation, mediation, negotiation, peer evaluation, settlement conferences, facilitated meetings, arbitration, grievance hearings, and, finally, legal services as options to empower participants in conflict management. We like the model of the "open-door courthouse," which allows people experiencing conflict to enter and choose from a variety of conflict management options, choosing the most appropriate for their own situation.

Process Management

Imagine four people competing for use of a copy machine. First of all, if they are lucky enough to deliberately sit down to talk about the issue, they are making progress. Most people in conflict will address it while in uncomfortable and inappropriate surroundings (such as while standing next to the copier with urgent material to be copied in hand). The conversation usually begins with an accusation, "You always use the copier first thing in the morning, and I get behind in my work." Or maybe the first statement is, "Why don't I ever get to use the copier when I need to?" What we offer in the Team Mediation System is a reminder that it is usually necessary to talk about process (the "how" of the conflict) instead of the content (the "what" of the conflict). For example, if the folks gathered around the copier could first say, "It looks like we often meet at the copier with urgent material.

Maybe we should sit down and have a conversation about copy machine use." Or someone could say, "I see we have conflicting needs in this workplace. Can I put 'Turns at Copy Machine' on the agenda for our next staff meeting?"

People need a process to work within as they address their conflicts. This could be as simple as a set time and place for the discussion, or it could be as complicated as a daylong meeting to determine ground rules for communication at staff meetings. Systems that offer this process management give participants a basis within which to operate. We like to use the saying, "Raise the umbrella under which you will be working." This umbrella is the agenda, the guidelines or ground rules, the facilitation or mediation process that is being used, and the expectations that accompany it. Common process considerations include the following:

- Who will facilitate, and what type of process will be used?
- What is the agenda for the meeting, and who will set the agenda?
- How long will the meeting be, and what constraints (such as time) do we have?
- What is the goal or objective we hope to accomplish?
- What should we do if we begin to veer off course, or move in a different direction from the goal?
- Should we take notes to capture the group's progress? How?
- What type of guidelines should we use to encourage constructive communication? How should we decide on these?
- How should we make decisions?
- What should we do with issues that we want to address but can't address at this meeting?
- How much time should we leave for determining next steps?
- What should we do with the final information or decisions resulting from this meeting?

These are just a few of the considerations for managing a process. Many groups and organizations have implicit ground rules or methods that work well for them, and it is helpful to bring these out and incorporate them explicitly. We enjoy stories of work at a particular electronics firm where employees work very well in a cubicle-centered environment. These cubicles are all centered in the middle of large rooms and surrounded by very nice conference rooms around the perimeter (eat your heart out, Dilbert!). All of the employees, including top management, are encouraged to meet often in these conference rooms to make decisions, work on projects, or discuss conflicts. A sign on the wall of each room reminds them **FIRST** to discuss the process they will use for their meeting before continuing on to the business at hand.

When we construct systems to manage conflict, we are reminded to keep the system simple. A funny reminder from Constantino and Merchant (1996) tells us,

> To make Alternative Dispute Resolution difficult to use and impossible to access, . . . require multiple levels of approval to use ADR . . . make people write numerous memos to justify their use of ADR . . . make it difficult to get approval to use ADR [and] . . . send messages that make it clear that the organization does not support ADR, that it is to be regarded as an anomaly, and that it is risky behavior to recommend use of ADR in any particular case. (pp. 130-131)

Process management is important at all levels of system design. When you first enter a system, the beginning question can be "How will we work together?" When we begin work on any project, we begin by establishing a process to work in, raising the umbrella under which we will work.

Face Management

One of the three teenagers mentioned at the beginning of this chapter is a particularly skilled "face manager." Lucy, a 14-year-old, was baby-sitting two boys, ages 10 and 7, and they were all swimming in the backyard pool. The 10-year-old boy, Trevor, thought he might be too old for a baby-sitter but was enjoying himself nonetheless. Trevor accidentally kicked a ball over the fence into a yard that was difficult to access. Lucy came to her mother and said, "The ball was kicked over the fence." They made plans to retrieve the ball later and continued the swimming fun. We know Lucy had many choices in how to relate the "ball over the fence" incident. She could have easily said, "Trevor kicked the ball over the fence." If that had been her comment, Trevor might have been embarrassed, angry, or withdrawn. Most important, he might have responded to that comment with disdain for his baby-sitter who "told on him." But Lucy saved face for Trevor. She responded in a way that helped him preserve his dignity and positive face. Nothing was lost in the exchange, but much was gained in this simple choice of words.

How do we construct systems for managing conflict that manage face? We can look at many different levels. First, we want an overall system that preserves the positive image of the organization. The system must flow efficiently enough so that all levels of the organization, including outside clients, neighbors, or observers, will see a respectful effort to help people address their conflicts. We know of one "dispute resolution office" that is very much centered in one person. This person controls all the conflicts in a very directive manner and the organization is often embarrassed by the reports coming from this office. A more positive example is the AMD program where they have created options for saving face. If a team member feels that a conflict is just too sensitive or humiliating to deal with inside the team, there is a confidential route to take that conflict to a manager who can set up an outside process to deal with the problem.

We also want systems that manage face on individual levels. The 8-hour training offered to all team members at AMD includes a section on skills to help "save face" in communication interactions. One example of quality attention to face management is a thorough discussion of agenda setting at the beginning of meetings. No one in the meeting should be surprised by an agenda item, especially if it is accusatory or demeaning. When differences arise that may disrespect a person or persons, the system should be able to attend to it constructively, without raising defenses or anger, *or* deliberately set up a time, place, and method to look at the conflict.

Systems for conflict management should utilize mediators and facilitators who can help participants save face in threatening situations. We know that if there is conflict, there is going to be opportunities for disrespect, embarrassment, and defensiveness. Mediators and facilitators can use skills to reframe these issues in ways that keep the conversation moving. We were recently at a workplace mediation that was tense and potentially accusatory. Fourteen staff members were meeting with their executive director and the CEO of their company. As mediators, we took the face-damaging comments we heard and reframed them in the following ways:

- "Our team leader does not respect my ideas and suggestions. I have lots of skills, and they are not used!" *Mediator: "You want an environment that has full team participation. Can you tell me what that would look like at a weekly staff meeting?"*
- "Our team is not empowered to make decisions. There is too much control at the top." *Mediator: "It sounds like you want the team as a group to have authority to make decisions about the project and procedures."*
- "Some people waste so much of our time at meetings, telling stories and dominating the conversation." *Mediator: "I hear you saying that you want efficient, well-planned, and organized meetings."*

With these reframings, the person who is dominating, the person who has been making unilateral decisions, and the person who is not respecting other ideas will all be able to continue in the conversation because their "face" has not been damaged.

Safe Environment

We know that the conflict management systems we are constructing in this chapter are probably not those in which we see spectacular results, with a big winner and a big loser, with the parties walking away afterward saying comments like, "We finally found out who is guilty!" The systems we are discussing utilize processes that involve hard work for the participating parties. These processes invite transformation, which entails a close look at our differences as well as our commonalities. This attention encourages a kind of communication that involves risk, sometimes stepping out on a limb. We earlier talked about "standing our ground while being profoundly open." If we are going to address our conflict in this manner, we need to feel safe. The communication must occur in a place where participants are willing to explore multiple perspectives without threat. How do we create such an environment?

As we construct the system, we must ensure layers of confidentiality. Programwide, these are sometimes difficult decisions to make. At the University of New Mexico, for example, confidentiality was a tough issue. Upper-level management, such as deans and chairs of departments, wanted to know if there were repeat offenders coming through the mediation program. They would wonder whether a professor could come to mediation every year on sexual harassment issues but the mediation never be brought to the deans' attention because it was confidential. We compromised on this issue, in the spirit of the gains and risks of a new program. If a person (the professor, for example) was sent to mediation by a university administrator, the Mediation Clinic would inform that administrator whether or not the person went through the mediation. We would give no information about the results or the issues discussed. We would simply inform them that so-and-so attended mediation on a particular date. If the person came to mediation invited by the other party, no one would be informed of the actual mediation.

Confidentiality clauses help participants feel safe in that they can share opinions, perspectives, and stories that they might not be able to voice otherwise. A system must protect participants from retaliation, guarding them from being ambushed for bringing an issue to the process. Mediators often discuss implications with the participants, exploring with them the possible consequences of bringing their disputes forward. The conflict management system must have safeguards so these consequences do not occur. For example, in a mediation we worked on recently, one person was afraid of harassment when he returned to work. We asked the manager, who was the other party in the mediation, "How can Orlando feel safe to return to work with the possibility that coworkers may know about this mediation?" The manager offered herself as a "first resort" if there was any hint of retaliation, and this offer was recorded in the mediation agreement.

Mediators and facilitators in these programs must be trained in skills where they can help the participants interact safely. We earlier mentioned the story of a divorcing couple who were continuously rehashing past hurts and painful stories. We offered a ground rule, to speak only of the present or future, not of the past. The couple could then continue discussing safely, with each person more apt to consider the other's viewpoint when working out a future working relationship. Agenda setting, clear introductions to the process, opportunities to ask questions or take a break during the sessions, skills such as summarizing and reframing—these are some of the methods that a mediator or facilitator should use to ensure safety.

We often tell the story of a case we mediated at the Metro Court in Albuquerque over money among family members. We had offered an introduction, building trust and ensuring a safe environment for the discussion. After 30 minutes of storytelling, the siblings began to raise their voices and accuse each other of very hurtful past events, such as abuse and dishonesty. As this exchange escalated, one of us stood up and respectfully asked them to consider their communication and the disruption it was causing in the mediation and in their relationship. We reminded them of some common courtesy guidelines we had offered for the communication in the mediation and asked them to consider a different kind of communication. They politely told us that they would prefer to talk in the loud and threatening way, as they had not had this conversation in many years. Because they were at least communicating, they wanted to continue. We sat down and let them continue. The mediation ended without an agreement, and we still wonder if the conversation was helpful to either of them.

Five Characteristics in Action: Working in Argentina

We are privileged to work with a wonderful group of people in Argentina. This is a country with a fairly new democracy, struggling to put a system in place that can offer shared decision making and deliberate choices about how to address conflict. Much of our work with the Argentines consists of training and consulting. We have worked with their blossoming school mediation programs, their challenging court-related mediation services, family and youth mediators, public issue facilitators, and organizational conflict management professionals. These are people who want to learn from our successes and our failures (us North Americans) and build a unique system that is appropriate for their culture.

One example of our work was a consultation with a community mediation program in Buenos Aires. This huge and very successful program is offered by the city government to serve many communities and neighborhoods in the metropolitan area. The program had completed hundreds of mediations in the past two years but wanted to bring the program to another level of organization by looking at the design of the whole system.

As they expressed their system design concerns to us, we began to think carefully about what we came to call the *assessment-evaluation cycle.* Assuming that assessment and evaluation are a necessary part of any system, we suggested that they should be considered systemically. As such, they are not distinctly different processes but are ongoing analyses of the current conditions, programs, and interventions. Instead of looking at a dispute and immediately asking "What should we do?" (or "What intervention should we choose to impose on the disputants?"), we suggested that a broader frame be considered.

Interventions should be evaluated in terms of how they change the current conditions, and current conditions should be used as a guide for creating programs and interventions. We played together with several different formats for this circular process. All of these are based on the five characteristics of constructive conflict management and basic communication goals. The conceptual structure we offered our friends in Buenos Aires is summarized in Table 5.1, and its applications are presented in Figure 5.1 (A-D).

We talked with our friends in Buenos Aires about several tools that might be used in the assessment-evaluation cycle. Assessment and evaluation data can be gotten from the providers, from clients, and from third parties. This diverse form of assessment and evaluation constitutes a kind of triangulation between self, participant, and observer points of view. At the same time, a number of data collection methods can be employed. Some sources and tools of assessment and evaluation are outlined in Table 5.2.

Let's say a neighborhood in Buenos Aires was experiencing numerous complaints about barking dogs. How might the mediation program begin to

Table 5.1   A Conceptual Structure for Assessment and Evaluation

---

Assess current conditions in terms of five characteristics of constructive conflict management:

> Collaborative communication
> Power management
> Process management
> Facework
> Safe environment

Then . . .

Develop **interventions** that achieved the following goals for participants:

> Empowerment and recognition
> Community consciousness
> Commitment building

Then . . .

Evaluate interventions in terms of how they affect **current conditions** in regard to the five characteristics:

> Collaborative communication
> Power management
> Process management
> Facework
> Safe environment

---

address this situation? Actually, they could begin from any point on the assessment-evaluation cycle. For example, they might do an assessment of the current conditions with a survey or interviews. They could establish a pilot program of animal-complaint mediations, perhaps relying on referrals from the police department. After a while, they would do another assessment, make adjustments in the program, and proceed. At various points, they might scope out by interviewing neighborhood representatives and city officials. Other times, they might scope in by, for example, asking disputants in barking-dog mediations to evaluate the process.

When this cycle is flowing well and working systemically, it becomes difficult to distinguish the interventions from the evaluations and assessments. Our colleague Elsbeth McAdam says there is no space between inquiry and intervention. Assessment and evaluation questions are a kind of

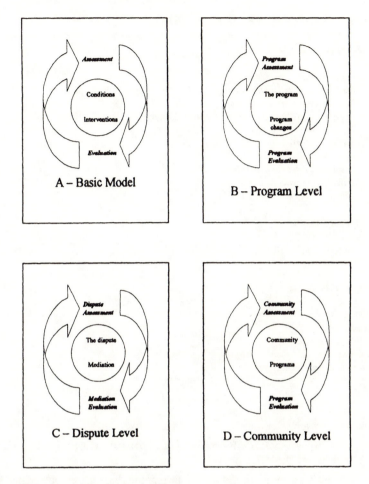

Figure 5.1. Assessment Evaluation Cycle

intervention that creates new possibilities for participants. When we are assessing the current conditions of a neighborhood, these questions enable people to think about and to articulate their perspectives in ways they might not have had the opportunity to do before. In mediation processes, this opportunity is an important step in problem solving. In our work, we often ask questions in an appreciative frame. Samples include the following:

• Tell me about some high points of working in your organization. When did you feel engaged or passionate about your work?

Table 5.2 Assessment and Evaluation Methods

The source of evaluation:
Self-evaluation:
For example:
Mediators or comediators evaluate their own performance in a case.
Trainers reflect on how they did in a training.
Program staff conduct a self study of their program.

Participant evaluation:
For example:
Disputants are asked to evaluate a mediation.
Participants evaluate a training.
Clients evaluate a program.

Third-party evaluation:
For example:
Observers complete a report on a mediation session.
Community members are interviewed regarding their perceptions of a program.

The form of evaluation:
For example:
Checklists
Rating scales
Observation guides
Interviews
Debriefings and reflections

- What do you value most about your community?
- What do you want for the future? What traditions, values, approaches, methods, or decisions would you like to see?
- Pretend it is ten years from now. You are reporting back to us about the status of your organization. What would you like to be saying?

Several examples of assessment/evaluation tools are included here in tabular form.

A System in Formation

As we mentioned earlier, a conflict management designer can enter a system through a variety of openings. Practitioners can be invited to design a whole conflict management system, or they can consult on one part of an

Table 5.3 Comediator Debriefing Form

---

1. How did we contribute to effective

   Listening
   Acknowledgment
   Responding
   Commitment

2. When we did these things, how did they contribute to improving

   Collaborative communication
   Power management
   Process management
   Facework
   Safe environment

3. When and how did we help the parties gain

   Empowerment and recognition
   Community consciousness
   Commitment building

4. What might we have done differently to help the parties listen, acknowledge, respond, and commit?

5. What might we have done differently to help the parties achieve the five characteristics of collaborative communication, power management, process management, facework, and safe environment?

6. What might we have done differently to help the parties achieve the three goals of empowerment and recognition, community consciousness, and commitment building?

---

ongoing system. It is even possible to create an opening, as we often do in our work.

At the time of this writing, we are in the process of helping an organization construct such a system, and we entered from a surprising opening. This organization is a nonprofit group that supports people with traumatic injuries by providing a meeting center and services. This agency was organized with a board of directors and a steering committee with the help of many community members who give them support. We were contacted to facilitate a board of directors meeting on certain challenging issues. For example, the group was struggling with a few individuals who seemed disrespectful and annoying in meetings. The group also had to give public presentations and became frustrated with some individuals who were behaving

Table 5.4 Disputant Interview Guide

---

1. At its best, mediation should be a safe environment in which the parties can discuss their issues. How safe did you feel? What did the mediators do to help build a feeling of safety?

2. Often disputants are able to develop a feeling of collaboration in a mediation. Did you ever feel that you and the other party were able to collaborate? What made this possible? How did the mediators assist?

3. We think that the mediation should include processes that work for the parties. Was the process helpful and comfortable for you? How might it have better met your needs?

4. Many people feel that mediations are successful if the parties have an opportunity to say what is important to them in a way that the other party can understand and recognize it. Did you have an opportunity to tell your story effectively? How did the mediators help with this? What did they do to help you understand the perspective of the other party? What might they have done differently?

5. We hope that each party is treated with honor and respect. Were you treated respectfully? Did the mediators help build an atmosphere of respect? Did they do anything that might have made the session feel less respectful?

6. What other comments do you have about this mediation session?

---

inappropriately during these meetings. We had many choices in entering this system. We could question them about these communication practices that were giving them such grief. We could do a small training on "communicating in public" and "conflict management in organizations." We even could have scheduled a group mediation session to discover and heal the differences that were causing them conflict. We decided to run this meeting with an appreciative turn in their conversation. Here is the agenda we offered:

1. Introductions: Members introduce themselves and answer this question, *What is one hope you have for the organization?*

2. Establishing a Goal: As a group, discuss what you would like to accomplish by the end of this meeting.

3. Exploring Successful Interactions: Privately, each person will answer two questions on a sheet of paper:

    • *If you were in a meeting where you were communicating effectively, making good decisions, and moving toward your goals, how would people be interacting?*

Table 5.5 Mediation Observation Form

As you watch this mediation, check the mediator behaviors you see and reflect on how these behaviors helped achieve the goals and characteristics indicated. Use extra pages if necessary.

Mediator Behaviors

☐ Acknowledging
☐ Active listening
☐ Agenda setting
☐ Agreement writing
☐ Caucusing
☐ Clarifying
☐ Closing the session
☐ Defining the problem
☐ Encouraging
☐ Establishing criteria
☐ Establishing guidelines
☐ Explaining the process
☐ Identifying interests
☐ Introducing mediation
☐ Inviting options
☐ Issue identification
☐ Microfocusing
☐ Questioning
☐ Reality testing
☐ Reflecting
☐ Reframing
☐ Remaining neutral
☐ Restating
☐ Summarizing

Mediation Goals	*How did the mediator(s) help achieve this goal?*	*How did the mediators detract from achieving this goal?*
Empowerment & Recognition		
Community Consciousness		
Commitment Building		

Conflict Management	*How did the mediator(s) help create this characteristic?*	*How did the mediators detract from this characteristic?*
Collaborative Communication		
Power Management		
Process Management		
Facework		
Safe Environment		

Table 5.6 Participant Survey

You recently participated in a mediation at the Community Mediation Center. We would appreciate your candid evaluation of this mediation session. Please answer each of the following questions by circling the appropriate response:

1. How effective were the mediators in helping the disputants work together to solve their problem?

| Highly effective | Effective | No opinion | Ineffective | Very ineffective |

2. To what extent were you given the opportunity to talk about what was important to you?

| Much opportunity | Some opportunity | No opinion | Not much opportunity | No opportunity whatsoever |

3. To what extent did the mediators give you an opportunity to help determine the process that was used in the mediation?

| A great deal | Some | No opinion | Very little | None |

4. How well did the mediators work to build respect within the mediation?

| They worked very hard at this | They tried somewhat | No opinion | They didn't try very hard | There was no effort at all |

5. To what extent did the mediators help build a safe environment in this session?

| They did a lot | They worked somewhat | No opinion | They did very little | There was no effort here at all |

6. What is your general evaluation of this mediation?

| Excellent | Adequate | No opinion | Inadequate | Poor |

Please write any comments you might have about this mediation:

- *If you were at a presentation with the public and it was going very well, what would be happening?*

4. Group Discussion: Discuss the responses from the questions and list them on a flip chart as "Characteristics of Successful Interactions."

5. Making the Characteristics a Reality: Discuss with the group this question, *"What would have to happen for these characteristics to be a reality in your work with the organization?* List answers on a flip chart.

6. Commitment Steps: Discuss the "next steps" the group could commit to, making the characteristics a reality.

7. Reality Test: For each of the commitments, determine who will initiate it, what will be done, when it will happen, where it will happen, and how it will be accomplished.

The tone of this meeting was positive and constructive. As participants discussed their stories of successful interactions, they revealed the value of clear agendas; respectful talk that did not attack, insult, threaten, or put others on the defensive; and environments of productivity and shared goals. For example, one member told about a time when a disruptive participant in a meeting was reminded of ground rules and asked to withhold critical comments until a later time. These stories began to paint a picture of the communication environment they would like to create at their organization.

When they began to discuss steps to make this picture a reality, the group became energized as they saw the possibilities. The discussion began to focus on boundaries or parameters for their meetings, a basis for communicating that participants could operate within. They mentioned that they needed a "tangible meeting process" and "agreed-upon principles for communication." They hoped to offer to participants "principles of effective and ineffective behavior" and "methods to handle violations of ground rules." Many next-step commitments were discussed, but the one the group agreed upon was to begin constructing a conflict management process. They would begin by determining some meeting guidelines or ground rules to provide communication parameters. A time, place, subcommittee, and agenda were decided upon. Here is the agenda they followed for this follow-up meeting:

1. Revisit the following aims of the process:
   - Work with difference as a positive resource.
   - Build good working relationships.
   - Collaborate to make a positive future.
2. Privately answer the following question on a piece of paper: *What ground rules or guidelines for communication have worked well for you in your work or life?*
3. Discuss which of these guidelines would work well in this organization.
4. Discuss ways of handling violations.
5. Decide on suggested language to use when addressing violations.
6. Appoint a subcommittee to prepare a draft proposal to present to the board of directors.

At the next meeting, we were astounded by their list of 31 possible ground rules, each and every one sensible in some way or another. Many of these rules had to do with disability management. During a break, we clustered these into about five categories and invited the group to talk about these and refine them.

One of the categories was conflict management, and this included a variety of ideas about what to do when conflict is experienced in the organization. This cluster of ground rules really became an opening for talking about a system for managing conflict. Based on this discussion, a subcommittee met to generate a final list of rules and processes for dealing with conflict.

Although not as grand as the system created at AMD, we like this case because it shows how a concerned group of people who must work together can acknowledge their constraints, establish constructive goals, collaborate on process, and create an innovative system that works. In short, it has all the elements of conflict system design.

▪ Resources You Can Use

Barker, J. R., & Domenici, K. L. (2000). Mediation practices for knowledge-based teams. In M. M. Beyerlein, D. A. Johnson, & S. T. Beyerlein (Eds.), *Advances in interdisciplinary studies of work teams*. (Product development teams, Vol. 5). Stamford, CT: JAI.

Campbell, D., Draper, R., & Huffington, C. (1989). *A systemic approach to consultation*. London: D.C. Publishing.

Constantino, C. A., & Merchant, C. S. (1996). *Designing conflict management systems: A guide to creating productive and healthy organizations*. San Francisco: Jossey-Bass.

Domenici, K., & Littlejohn, S. W. (1998). *The team mediation system: Effective communication in teams* [Video]. (Available from Domenici Littlejohn, 504 Luna Blvd. NW, Albuquerque, NM 87102, 505-246-9890)

Fisher, R., & Ury, W. (1991). *Getting to yes: Negotiating agreement without giving in*. New York: Penguin.

Gleason, S. (Ed.). (1997). *Workplace dispute resolution: Directions for the twenty-first century*. East Lansing: Michigan State University Press.

McDaniel, G. L. (1999). Designing a team management system that really works. In *The Best of Teams 99* (pp. 248-262). Lexington, MA: Linkage, Inc.

Nicotera, A. M. (1995). *Conflict and organizations: Communicative processes*. Albany: State University of New York Press.

6

Large-Scale Interventions

One of the most commanding issues in our city in recent years was the construction of a bridge. The project was designed to ease the congestion on major city streets and connect portions of town not easily accessible to each other. Despite some advantages, many members of our community felt threatened by the proposed plans. They saw this bridge as an intrusion that could create more problems than it solved—increases in traffic, crime, pollution, accidents, and taxes. The bridge is now a reality, but it was interesting to watch how this controversy unfolded over the years.

At one point, the mayor convened a town meeting to communicate information about the plans. In the local gymnasium, community members listened to a "report" on the proposed bridge by city planners and the developer in what was to be a classic "monologue." This meeting was all too typical. It took about an hour and informed people that they could write to the city to voice any complaints. Needless to say, community members left feeling frustrated, not listened to, and helpless.

A second town meeting was arranged, and those community members willing to try again were pleasantly surprised that they were actually heard. An agenda was agreed upon at the beginning of the meeting, with input from the community members. After a brief review of the bridge plans, the community members had a chance to speak of their fears, hopes, and concerns. The planners and developer also spoke of pressures they were experiencing and the benefits they anticipated from the bridge. This respectful communication gave participants a chance to understand the many different perspectives in the system and to discuss them without confrontation. Results of the meeting were compiled in a report to be addressed at the city council meeting.

The bridge controversy continued for a number of years with some public events being more successful than others. But we imagine another kind of event that might have been held, a format we have used successfully with many other public issues.

The event might have looked like this: Representatives from the many groups with concerns about the bridge project would have gathered again in the gymnasium, this time organized in teams according to their interest area. These would have included such groups as the city government, state government, schools, churches, neighbors, and traffic management experts. Participants would clarify their interests, fears, ideas, and challenges. Based on this exploration, each team would actually plan action steps that affect other teams in the room. Throughout the afternoon, they would approach one another, negotiating and collaborating about the plans they had made. The closing session would offer a look at the system, noting where teams intersected each other and places where collaboration was possible. Each team would reflect on the results of their negotiation and the learning they experienced.

We do not know what the outcome of such an event would have been, but we are confident that it would have created a place to acknowledge and use the unique perspectives of each stakeholder group. It would have held out the potential for participants to experiment in a safe environment with their own future.

As we move from small systems to larger, more complex ones, we bring the same toolkit to the interventions. We may use our tools in somewhat different ways, but we still focus on the communication patterns within and between systems. Our large-scale interventions are designed to illuminate larger systemic patterns while addressing the complexities of smaller systems at the same time.

If you take a nonsystemic view, you will concentrate on what parties to a dispute are saying and how they act toward one another. You will look at the "one-way" communication flow as *monologue,* like the first bridge event mentioned above. Your intervention will consist of advice on how the parties might communicate more effectively. In the case of the bridge, a consultant would critique the presentation and tell the bridge advocates how they could have been more persuasive.

When you begin to take a systemic view, however, you start noticing the "two-way" interaction between parties, and your intervention aims toward creating an environment of *dialogue.* In dialogue, people say and hear things that may not get disclosed in other adversarial situations. Listening is as important as speaking, and personal stories and perspectives can be shared in an interactive environment. The second bridge meeting came closer to being a dialogue.

As more and more stakeholder groups are involved, the interactional patterns become complex and offer the possibilities for *multilogue,* in which parties can manage and learn from multidimensional connections among parts of the system. The systemic practitioner aims to help parties communicate from a variety of vantage points and to enter the conversation at many fruitful places.

In this chapter, we present a systemic method that can work well to promote healthy multilogue in a complex system. Based on game theory, this intervention makes it possible for people to experience the spirit of multilogue while engaging in long-range planning.

Interventions in large systems offer a focus on the dynamic interaction of the whole rather than just the parts. In these days of rapid change, fast pace, and often scarce resources, we frequently see a competitor one day emerging as a collaborator the next. Methods that invite multilogue create opportunities for a clearer picture of potentially constructive patterns of interaction between and among systems.

In this chapter, we feature one of the many ways of creating multilogue—gaming methodology. When we use gaming methods in large system interventions, we see the opportunity to create a critical mass for change in the midst of difficult large-system issues. Here we will explore game theory and its evolution in Prosperity Games™.

▪ A Gaming Metaphor

Game theory originated as an application of mathematics to the study of rational decision making. Assuming that human beings act rationally, game theorists wanted to know what choices players would make to achieve their interests in light of the choices of others. Mathematical games have a set of rules that define possible goals, control the interaction of the players, and provide methods of assessing outcomes. Participants may have one or more goals that address different levels of the system in which they are interacting. In classical game theory, players study a matrix of payoffs and make "moves," or choices, based on the anticipated actions of other players.

Imagine that you and an accomplice are arrested for a crime. After being separated, each of you must choose whether to confess or not. If you confess and your accomplice does not, you will be allowed to go free, and your testimony will send the other person to prison for 20 years. If you both confess, both will be sent to prison for 5 years. If neither confesses, both will go to prison for 1 year on a lesser charge. This is a classic game scenario called the "Prisoner's Dilemma." Here you face a true dilemma between cooperating or competing with your accomplice. There are good reasons to do both, and you cannot really decide what to do until you see what your partner does. We call this a "mixed-motive game." In the Prisoner's Dilemma, the payoff matrix is years in prison, but in other games, the payoff can involve dollars, happiness, or any other relevant resource. In more complex games, players actually look ahead and invent strategies that could be used to respond to the different possible moves that an opponent might make.

As the Prisoner's Dilemma illustrates, the result of cooperation can be disastrous, so choosing to cooperate is a decision of trust. This is why communication is so important in games: If parties recognize they have common interests, cooperation is more likely to occur.

Games and Communication

In traditional games of the type described above, there is no communication between the players other than watching one another's moves. Such games are highly mechanistic and individualistic. In real life, the potential costs and rewards are mixed, changing, and often unclear, and they make it difficult to assume rational motives. Looking at games from the communication perspective, the participants can create and define a situation by engaging in critical thinking and decision making. The participants are then able to execute moves based upon decisions made. Consequently, the participants can be both producers and products of the reality they construct. In the hypothetical "Bridge Game" described above, participants could contribute to the ongoing conversation about this divisive issue on many levels.

Using the communication perspective, several terms describe higher levels of sophistication in game play. In his book *Interpersonal Communication: Making Social Worlds,* Barnett Pearce distinguishes between *game playing* and *game mastery.* A game player knows how to follow the rules well and will probably win a lot but does not understand the larger values or frames that give meaning to the game. A game master is one who has a larger view, knows not only how to play but also when it is appropriate to play, when the game needs to be changed, and how to construct new frames and futures that will benefit everyone.

Many of the participants in the "Bridge Game" probably would make excellent moves, negotiate effectively, and collaborate to build future plans exceeding what any of them could have done alone. These game players are necessary and integral to the system exploration. But other participants might have taken game play even further. They might have constructed an agenda that encouraged deliberate attention to the patterns of interaction between and among teams. They would have had an overall view of the potential for movement in the system. They probably would have seen this system's place in an even larger system such as national traffic management plans. They would have looked for the "stuck" places in the game and created ways to work out of these and move the game forward. They might have noticed the "overlap" areas where positive resources might be harnessed in the future. These participants would have been the "game masters."

We once helped coordinate an Entrepreneur Prosperity Game™ that dealt with the challenges and problems of starting a business and the actions needed to address these. The game offered nine startup companies in which "entrepreneurs" pursued and advanced their business plans. Expert teams of consultants, licensing offices, corporate partners, and investors were available to implement these plans. We were struck by the engagement of the participants, who commented that this "real-life" scenario allowed them to learn so much more that they could have from books and classes. They received initial exposure to what is required to start a new business and realized the need to network and collaborate with other players to make the business work. A systemic view of the process was illuminated and evaluated by their interactions. "Game players" noted the steps they could take in business start-up. They attempted some of those and noted the implications on their plans. A few of the participants proved to be "game masters" and developed plans that included components such as (a) balancing their team by including management skills, financial skills, negotiating skills, and interpersonal skills; (b) encouraging sophisticated strategies that allowed risk taking and contingencies; and (c) investing in relationships with their potential investors. We agreed with one participant's parting comment: "This game did not feed us, but taught us to fish."

In Chapter 1, we wrote that the communication perspective helps us see the connection between "resources" and "practices" of a system. As the members of these game teams interact with one another, they literally construct resources such as understandings, values, ideas, goals, challenges, and strategies. These resources are not just "made up" but are constructed by talking, making joint decisions, making proposals, working on a strategy matrix, and any number of other joint actions.

If a game is successful, several things will happen. Players will create positive, forward-moving resources by highly productive interaction. By the end of the game, their resources and practices will have changed because of this interactional process. New views will emerge, new practices will be learned, and the resulting roadmap will be richer than what any one stakeholder group might have imagined before the game.

Prosperity Games™

With the end of the cold war, the future of the Department of Energy's national laboratories became a major topic of discussion in Washington. Some have forecast that federal support for research will be reduced by 30% by the year 2001. The original mission of the national laboratories was the creation and maintenance of the nuclear arsenal, but over the years, new missions have been created, such as energy use, environmental research, and waste management. At the same time, the resources for this work have decreased, and competition has increased. To explore the implications of these changes, the "Future@Labs" Prosperity Game™ was developed. It explored the roles of industry, government, universities, and laboratories in this rapidly changing environment. The game was designed to increase collaboration among stakeholders in this large system and create a network to develop policy options.

Eleven teams were included, representing the U.S. Congress, Department of Energy, other federal agencies, U.S. industry companies, foreign countries, universities, Department of Energy laboratories, other labs, and the U.S. public and investors. Over 80 players participated. This game was fascinating to watch. We saw a system in action, managing its plans for the future, testing options for change, and observing outcomes. One particularly engaging scene occurred during a negotiation period when the director of a large lab was telling the Department of Energy team why his lab should stay open. We eagerly watched the reaction of the Department of Energy and noted with surprise and pleasure when the department team brought in the public and investors team to consult on this issue. The outcome of this event and the many other Prosperity Games™ depended on the players. As they faithfully represent their roles, their creativity and commitment provide a major learning experience for a critical mass of people.

War games were invented about 200 years ago to simulate the forces at work in a strategic war situation. In such games, participants safely learn about themselves and their enemy and try out various tactics and strategies. When the cold war ended in the 1980s, some members of the defense community realized that the ambiguities of global business are at least as challenging as the ambiguities of war. Pace VanDevender, from Sandia National Laboratories, explored the potential for industry-led, government-partnered, and university- and national laboratory-supported gaming events. In collaboration with Marshal Berman, also of Sandia, he pioneered Prosperity Games™ to explore partnerships in the context of the global economy. The games have since been adapted to address many different systems, including biomedicine, industrial ecology, community development in Argentina, and international competition.

Prosperity Games™ are an adaptation of strategic war gaming applied to peaceful means. We have explored the potential in these games to meet challenges in industries, communities, and organizations by helping to create and sustain growth and change. The games, tailored to these unique challenges, are highly interactive, competitive at some points, and collaborative at others. The players plan and construct strategies, implementing them through negotiation, joint ventures, alliances, and market creation. Players are organized into teams, representing the various stakeholders in the system. We often provide a Rest of the World (ROW) team, which manages processes and gives feedback to maintain the momentum of the play and is available to "play" a team not represented. The tightly packed agenda keeps the action moving. Prosperity Games™ explore cooperation and confrontation in a setting where many strategies are under way simultaneously. With the opportunity to involve up to 100 participants, the resulting learning is relevant and immediately useful for the participants. Let's take a closer look at developing Prosperity Games™.

▪ How Prosperity Games™ Work

As systemic practitioners, we design games in collaboration with the clients or concerned stakeholders to create a systemic event. The following principles guide the design of a game.

We are not searching for the "right" way to proceed but exploring many plausible avenues for systemic change. As the participants tell stories and offer examples, they make connections and begin to envision the story they wish to see in their community, workplace, marketplace, or world. We will be looking at the patterns of interaction, illuminating similar and differing interests and responses. In many of our games, we offer a time for teams to hear what other teams are planning, offering a chance to adjust plans and rethink options. We often call this an "elevator speech," in which the teams gather in a common area and take turns giving a 1-minute presentation of the results of their first planning period. This is a speech that would be given to the president of their company if they met momentarily on an elevator. Participants get a look at the range of plans that reflect a more cohesive system ready to move forward into a round of negotiation.

Our collaboration with the client is interactive, not prescriptive. We ask questions and then offer suggested directions for game design and evaluation based on their answers. The design they want may not always be what we would suggest, but we know that people support what they create, and we want an event that builds commitment from all involved. We continue to check with the participants throughout the process. As we design games, we often work with the client or stakeholders in creative ways. For two of our major events, we had a person from the client company actually come and stay in Albuquerque for a period of time, and we collaborated on designing the games, learning from each other and ensuring an event that had buy-in from the client.

We work organically, listening and observing carefully and responding as appropriate. This means that the whole process of designing, implementing, and evaluating a game will consist of observation and listening, with readiness to change or adapt as needed. Anticipating on-the-spot adjustments to schedule or design is done with confidence, as we know that this flexibility is an important element of a fluid system. Even determining the best place to enter the system is a search for an "opening" with knowledge that this entrance will affect the system of interacting parts like ripples on a pond.

Designing a Game

One game sponsored by a major multinational imaging company was designed to alternate planning, implementation, and feedback over and over again for three days. The repeated cycle gave players a chance to test and revise their ideas, to continually refine their plans. The first two feedback sessions were done by peers and measured "ease of doing business" with each team, the sense of "business savvy and understanding" that was evolving, and the "sense of urgency and competitiveness" experienced in the game. Later, a consultant team gave assessments on the game play and the game flow, in this case, urging participants to build a deeper emergence in the issues. The game director then gave feedback on the level of strategies experienced thus far in the game. We also spoke individually to participants during breaks and meals and utilized a written and oral process evaluation at the end.

Several feedback methods have been used in various games. One method is a town meeting, with a facilitated question-and-answer session. In another, participants periodically fill out diversity/inclusiveness check sheets to judge their team's attempt at utilizing the team's diversity. Another method is "pulling the string" debriefings, in which a facilitator with a microphone roams the room, extending a participant's observation with two or three more questions to be answered by the audience. We often use electronic anonymous voting with handheld data organizers that transmit player judgments to a central computer, providing nearly instantaneous results on a large screen. These many levels of feedback and evaluation help us minimize complaints and abstractions while maximizing participants' buy-in and commitment.

We have learned that the "frame," or conceptualization of the issue(s) to be addressed in the game, has a significant impact on the game's outcomes. Framing the issue in a positive way helps participants move into game play motivated to contribute rather than complain. The frame can also move the perspective from that of a small system to one of larger views. In a game with a large aerospace company, we had to reframe the problem the company was facing. The problem was originally presented as stiff competition for a huge global satellite component contract. By taking a systems view, however, we were able to reframe this problem into an opportunity. We asked, "How can the stakeholders in the aerospace industry build on their combined strengths and manage their weaknesses?" The game then moved from one in which teams competed to win to a game in which teams creatively explored a system of opportunities and barriers, discovering ways to move forward together.

As we frame the issue to be addressed, we are also determining the game's stakeholders, identifying the teams that need to be represented. When planning an intervention or consulting on a systemic situation, it is important to define the stakeholders clearly. We are confronted with questions such as: How do we identify the microsystems that need to be addressed and included in the macrosystem? What participants need to be included in the system, and how large of a system should be addressed in the game? Who can we safely "leave out" as a stakeholder team? Can we include their "voice" any other way? In this way, a clearer picture of the system begins to emerge. Early game design decisions and research can alert the practitioner to both internal and external stakeholders who may be a part of a larger system.

We often begin by listing all the potential people or groups that have an interest in the issue. The first that come to mind are usually the ones in the forefront. In the bridge issue, we know that the *city government* and the *developers* definitely have an interest. The *concerned citizens* represent another group, and depending on the plan for the intervention, they could remain one stakeholder group or be divided into many (*schools, churches, neighbors,* and *community groups*). After determining the most obvious groups, it is helpful to ask questions that identify others in the system that have interests in the issue.

We begin *scoping out,* or asking: Who else might be affected by this bridge? Are there other city residents who do not live close by but might be interested because of the precedent it sets? Are there any other legislative or government bodies that will impact the system in some way? Are there any environmental or activist groups whose voices might be needed to ensure a whole system? Are there some experts in this issue who could offer resources to move forward during the game play? We sometimes address the questions to focus groups or individuals in interview settings. A set of systemic questions assists us as game designers by looking as far out in the system as is needed to ensure a significant event. In the game for the imaging company, we had individual interviews with many of the executives in the company. We discussed the context of the game and made queries concerning the teams to be represented and the participants to be invited. That game had a mixture of people internal to the company and actual representatives from the other companies represented in the game.

A method we often use in designing business games to gather a more complete picture of the larger system is a concept called the "value net," introduced by Adam Brandenburger and Barry Nalebuff (1996) in their book *Co-opetition.* This approach works well in the business world and can be applied directly to other types of systems, such as communities, sectors of industries, or other geographical areas. On one dimension of the value net are the *suppliers* and *customers*. In a typical business, suppliers bring the resources to the company and the customers consume the products and services of the company. Along the other dimension are the *competitors* and *complementors*. Competitors have long been seen as the "enemy," those other forces in the industry that want your customer's attention. Complementors are the reverse case. They have a product, service, or action that makes your product, service, or action more attractive. The main difference between competitors and complementors is spelled out by Brandenburger and Nalebuff:

> A player is your competitor if customers value your product *less* when they have the other player's product than when they have your product alone. A player is your complementor if customers value your product *more* when they have the other player's product than when they have your product alone. (p. 18)

Coca-Cola and Pepsi are definitely competitors. One business does not add to the business of the other. Oscar Mayer and Coleman's are complementors. People value hot dogs more when they have mustard than when they don't and vice versa.

After agreeing on the issue for the game involving the aerospace industry, we used the value net process to determine the stakeholder teams. Since this company has experienced consolidation and acquisitions in recent years, two of its subsidiary companies were seen as complementors. These smaller companies represent work with large-scale infrastructure projects owned by the private sector, as well as state and local government work. The work of these companies is enhanced by the parent company and vice versa. They were also seen as suppliers because they provide goods and services to many of the stakeholders in the game. It is usually easier to identify the competitors. The problem is narrowing the competitor list down to get the appropriate combination for the game. In this case, we included the company that was competing for a major contract and a second company that would align closely with the winner of the contract. The final team was the government entity that was offering the major contract, the customer. The face-to-face interactions that occurred in this system led to negotiations that challenged each other's conclusions and reconceptualized and reorganized conclusions about the "pie" in the aerospace industry and creative ways to divide it.

Levels of Game Play

We have analyzed how executives and key stakeholders approach development and long-range planning to figure out what levels of strategies can be expected in these games. These levels of play reflect different levels of sophistication in the larger collaborative frame in which strategic moves are understood. We verbally encourage four levels of play, and we promote the levels with a Strategy Matrix™ chart, an intriguing tool for recording planning and strategic moves. The chart gives players a chance to look carefully at team moves, discover mistakes, and make corrections. The game staff can also use it later as an assessment tool to evaluate the sophistication of play.

In a *"seize the day"* context, every move is understood only in terms of the immediate gain with little view of the larger environment or a future beyond the short-term payoff. Teams that want to pick the low-hanging fruit rush out to make the first negotiations they can think of with little vision.

The second type of strategy we see in the games is called *"parts for the whole,"* in which teams may plan parallel moves. These action steps move in the same direction and have a degree of connectivity. These strategies remain within the team and move linearly out in time.

If a strategy has a series of moves that build on each other, creating new trends and new markets, we have identified it as *"it grows as it goes."* This type of planning and implementation has much potential for growth and looks fairly far out into the future. We have seen this level of strategy in our games that feature high-level executives interested in the global marketplace.

Hinted at in a few games but never successfully achieved in a Prosperity Game™ is a fourth strategy called *"force for the future."* In this level of play, stakeholders realize that they can create their own new ways of framing industries, markets, and events. With newly conceived social and economic values produced, the context guiding the games, rules, and moves will be affected for years to come. Many teams will jump on board to carry out such strategies because of the power of the idea.

We have found, through both research and experience, that learning from cooperative team situations can be highly effective. In contrast with competitive or individual learning situations, the gains are much enhanced when individuals can observe skilled team members and work with them to accomplish tasks. In Prosperity Games,™ teams are primarily composed of appropriate work groups from the real-life issue they are addressing. Occasionally, in order to model desired team skills, experienced external participants are placed on each team. We also sometimes aid the process by using facilitators, one or two per team, or "process managers" who visit and serve two or three teams. These people clarify communication, prevent miscommunication, manage conflict, and encourage the agenda for their team. Systemic practitioners have proved to be excellent facilitators, as they can help their group operate in their smaller (team) system while recognizing the larger game system represented. By following constructive communication and conflict management guidelines, the facilitator creates a safe place for participants to share points of view, negotiate options, and discuss issues. We always use a flip chart to record the group's progress and ask for a report from the facilitators after the game. The recorded information helps the group focus on ideas rather than personalities. Flip chart records also provide a group memory, so the team is not burdened with having to recall discussions and agreements.

Playing a Prosperity Game™

We worked with the group that produced the U.S. Infrastructure Assurance Prosperity Game™ and Planning Event in 1997. Sponsored by the President's Commission on Critical Infrastructure Protection, the National Communications System, and the Department of Energy, the two games held in January and March helped the President's commission recommend national strategy for protecting and securing the U.S. infrastructure over the next 15 years. Stakeholders were determined after much collaboration with the sponsors, resulting in the following teams: Telecommunications, Electric Power, Finance & Banking, Insurers, Government, Emergency Services, Oil & Gas, and Transportation. These teams explored options for protecting the U.S. infrastructure while identifying insights on the most effective relationships in the system. Each participant received a player's handbook about ten days before each event. This handbook included objectives of the event, an overview description of each team, available resources, and a game schedule.

To get an idea of how this event worked, imagine that you are the president of the State Electric Power Consortium and very concerned that power grids in the area are not upgraded in a timely manner. This situation can endanger many local residents if power disruption occurs. You have read your handbook and have anticipated the fast pace of the game and the need to be fully engaged in the process. You enter a large ballroom, where you see banners hanging from the ceiling indicating the stakeholder teams. After identifying the "Electric Power" banner, you enter that cubicle and see a table for eight people. A loudspeaker announces that everyone is to gather in the town meeting area, and you grab a cup of coffee and a bagel and assemble with 100 other players for the inbriefing, or game orientation.

Less than an hour is spent with introductions of sponsors and game staff and an explanation of the context of the game. Instructions conclude with a request to represent your "real-life" interests, helping to create new insights and options for developing postgame opportunities. Your team gathers back in the attractive cubicle called the home base area. Here a facilitator introduces herself as a "process manager" and reminds you of the group's responsibility for the content and plans. A brief round of introductions helps the team to note the individual strengths and weaknesses this particular team has. You notice that you have many people from industry on your team and only one regulatory representative. The facilitator assures you that this imbalance will be managed as the play proceeds. Your team discusses the ground rules and decision-making methods you will use over the next two days. The facilitator gives an overview of the agenda, emphasizing the movement from identification of challenges and strategies to action plans.

As your team begins discussing challenges to the electric power industry in the United States, your facilitator begins using skills that she exhibits throughout the game. She restates important comments and writes them on a flip chart. She gives attention to all members of the team, inviting the quieter members to share their perspectives and helping the dominant members to listen. Challenges are identified by a discussion of the strengths and weaknesses of the electric power industry with respect to protecting the infrastructure. Discussion veers off into a local political issue with a power company, and the facilitator redirects the conversation back to identifying challenges. A consensus is reached on the challenges, and they are recorded and given to the game director.

After lunch, the team meets again briefly in the town meeting area to give "elevator speeches." These 1-minute presentations recap each team's challenges to alert other teams in the system to the concerns of others. Possible overlaps and common challenges are noted. You are interested to hear that the Emergency Services team recognizes their dependency on Electric Power.

Your team meets back in the cubicle for another round of discussion, this time focusing on strategies. What strategies can our stakeholder team create to meet the challenges we identified? You notice that the facilitator encourages the team to look for strategies that require the cooperation of other teams. The discussion becomes heated as the team debates the increasing pressure in the new deregulated industry. It has been difficult to keep trained personnel to operate the increasingly complex systems. You feel this vulnerability could result in disgruntled employees who could use their knowledge or skills to disrupt operation. Others on your team see that your concern is not as important as a potential cyber attack on the automatic switching systems. The team can try to implement the resulting strategy and note the results and implications in a negotiating period later in the day.

The last planning session on the first day is dedicated to creating moves, or action steps to implement the strategies. Your team sees many areas of overlap with other teams and discusses ways to collaborate with these other teams. For example, you would like to approach the Government team and ask for help in training and hiring operators who receive incentives to help callers make their way through the complex electric power system. Various team members receive their negotiation assignments. Government is one of the stops on your list.

The first negotiating round begins, with many of the teams rushing to cubicle areas to grab team representatives. Some of the teams are still planning and are not ready to talk to you. You decide to go on to the Government team but see that the Government table is mobbed. Everyone wants to get Government to help. You make an appointment for 15 minutes later and return to your cubicle to refine your proposal. You realize that many people are probably asking Government for money, so you ask a teammate to help you brainstorm a win-win situation that the Government team might like.

When it is time for your appointment, you meet with the Government representative and negotiate a deal. You suggest a government-industry consortium for training workers and providing incentives for workers. It turns out that Emergency Services and Telecommunications have already approached them with similar ideas, so you gather those representatives together and craft an agreement to form a consortium. Your facilitator helps you fill out an official agreement form and you turn the form in to the game director. As your team reconvenes at the end of the negotiating period, you find out that some of your team members were continuing negotiations after dinner, some had hit a brick wall, and some had proudly forged agreements.

Immediately after dinner, each team gives a 7-minute report on its successes, obstacles, and learning about this infrastructure system. Teams listen carefully so that they can adjust their own plans later. Then it is back to the cubicle and preparations to begin the second negotiating round.

Another day of negotiating, adjusting, and responding gives you and the other players a better picture of the system and the impact of stakeholders on each other. Many strategies are tried. Some have a negative impact on the system and fail; they are either scrapped or revamped. Those that succeed are expanded and carefully recorded for postgame work.

As the game winds down, you and the other players are encouraged to begin the transition from the game to reality. What are the highest priority opportunities that developed here? What are the barriers to implementing these opportunities? What is the most pressing issue to address when you go back to work? The answers to these questions are presented at the final town meeting, emphasizing the interdependencies between stakeholders as they address these pressing issues. Final feedback and group discussion is facilitated to identify total infrastructure system opportunities, barriers, and pressing issues to be built into an infrastructure roadmap by the game developers. This roadmap will be sent to all participants when it is ready, and you will have the chance to offer suggestions or advice for the final product.

You leave the game exhausted yet invigorated. You now have a better picture of the larger system in which electric power exists. You have made some invaluable contacts, and you have some plans to present to your boss back at work. You have recognized some of your priorities and seen them in light of a larger system of priorities. And best of all, you had fun!

Evaluation

The success of a gaming event can be measured in many ways. The first place to look is at the objectives, which were set in pregame collaborations. Judging whether these were met is an important learning from the practitioner's perspective and from the perspective of the client, who holds the content interests. Participant satisfaction in the event can be evaluated to get a picture of the level of ownership and commitment to the potential roadmap. Process evaluation helps the practitioner learn which components of the gaming methodology worked and which did not.

All of these variables can be measured in a variety of ways. As mentioned earlier, frequent questions during the game to the client and to game planners can indicate "how things are going." The practitioner should anticipate the need for real-time change or adjustments to the schedule or game design. A team evaluation session can be scheduled for the end of the game, where a facilitator leads the team through questions evaluating the process and content learning of the game. These can be presented back to the whole

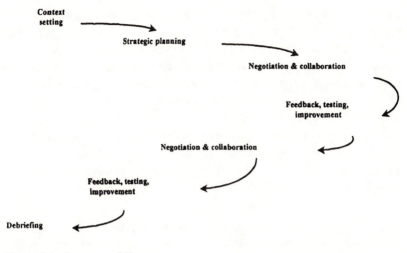

Figure 6.1. Sequence of Play

group and concluded with a whole-group discussion. Comments can be recorded on flip charts at the front of the room. Paper or computer questionnaires can be given at the end of the game measuring the variables mentioned earlier, or electronic voting might be used. Although each game is unique, all games follow a similar process, depicted in general form in Figure 6.1.

Other Prosperity Games™

Of the 17 Prosperity Games™ that have been held thus far, most have followed a schedule similar to the one described above. Of course, as a result of ongoing collaboration with the client, many variations can occur. The following examples briefly describe some games and some highlighted design components:

The Industrial Ecology Prosperity Game™ invited participants to explore a very systemic view of the interaction of industry and the environment. Presented as an interactive whole, "Industrial Ecology" seeks to enable management of human activity on a sustainable basis. The series of two 3-day games sought to shift the linear flow of resources in industrial use toward closed-loop systems. For example, "waste" in the game is seen as input for other processes. These games were a major learning experience, utilizing five stakeholder groups subdivided into 13 teams. The stakeholder groups were: U.S. Government, Industry, Research & Development, Public Stakeholders, and Foreign Countries. As in many games, the Rest of the World (ROW) team is the control team that conducts the game, manages disputes, and plays other roles not assigned in the game. The concept of resource scarcity was modeled by introducing a number of "chits" into the game. These chits represented not only money but also other intangibles, such as technology, political influence, and regulatory, or legislative, action. Chits were used during negotiation periods during which teams attempted to test their strategies. The following are examples of challenges from the game that were "played out":

- Developing countries are choosing automobile-based transportation systems, which use oil inefficiently, contribute to air pollution, and require highway systems covering valuable agricultural land.
- Materials themselves move relatively rapidly through the economy. In spite of industrial waste prevention and municipal recycling, most materials extracted still end up as waste in landfills or dispersed in the environment.

The Sports Complex Prosperity Game™ was played in Rosario, Argentina, to help the Centro de Asistencia a la Comunidad (CeAc), or the Center for Community Assistance, plan a sports complex. The game offered a forum for the community to mobilize and collaborate on providing recreational opportunities in the neighborhood. The community being served included a highly impoverished area on land owned by the university in Rosario. CeAc's mission is to promote collaboration between the university and the community on all matters relevant to the improvement of life conditions in the area. Playing for 1 day around this issue were eight stakeholder teams: Neighbors, Funding Agencies, University, CeAc, Political Parties, City Hall, State Government, and Schools and Clubs. Using a basic Prosperity Game™ format, the game was set up for participants to explore their concerns, visions, and actions. They moved through a process where they discussed their current concerns, constructed visions for the future, and created action plans to alleviate the concerns and achieve the visions. The motivation of the community to improve itself was very evident as the participants negotiated and collaborated and worked out their visions for the future. This game also used bargaining resources in the forms of money, know-how, regulations, influence, and hope. The last resource, hope, was seen by the Argentines as a very important and powerful resource for certain stakeholders that do not have access to traditional sources of power. These resources were determined by the game planners in collaboration with the community to ensure that the real system was represented accurately. An innovative, cost-effective approach was needed for this event, as resources were scarce. Taking place in a school cafeteria, the participants had no background information (no player's handbook) and relied entirely on the information, intelligence, and judgment of the participants.

The **Biomedical Technology Prosperity Game™** helped explore existing and future biomedical technologies with emphasis on lowering costs and maintaining quality. The game focused on major diseases and accidents that provide opportunities for improving quality and lowering costs through new technologies and policies. Three points of view were represented in the game. "Consumers" represented patients. "Providers" included doctors, hospitals, research organizations, and manufacturers. "National Stakeholders" included legislators, insurers, government customers and payers, and lawyers. Over the course of the game, patients developed diseases, disabilities, and aging problems that were treated by doctors and nurses using available technologies and new technologies developed during the game. Suppliers, manufacturers, government, lawyers, insurance, finance, and news media all played their real-life roles in these scenarios. Results of the game were combined with the expertise of a large group of health care professionals to help create a Technology Roadmap for the future of the health care system in biomedical engineering. The game looked 8 years ahead, and players were able to develop innovative biomedical technologies. The patients were provided with D/D (Disease/Disability) cards that described their age and symptoms, treatment options, and estimates of cost to society by either dying, remaining ill, or completely recovering and returning to the workforce. The following description of the Consumer team (from the player's handbook) will give you a flavor of the game:

The U.S. health care system is vitally important to you and your family. You recognize that costs have been rising dramatically, but you want to preserve and improve the current system. You differ among yourselves in values. Some of you demand freedom to choose your own doctors; others are willing to sacrifice some choice in exchange for the lower costs provided by managed care. Some believe that health care is a universal right and entitlement; others that it is a commodity like food. Some of you enjoy stable employment, and employee-funded insurance. Others are elderly or poor. Many among you rely on government insurance programs and are concerned about the future benefits of Medicare and Medicaid.

This team interacted with Provider teams who were dedicated to high quality care for their patients, but rising costs were eating into their profit margins and creating conflicts with public and private insurers. Government was pushing them into more managed care systems. The teams in the game developed partnerships to manage challenges like those described above and built an increased awareness of the needs, desires, and motivations of the different stakeholders.

Other Prosperity Games™, such as Electronics Manufacturing and International Competition, simulate real-world systems, offer a safe environment to explore those systems, and reduce the cost of error as participants try out strategies and action plans in concert with other stakeholders. As a multitude of issues are dealt with simultaneously, the games provide a learning and predicting environment. It is a powerful learning for the citizen, for the policy researcher, and for the decision maker to be able to comprehend the whole, or the system, before the particulars are dealt with in our world with its complex nature of public and private issues.

▪ Beyond Prosperity Games™: Advancing the Communication Perspective

At the time of this writing, we are experimenting with new forms of games in which the goals of the traditional Prosperity Game™ are transcended. Here is what we hope to achieve:

• *Allowing game rules to emerge from interaction among teams.* We imagine games in which the players themselves invent the rules as they go. One way in which this might happen is to have each team send a representative to confer on a "Game Process Committee" at different points to redirect the game. Here teams would need to cope with systemic change, very much like real life.

• *Setting up processes to encourage "force-for-the-future" play.* Teams would be challenged to think of ways in which they could cooperate in creating a force-for-the-future outcome. Special cross-team communication opportunities would be provided specifically for this purpose.

• *Providing for communication forms other than negotiation.* Here, teams would have a chance to "talk" with one another about larger game concerns and goals prior to or in addition to negotiating. For example, teams might have an opportunity to ask one another appreciative questions about their challenges, strategies, and moves.

• *Creating new, nonfixed resources.* In addition to the finite resources provided each team, participants could be encouraged to create their own resources or figure out a way to create a environment that isn't zero-sum. When we played the Sports Complex game, the Argentines insisted that we include hope as a resource. It fit their culture and gave power to those groups that do not have traditional resources. This new resource energized the players, and we stood by fascinated as players traded hope like a commodity and gained even more hope in the process.

Gaming methodology provides a flexible method of intervention with great constructive potential. We have experienced tremendous enjoyment and satisfaction helping to design and facilitate these games, and we look forward to numerous creative iterations in the future.

▪ Resources You Can Use

Brandenburger, A., & Nalebuff, B. (1996). *Co-opetition.* Garden City, NY: Doubleday.

Davis, M. (1970). *Game theory: A non-technical introduction.* New York: Basic Books.

Pearce, W. B. (1973). *Interpersonal communication: Making social worlds.* New York: HarperCollins.

Prosperity Games™ Design Manual. (1997). (Available from Prosperity Institute, 7604 Lamplighter Lane NE, Albuquerque, NM 87109)

Rapoport, A. (1960). *Fights, games, and debates.* Ann Arbor: University of Michigan Press.

Rapoport, A. (1967). Strategy and conscience. In F. Matson & A. Montagu (Eds.), *The human dialogue: Perspectives on communication* (pp. 79-96). New York: Free Press.

Steinfatt, T., & Miller, G. (1974). Communication in game theoretic models of conflict. In G. R. Miller & H. Simons (Eds.), *Perspectives on communication in conflict* (pp. 14-75). Englewood Cliffs, NJ: Prentice Hall.

von Neumann, J., & Morgenstern, O. (1944). *The theory of games and economic behavior.* Princeton, NJ: Princeton University Press.

7
■ ■ ■ ■

Working With Public Issues

Cupertino is a suburban community in the Silicon Valley near San Jose, California. This city of 40,000 has seen tremendous change over the past 30 years. Once primarily agricultural land with walnut groves and farmhouses, Cupertino now consists of city streets, strip malls, housing developments, and office buildings.

Several years ago, we met with a group of citizens from Cupertino to find out what life is like in their community. One woman told us that she used to mark the seconds at a certain stoplight by watching the grain fall from a tall conveyor belt at a mill located at that corner. Now, she told us, she looks up at the same spot and watches a huge digital clock flash outside the corporate headquarters of Apple Computer.

Change is one of the many things that can bring conflict to a community. Indeed, the health of a community is reflected in the extent to which change and difference are managed effectively and constructively. Cupertino is a great success story in this regard, and we will have much to tell about this remarkable community later in the chapter.

Difficult public issues are always a challenge. Passionate engagement on a issue shows commitment and concern, but it can also tear a community apart. Whether the issue is education or natural resources, social services or housing, transportation or industrial development, conducting the public's business can be difficult. The traditional processes used to manage public conflict often make the problem worse. Too often, policy makers, agency personnel, and professionals dread mandated public meetings because such hearings can be unproductive, wearing, and downright demeaning. Public

168

participation is sometimes considered an obstacle to be rushed through, bypassed, or ignored, an attitude that exacerbates mistrust.

In recent years we have met a number of people who, exasperated by such struggles, are asking whether there is a better way. And of course there is. This chapter presents a different picture of how the business of common public issues might be done. To get there, though, we need to take a more careful look at why public issues can be so difficult.

▪ Camping Up and Striking Out

Catron County is a beautiful, sparsely populated region in the pristine Gila National Forest in southwest New Mexico. Many of the residents, mostly lumber workers and ranchers, have lived and worked there for many generations. In the early 1990s, the community's only physician retired, and a new country doctor had to be recruited. The citizens were successful in finding a young man who had recently completed his residency in Family and Community Medicine at the University of New Mexico, and by 1993, "Dr. Mark" and his family had settled in Reserve, the county's only real town.

Almost immediately, the new doctor began to see many stress-related cases, including depression, drug and alcohol abuse, domestic violence injuries, and stress-related diseases. He realized that the community itself was in distress, and he contacted his former professor Dr. Ben Daitz to explore what might be done.

By the mid-1990s, Catron County had made national news. Tension among the timber industry, ranching, the federal government, and environmentalists had reached a peak. Pipe bombs were found on hiking trails, the commissioners passed a symbolic law requiring every household to own a gun, and some residents spoke openly about armed defense against the federal agencies that had threatened their livelihoods with increased regulation on land use. A law was passed to require "environmentalists" to register with the county.

The case of Catron County is less known than higher-profile national and international conflicts, but it is no less illustrative of the negative outcomes of a struggle over issues that matter to a community. When various interests in a community come to clash, people take sides. Clear and polarized identity groups get established, and the situation quickly turns into a struggle between "us and them." The value of the rich texture of difference gets lost, and shared goals evaporate.

In Catron County, the ranchers and timber workers felt that their ways of life were threatened by new government regulations fueled by environmental interests. Environmental groups were also taking a stand. Viewing the Gila as one of the country's most endangered areas, they vowed to fight back. Successful in lawsuits to require the forest service to shut down logging operations, they made their move on the ranchers to reduce grazing on federal lands. Resident employees of the forest service were stuck in the middle and were even concerned about their own personal safety.

In cases like this, the parties are fighting a metaphorical war in which the only imagined outcomes are winning or losing. The processes employed by the parties are designed to prevail. Each side greatly fears that its own interests will be subverted and lost. Each believes passionately in its own position and struggles to be heard. More and more extreme actions are taken, and more and more lawsuits are filed in federal court.

Since winning means everything, power assumes tremendous importance. The camps dare not show weakness, inconsistency, or lack of resolve. They must demonstrate a unified front. They employ the most effective resources available to them. Litigation is often critical, and good lawyers are a must. Sometimes, parties make use of the clout of national organizations and "outsiders." Legislation is another weapon. Even violence or the threat of violence can become part of the arsenal. In the end, neither side wins, but the community loses.

These kinds of community struggles are usually viewed as interest based. Indeed, they are, but they frequently involve more than a fight over resources. These conflicts are difficult in part because the very identities of the parties are at stake. Losing means more than having to give up water rights, employment opportunities, money, minerals, or an endangered species. It also means giving up some part of ourselves, our history, culture, and traditions.

A big part of a group's identity is how it thinks about and acts in the world—what it considers right and good. In their book *Moral Conflict: When Social Worlds Collide,* Barnett Pearce and Stephen Littlejohn use the term *moral order* to label the way in which a group understands and enacts human experience. The most serious and difficult conflicts are usually *moral conflicts,* because they involve a deep clash between opposing and incommensurate moral orders. Moral conflicts are difficult because traditional methods of conflict resolution just don't work. No matter how hard each side tries to prevail, the situation gets worse, frustration grows, and discourse degrades to reciprocated diatribe, sometimes even violence.

No matter what factors precipitate difficult public conflicts, they require creative thinking and new forms of communication. Certainly not all community disputes are as strident and difficult as Catron County's, but regardless of the issue, we believe that communities must imagine better ways of exploring their differences and shared concerns. Even before conflict surfaces, way upstream, communities can set processes in place that make collaboration possible. And when open conflict does erupt, it is often possible to find ways in which disputing parties can manage their differences constructively.

After his former student talked to him about the medical problems of Catron County, Dr. Ben Daitz contacted the New Mexico Center for Dispute Resolution (NMCDR) based in Albuquerque. Melinda Smith of NMCDR formed a small team and approached the community through the auspices of their doctor to begin discussions about new forms of communication within the community. About 20 people, including ranchers, forest service personnel, an environmentalist, county officials, and others, attended the first meeting and formed a dialogue group. Their stated purpose was to "come together to openly and honestly discuss and deal with the diverse situations we face, finding common ground from our different points of view to ensure an economic, social and an environmentally sound future for us all."

The group later sponsored public meetings, mediations, field trips, community visioning, a youth project, forest negotiations, and a conference. The results have been remarkable, but the process has been difficult. There is no magic bullet for these hard conflicts, and the progress in Catron County was rough going. They experienced many setbacks, and the struggle continues today. We learn from the Catron experience that good community conflict management is a never-ending process. It is always something you work at, never something you work out.

▪ Community as System

Although it often appears to be an undifferentiated mass (or mess), the community is actually a complex, open system. It consists of innumerable linked conversations, in which many social worlds are made. Nothing that happens in a community is unconnected. Each conversation, each turn of events, emerges from and leads to other turns. The many groups composing the community have different ideas about the community and its future, and these groups interface with one another in many fascinating, constructive (and sometimes destructive) ways.

From a distance, these systemic features are obvious, but when we are members of a community, we often find it difficult to "see" the system. Acting from our own perspectives and interests as community members, it appears more like an aggregate of individuals and interest groups. Especially in the heat of dispute, we almost always fail to see the role of communication patterns in the social worlds we make. How would things be different if we did?

If community members took a communication perspective, they would pay close attention to their own patterns of communication, apart from the actual content and issues. They would stop to consider the effects of certain forms of communication before engaging in them. And they would imagine forms of interaction that could lead to constructive futures for the entire community. This is precisely the challenge of the systemic practitioner—to engage the community from the communication perspective and to collaborate with the community in building a system consciousness.

We recently facilitated two public engagement events for the Department of Energy on a fascinating scientific research project called NABIR (Natural and Accelerated Bioremediation Research). The subject of the project was bioremediation, the use of microorganisms in nuclear waste cleanup. A group of professionals associated with NABIR had received a grant to improve communication with the public and hired us to design and facilitate a process for this. We worked with three groups—(1) the professionals, (2) community activists, and (3) concerned citizens not formerly involved in science issues. Our goal was to engage representatives from these three groups in a dialogue.

Our sponsors insisted that the event should begin by having each group meet separately and talk about their separate concerns. They had a point. If you push people too rapidly into new groups, they can feel vulnerable and unsafe. At the same time, staying the conservative course risks reproducing the old patterns you are trying to change.

We decided to have each group meet separately for an hour or so, but we asked them to talk in a new way by considering the "community" as a system. Each group discussed five questions:

1. Who are we in the system? What are our roles, interests, responsibilities, and connections?

2. What do we have the most to gain by interacting with the other groups here today?
3. What assets do we have as a group to contribute to the interaction?
4. What do the three groups need to do today to make this a highly successful event?
5. How will we know if this event is successful?

We put a "system map" on a large piece of butcher paper on the wall and asked each group to write in their roles, assets, gains, and hopes for a successful event. In other words, we asked the groups to think consciously about their community as a system.

■ Safety and Appreciation

In our work on public issues, we have found two principles repeatedly important. The first is to establish safe environments for dialogue, and the second is to show appreciation for difference.

Constructing Safe Environments

We wrote in Chapter 2 about the need for safety in promoting dialogue. When you ask people to communicate in new ways, you are really asking them to take a risk, which they normally will not do if they feel threatened. If establishing a safe environment is hard in private disputes, imagine how difficult it can be in public. It is challenging for sure, but quite possible in many cases. Here are some things we have learned along the way:

Involve the public early, when the atmosphere still feels safe. Some of our most rewarding and productive public issue work takes place long before conflict breaks out. This work is extremely important because it introduces new forms of communication before groups can "camp up and strike out." Participants can explore their concerns, ideas, differences, and common ground precisely because they are not in a posturing, argumentative mode.

Community visioning is an example of this kind of participation. Citizens are asked to talk about their hopes for the community. They collaborate with one another to produce creative ideas about how the community might be improved. In the process, many differences arise, and "conflicts" might become apparent, but since community members have not had the opportunity to become identified with one side or another, they typically acknowledge the difference, explore it a bit, and then move on.

Strategic planning is another "platform" on which good dialogue can occur. Especially when a community will be facing difficult policy decisions in the future, agencies can solicit the help of the public well in advance. We have seen this kind of activity work on such issues as land development and transportation. In Albuquerque, the city in which we live, the local Council of Governments has sponsored a significant 3-year strategic planning process on growth, in which citizens have played a vital role at all stages. By the time the council is ready to present its recommendations to the various governments of the region, the wisdom of ordinary citizens will have been tapped in very creative ways and without a great deal of rancor. This does not mean that serious conflicts will not erupt during the implementation stages, but it does show the value of involving citizens in new forms of communication early, when the environment still feels safe.

Invite people into "a new kind of communication." If participants in a public issue event expect old patterns of interaction to be used, they will prepare to act in protective, combative ways. On the other hand, if they expect that a better form of communication is going to take place, they will be more open to innovation. Some activists are simply not interested in participating, but others are quite willing to do so. Especially after experiencing the repeated frustration of unproductive public meetings, constant attempts to win the favor of the press, and exhausting struggles, many participants welcome a new way of doing business. This was certainly the case in Catron County.

When the Public Conversations Project first invited activists into a radically different kind of conversation on abortion back in 1990, the project leaders did not know if anyone would be willing to participate. But almost everyone they invited accepted, and many were even enthusiastic. Almost everyone was glad to have participated, and they heard again and again in debriefing interviews that participants had gained an appreciation for talking about difficult issues in new ways.

Periodically over the years, we have experimented with an innovative format for a public forum called Kaleidoscope. We designed the Kaleidoscope sessions in various ways, but they always involved public interviews of advocates on two sides of a significant public issue. The participants were invited to try out a new kind of communication designed to change the pattern of interaction in the dispute. We sponsored Kaleidoscope sessions on animal rights, the Central Intelligence Agency, U.S. involvement in Central America, gay and lesbian rights, multiculturalism and affirmative action, and other issues. Not all of these sessions were equally effective, but we have always been successful in recruiting advocates who are willing to try something new.

Deal with the most difficult issues in small, private groups first. Large public meetings feel basically risky to most people. Especially when emotions are high and commitments are deep, the risk of uncomfortable interaction is major. But public issues do not necessarily have to be explored in large public meetings. On some issues, dialogue is best achieved in private settings. This is especially true when the group can make agreements to achieve a safe environment.

We were recently invited to facilitate a group of Jews and Arabs interested in planning a dialogue event on the Israeli-Palestinian peace process. We were told that there was potential conflict in this group and that a facilitator was necessary to help make the planning go smoothly. We met in the privacy of a member's home and spent the entire first meeting, about an hour and a half, negotiating process agreements. Eventually, this small group did build a safe environment and ended up planning an excellent public event that attracted 300 participants.

The facilitators in Catron County did not begin by calling a large public meeting. They started by inviting a small group to explore the possibility of dialogue. Only when a feeling of relative safety was accomplished there did the project expand to involve the entire community.

Even when we do hold large public meetings, we most often break them into small groups around tables. These semiprivate groups can begin to explore the members' experiences and perspectives in ways that are not possible in a large plenary session. Often, we work back and forth between the large group and the small group, and we have found that this movement tends to increase a feeling of safety at many events.

Create distance by using "simulations" or "games." Our friend Coco Fuks, a community psychologist in Rosario, Argentina, works in the most difficult communities—disempowered, impoverished, and conflicted neighborhoods. We asked him recently how he manages to get people with serious conflicts to talk in productive ways about their differences.

He told us that he asks participants what they can talk about safely and how they might do so. He offers a variety of techniques with which they might explore difficult issues safely. Sometimes he asks participants to create fictional stories that symbolically represent their situation. Participants work with their stories, changing details and writing alternative endings. You can work with metaphors the same way. Ask participants to create metaphors that represent certain issues or situations and to explore problems and solutions metaphorically.

Each summer, our friend Mary Jane Collier hosts a summer camp in the Rocky Mountains for Israeli and Palestinian girls. In one of their most intriguing activities, the girls work in pairs to design and construct a model bridge. They must collaborate in planning, finding materials, and building the model. When they present their bridge to the other girls, they talk about what the bridge means symbolically and the process they used to plan and build it.

We have had very good results by using gaming methodology, which is described in detail in Chapter 6. Gaming engages stakeholder teams in a highly interactive, simulated environment. The teams make strategic plans and negotiate agreements with one another. This method has many advantages. One of the chief benefits of gaming methodology is that it can be viewed as a simulation, in which participants are playing roles. In fact, the most successful games involve participants playing themselves, but there is something about the language of gaming that feels more like an experiment or a laboratory than real interaction. Participants are usually quite willing to try new forms of communication in this context, just because it feels somewhat removed from reality.

Ask people what they need to feel safe. One of the best things you can do in difficult situations is to have participants collaborate in making the environment safe. We do this in private mediations all the time, so why not do it with public issues as well? It might not be practical to negotiate process agreements with a teeming throng of hundreds, but you can always meet with representatives and stakeholders in advance. This is exactly what the Jewish-Arab dialogue group did. They carefully considered what would need to happen at the public meeting to make it safe and successful. They decided to have live music as people arrived and to offer an interesting, ample, and delicious array of ethnic foods from the Middle East. They made sure that the keynote speakers represented a spectrum of opinions on the issue, and they recruited facilitators for the discussion groups.

Provide structure and strong facilitation. Again and again, we have seen what a difference structure can make in establishing a safe environment. What do people most fear about large public meetings on difficult issues? They fear emotional outbursts, personal attack, disorganization, lack of focus, lack of progress or forward movement, and a host of other worries that good facilitation and structure can prevent.

A clear and appropriate meeting structure can prevent the disruptions and disorder. Equally important, such processes can encourage positive, constructive, and respectful interaction; promote creativity; and allow participants to try new forms of communication. Just the presence of a skilled facilitator can lead to increased comfort, and the interventions a facilitator might employ can also help promote safety.

We must introduce an important caveat at this point. Structure and facilitation alone do not necessarily build a safe environment. Indeed, processes that seem oppressive, stifling, culturally inappropriate, or arbitrary can make the situation worse. There are at least two reasons to involve participants or their representatives as collaborators in process design. One is to build ownership, and the second is to make sure that the structural arrangements are appropriate for the community.

Treat participants as collaborators rather than competitors. When a public event is understood primarily as a place for venting feelings, expressing opinions, and persuading others, you can predict that old, destructive patterns will continue. On the other hand, when an event is understood as an opportunity for participants to work together toward a commonly valued outcome, the conversation will take on a different tone.

Consider: A city is experiencing tremendous growth problems and wants to seek public input into the situation. One way would be to hold a "City Growth Forum" and allow people to debate competing points of view. Another way to frame the session, in contrast, would be to establish a collaborative goal, such as developing a growth policy. Here, stakeholders would be asked to work together to frame the issue, define various positions and interests, and explore creative options. Even when stakeholders express significantly different points of view, they feel that they are participants in a planning effort rather than advocates pleading their positions to a court of policymakers.

Participants can be viewed as collaborators in trying out experimental forms of public communication. We have taken this approach on several occasions: Tell people that we want to see if an issue can be discussed in a

different way and ask them to come and try it out. Here, participants are
working together to see how this new format works. They will state clearly
what they think, what they want, and what they hope to achieve, but the purpose is not so much to persuade one another as to see how a new form of
communication works. Often, they engage a creative process enthusiasti-
cally and are intrigued by it. At these moments, the focus shifts from positions to processes. Sometimes our best ambassadors turn out to be people
who participated in our innovative public meetings in the past. Indeed, one
of our clients recently told us that he had become "a dialogue convert."

Put community leaders and authorities in a serious listening role. Often,
community leaders and other authorities are actively engaged in persuasion
with the public. They present proposals, defend actions, justify policies,
and advocate courses of action. Using the DAD model, policy makers
decide what should be done, *announce* it to the public, and then *defend* their
plans against a storm of protest. Under DAD, public involvement is strictly
pro forma, accomplishes little of value, and serves only to frustrate both the
public and the policymakers.

Sometimes, officials are genuinely interested in public input, but often
they are not. Indeed, they often use public hearings to gauge support for
their political positions. The traditional setup for public hearings merely
reinforces this feeling. The council, board, or commission sits at the front
facing the audience, and members of the audience make their appeals one by
one.

When alternative processes are used, leaders can take a different role.
They can "listen in" as citizens deliberate on issues. It is sometimes necessary to "train" leaders how to listen in a new way, to listen for stories, experiences, values, shared concerns, common ground, true differences, different
perspectives, and creative ideas. In this kind of format, the leaders do not
dominate but take a backstage role. Indeed, they may be called upon to
respond to what they heard, but only after the participants themselves have
had ample opportunity to talk through an issue.

We recently facilitated a very interesting conference for Los Alamos
National Laboratory. Management wanted to know how to build trustworthiness with employees on matters of safety and health and called together
15 employees in a small conference to talk about this issue. We asked the
decision makers to watch the deliberation on a closed-circuit television in
another room, with the full knowledge and permission of the employees.
These managers listened intently for 3 hours, while the employees talked

through a number of options for building trust. The employees were extremely honest and even critical of management at several points. Clearly, the environment felt safe enough for them to open up about their concerns and ideas. We were in the room with the managers as they listened in to this conversation. One director was so surprised at the employees' candor that he approached us and whispered, "Do they realize we are watching?" At the end of this event, the managers talked to the employees about what they had heard. They showed that they were listening well, that they took employee concerns very seriously, and that they would follow up with constructive action.

Our colleague Jeff Grant once suggested the use of "keynote listeners." We recently had the opportunity to use this concept at a 1-day conference in Richland, Washington. The conference was designed to begin collaboration between the institutions of higher education and the Hispanic communities of the Tri-Cities area. We asked the heads of both campuses in the area, Dr. Larry James of Washington State University—Tri-Cities and Dr. Lee Thornton of Columbia Basin College, to serve as keynote listeners. At the beginning of the day, we introduced them to the 100 participants and explained that they would be listening in to the various groups and plenary sessions of the day. We met with Drs. James and Thornton before the event to talk about how they might listen and what they might listen for. We were delighted that they embraced this unusual role and did an excellent job of listening without interfering. At the end of the day, we invited them to join us in a small circle in the middle of the room and asked them to reflect on what they had heard. They told us what most surprised them, excited them, and what commitments they were willing to make. As the participants left a few minutes later, it was clear that they had felt heard, were excited, and were ready to continue the collaboration on several fronts.

Plan ongoing processes in which safety and trust can develop over time. A safe environment is not necessarily something that can be achieved immediately. Often, safety builds as participants gain experience with the methods employed. One-shot events can sometimes be very effective, but more often, we want a series of events or connected processes. Especially in very conflictual environments, trust may have to grow gradually.

At the time of this writing, the Public Dialogue Consortium has been sponsoring public issue processes in Cupertino, California, for three years. We started off tentatively, meeting with small groups to explore their concerns and visions. At first, participants and city leaders were suspicious and watched closely. Over time, however, they began to feel more comfortable with our work, and many people returned several times to participate in our events. In general, we think they have found the process employed in our meetings to be fresh, interesting, helpful, and safe.

We advocate designing processes that span several days if possible. You can have a multiday event or series of events held periodically. One 3-day community-visioning event we facilitated had a rocky start because participants were unsure about what to expect. By the next morning, however, they were feeling much more comfortable with the process and participants, and by the third day, they were wildly enthusiastic about what was happening.

Build on prior success. An important learning from the Cupertino Community Project is that success breeds greater success. When people see that new processes work and come to be comfortable with them, they trust those processes even more. In Cupertino, we have hosted many different kinds of events, groups, and processes. We have had small groups, large town meetings, trainings, interviews, school-related projects, and much more. Because Cupertino has become infused with this kind of communication, citizens are increasingly comfortable attending and participating. A sure sign of success occurred when the work started to be taken over by the citizens themselves. One group, the Citizens of Cupertino Cross Cultural Consortium (the 5Cs), now creates and facilitates processes for communicating about community issues in this city.

Frame issues in safe ways. How an issue is framed can make a big difference in the felt safety of a discussion. This means thinking carefully about how topics are phrased. Some wording promotes negative, complaint-oriented talk. Alternative wording, in contrast, can help participants talk in a new way about the issue.

Two of the central issues treated in our Cupertino work are *cultural richness* and *community safety,* originally framed as *racial tension* and *crime prevention.* There is nothing really wrong with the latter, but they do call attention to the problem rather than to the solution. In the case of racial tension, the phrasing of the issue was critical because this issue had become undiscussable. In other words, the issue itself was unsafe. Citizens just didn't know how to discuss it productively, so they did not discuss it at all.

Community safety is an interesting framing. We found that it opened the discussion significantly so that citizens were able to make connections with many things. Indeed, some did talk about crime and violence, but participants were also able to explore many dimensions of a safe community and to talk about specific actions that might be taken to achieve the vision. *Cultural richness* took the focus off the problem associated with the changing demographics of the community and called attention to many ways in which cultural diversity is a community asset. In our meetings and discussion groups, participants discussed many ways of achieving cultural richness in the community.

The Appreciative Turn

In our work in private and public settings, we have come to appreciate conflict as a rich, positive resource. Our mentors have taught us that inquiring after the positive can be one of the most powerful moves a third party can make. Typically, those embroiled in a conflict have a very hard time seeing anything positive in the situation. And yet, behind every "negative" circumstance is a positive shadow, a vision of what might be. We cannot know what is bad if we do not have an ideal for the good.

Our colleagues Barnett Pearce and Ralph Banks demonstrate this principle through Aikido, a marshal art. Aikido practitioners look for the energy of struggle. Rather than strike against a moving source of energy, they find ways to move with it, to direct it, and to use it to achieve a positive outcome. The challenge for the public issues facilitator is the same—to direct passion, energy, concern, and involvement in positive, constructive, and humane directions.

When we started our work in Cupertino, we did not initially ask group members to itemize their problems. Instead, we asked them what they most appreciated about their community. We asked for positive stories and began to make a list of the resources on which they could rely. They told us how neighbors helped one another after a devastating earthquake. They told us about the fine schools in the community and their appreciation for culture and education. They told us about the friendly atmosphere and youth activities.

One of the most interesting things we did in Cupertino was a series of intergenerational interviews. We trained high school students to conduct appreciative inquiry and asked them to interview adults in the community about race relations. The students asked their parents, neighbors, church friends, teachers, and other adults to recount positive stories of interracial relations in the city. They collected many stories and shared these on posters and in presentations at a town hall meeting. This was just one way for participants to get in touch with many positive resources for building cultural richness in their community.

One of the most effective ways to make an appreciative turn is to explore the future. After itemizing problems and concerns, participants can talk about the future they want to build. Then, they can use their energy and passion to plan concrete actions to alleviate the concerns and build the vision. For example, participants in groups can construct scenarios. Using creative imagination, they can paint a rather specific picture of various hypothetical futures. After several alternative scenarios are developed, the participants can step back and evaluate them critically and then deliberate on the pros and cons of each. This technique is a very constructive and appreciative way to identify shared and differing values, experiences, and goals.

Of course, groups are not always ready to be "appreciative." Often, citizens need time to work through their concerns and complaints. As they do so, we can make mental (and sometimes written) notes of the hidden visions in the negative so that we can help the group find a positive path later, when ready. One way to make a transition from the negative to the positive is to broaden the context of the discussion. If a group seems to be stuck in a conflict about building a hospital near a particular neighborhood, you might say, "I'm struck by how important the quality of life is here in this area. Could you talk for a while about what is important to you in this high quality of life?" You acknowledge what the group has been fighting about, redefine it as positive energy, and broaden the context to allow this positive vision to be explored. Then, using the criteria of good community life, the topic of the hospital can be revisited in a new way.

This technique was used effectively in the formation of the 6-6 group, discussed in Chapter 1. Recall that this organization developed out of a heated dispute between ranchers and environmentalists in Arizona on legislation permitting cougars and bears to be shot. A group of six environmentalists and six ranchers met privately to discuss this issue. The facilitator refused to let them begin by reiterating their respective arguments. Instead, she asked them to list what they wanted for the land. Discovering that they wanted the same things, they realized that they could collaborate to achieve those goals. The 6-6 now sponsors collaborative ranching teams to solve "on the ground" problems on actual ranches throughout the West. They do not worry that they may have significant disagreements but concentrate on what they can do together to achieve their common goals.

- **Making Spaces for
Constructive Public Conversation**

We owe a great deal to our colleagues in the Public Dialogue Consortium (PDC) for teaching us many creative ways to work through difficult public issues. The PDC is a group of professors, students, and practitioners, mostly schooled in communication, dedicated to helping communities develop superior new forms of public communication. As in hundreds of similar organizations throughout the world, the members of the PDC worry about destructive patterns commonly seen in communities. The organization works with a systemic, communication orientation in a variety of settings to establish effective processes for dialogue.

The PDC has an evolving set of methods for achieving these goals. It networks with other practitioners and organizations to learn techniques and stimulate its own creativity. In this section we discuss several practices we have learned through our work with the PDC.

*Gaining Ownership:
Collaborative Issue Framing*

We first learned about issue framing many years ago when we attended a training of the National Issues Forums (NIF). The NIF is a remarkable organization. In conjunction with the Kettering Foundation and the Public Agenda Foundation, the NIF each year identifies certain national issues for public consideration. For each issue, a small number of policy options are identified, and background materials are drafted. Participants in forums and study circles throughout the country then deliberate on the policy options as outlined in the NIF materials.

Issue framing involves identifying and phrasing a concern, or policy problem, and generating various options that might be adopted. The policy options are general approaches that differ from one another in important respects. If the issue is well framed, the options reflect realistic proposals actually encountered in the national debate. NIF issues are framed very carefully using focus groups.

We once sponsored an NIF forum on affirmative action using the standard NIF booklet. The forum worked out OK, but we were surprised to hear from many participants that the issue somehow did not feel quite right, that it was strangely distant from their own experience. This experience made us aware that how an issue is framed affects the quality of deliberation that takes place.

If participants do not recognize this issue as "their" issue, the meetings will probably not work out. We do not mean to imply that nationally framed issues are always ineffective. Indeed, NIF-framed issues have worked effectively in thousands of forums and study circles over the past 20 years.

In many communities, nationally framed issues will spark intense and productive discussion. We helped to sponsor a project called Community Conversations on Violence, a month-long series of study circles produced by the Study Circle Resource Center based in Connecticut. The project was quite successful, as reported by many of the over 200 participants in numerous dialogue groups that met throughout the city. Although the format and materials were "canned," they left open much opportunity for each study circle to redefine the issue and options in its own way.

Issue framing is not always easy. In preparing for the employee conference at Los Alamos National Laboratory described previously, we worked with the Public Involvement Design Study group, or PIDS. We worked with PIDS for months trying to frame just the right issue to make this a successful event. Going through several iterations and exploring several different issues and options, the group settled on Trustworthiness in Safety and Health. They carefully crafted three quite different approaches for gaining employee trust, wrote a booklet describing each, and recruited 15 employees to deliberate on this issue. The conference was quite successful in many ways, but there was one problem: The employees had a hard time grasping and coping with the issue as we had framed it. Despite their hard work, PIDS was really not the right group to help us frame the issue. We should have had at least one focus group, or a series of interviews, with line employees to help define and draft the issue.

There is no one process by which issues should be framed. Sometimes, it is best to leave an issue open and somewhat vague. Other times, you want a very specific and clearly defined statement. Sometimes, talking with a variety of people in the community about their concerns and listening closely to the language or "grammar" they use in describing these concerns can accomplish the issue framing. Other times, a rather formal and explicit issue framing should be used. Often, we let the issues emerge organically from the discussion of a group.

Although it requires a great deal of facilitation skill, an inductive meeting format can be a productive way to encourage collaboration on issue framing. Such meetings usually begin rather openly by having participants address a general question such as, "What challenges does this community face?" Facilitators then make note of the issues and concerns that flow out of this discussion, work with the group on how to cluster and phrase the concerns, have the participants select those issues they wish to explore further, and provide a creative process whereby these self-defined issues can be discussed.

Other times, a more formal method is called for. In these situations, the following procedure is helpful:

1. Begin by asking the group participants to make a list of their concerns.
2. Work with the group to cluster these into meaningful categories.
3. Identify one cluster on which the group wants to work.
4. Have the group discuss how this issue should be worded. (We often encourage groups to phrase the issue as a question, such as, "How can teacher-parent relations be improved?")
5. Brainstorm many possible actions for addressing the question, and eliminate the obviously unrealistic ideas from the list.
6. Have the groups cluster the ideas into categories or general approaches and decide what to call each category.

When we talk about issue framing, it often sounds as if it is a separate process, preliminary to the "real" dialogue that will follow later. This is a false distinction, of course, and we would prefer to think of issue framing itself as an integral part of public dialogue. When citizens begin to talk about what their issues and options are, they are already engaged in an important form of public communication.

Avoiding the Commonplace:
Creative Public Meetings

We have been blessed with many creative colleagues. From them, we have learned that new and effective forms of public communication require creativity, and we have learned how to be innovative in designing public issue processes. Indeed, event design can be one of the most fun and rewarding parts of public facilitation.

We recently taught a university course in facilitation at a branch campus and attracted a number of experienced professionals. We used a collaborative learning format and had a truly enjoyable time. Everyone seemed to gain from the experience, and we all learned from one another. The largest class assignment was a creative event design project. Each student identified an issue or situation that could benefit from public participation, imagined that he or she had been called upon to design a meeting or series of meetings around this situation, and created a format for the meeting. Almost everyone reported that he enjoyed the assignment immensely and had learned a great deal about how to create specific processes to accomplish high-quality communication.

When we accept a facilitation job, we put together a creative design team, set up a flip chart, roll up our sleeves, and get to work. Sometimes, it takes just a few hours. Sometimes, we may work at it for several days, and for more complex processes, the design process may go on for several weeks or months. We often involve our clients or participants in the design process, and a back-and-forth revision process almost always occurs.

Although we enjoy this process very much, pleasure is not the point. If you take a communication perspective, you are looking for forms of communication that allow participants to engage in the most effective interaction possible while experiencing the power of new ways to communicate. We want participants to say, "This is fresh and different, and it worked in a way we have never seen before." We want participants to see that there are better ways of doing the public's business. We want them to experience the power of dialogue.

We received just such a reaction to the two public engagement events we facilitated for NABIR, the bioremediation project mentioned earlier in the chapter. The NABIR committee knew what it wanted to accomplish. It was interested in experimenting with an interactive dialogue format in which participants could learn significant new things from one another without the domination of experts. They wanted good two-way communication flow, and they wanted to identify facilitation skills necessary to continue having such events in the future. As a pilot, the committee arranged for two 1-day events, one for the Pacific Northwest Laboratory in Richland, Washington, and the other for the Oak Ridge National Laboratory in Tennessee.

After learning more about what they hoped to accomplish, we put together four design possibilities. They studied these and selected one they felt would fit the culture. We developed this design in more detail, and they gave us good feedback on how it might be improved. We ended up with a unique communication experience that was a real eye-opener for most of the participants. It was not perfect and will certainly be improved in the future, but as a first attempt, the format worked very well.

Each event involved three groups of eight participants each. The *professionals* were the scientists and staff members of the NABIR project. The *stakeholders* consisted of individuals who had been community activists on science issues in the past, and the *newcomers* were involved members of the community who had never participated on science issues before. We began by having each group reflect on its role in the system and talk about the group's assets, potential gains, and hopes for a successful event.

Then we divided the group into triads—a professional, a stakeholder, and a newcomer. In these small groups, the professional told a story about his or her work, being careful to talk in lay terms and use a narrative format. Then, the newcomer interviewed the professional to learn more about the work. The stakeholder observed this process and later shared his or her observations with the other two. This interviewing activity turned out to be one of the most successful parts of the meeting. The newcomers learned a great deal about the subject, the professionals gained insights from the newcomers' questions that they could not have gained in a typical presentational style, and the stakeholders gained insights by listening to these unique conversations. By the end of this segment, the three groups felt they were on an equal footing, and good dialogue had already begun.

We debriefed after the interview segment, then formed three new groups, each with an equal number of professionals, stakeholders, and newcomers. Here, they discussed their concerns about bioremediation and the siting of field research centers, a somewhat controversial topic. After sharing these concerns in a plenary session, the group continued to work on visions and scenarios. Later, the scenarios were presented in a plenary session, and the whole group deliberated about the pros and cons of each. We encouraged them to discuss the following questions:

- What opportunities and benefits would this scenario make possible?
- What would be lost if this scenario became a reality?
- What would be the costs of pursuing this scenario?
- What tradeoffs would be necessary to achieve this scenario?

The groups then talked about next steps and spent time at the end of the day harvesting what they had learned.

At the end of the day, many participants told us that they had never experienced anything like this, that they found it a dynamic and refreshing approach, and that they had learned a great deal on many levels.

Although we have used many of the same tools over and over, we never use them exactly the same way twice, and we have learned to combine our methods in creative ways. We have had participants create posters and maps on butcher paper; we have taught process tools to participants during actual engagement events; we have had onstage interviews; we have used numerous types of dyadic and small group exercises; we have had speakers; and we have used closed circuit TV, reflecting teams, simulations and games, and numerous other features.

Giving Careful Consideration: Public Deliberation

As we use the term, *deliberation* is a systematic and careful discussion of an issue. In our minds, a series of speeches advocating different points of view, one after another, does not really qualify. What makes deliberation different?

First, deliberation is focused on a well-defined issue and options. Everyone is asked to concentrate on the issue as defined and to think critically about the options. Second, deliberation is organized around the aspects of the issue and action alternatives. Third, participants are asked to weigh the pros and cons of various alternatives. And fourth, deliberation connects the issue to actual personal experiences, perspectives, and values.

There may be a good deal of advocacy and argument in a deliberation session. Participants will, and should, disagree on what course of action should be taken. At the same time, however, they are asked to do two important things: They should listen well to different points of view, and they should weigh the pros and cons of every alternative, even the one they most favor. In deliberation, the goal is mutual learning, not winning. Eventually, policymakers and even individual voters will make their decisions about how the issue should be handled, and deliberation is a way to make those decisions more informed.

Our colleague John Gastil created one of the most productive formats for deliberation. Called Citizen Conferences, this process involves small groups of representative citizens deliberating on policy options on an important public issue. A representative sample, using polling techniques, is selected to participate. The citizens, called advisors, are paid for their time, and they spend a day learning about and deliberating on the issue at hand. Because they may not have dealt with the issue before, their perspectives can be fresh and reflective of the wisdom of the community at large.

Usually, the event begins with a series of short presentations by a resource panel composed of individuals who have some knowledge of and interest in the issue. The panelists must represent diverse points of view and may disagree vigorously among themselves on certain points. Although they may give a very short presentation, most of the time with the panelists is guided by questions from the advisors themselves. After talking with the panelists for a couple of hours and reviewing written materials on the issue, the advisors retreat to a deliberation room and talk for as long as 3 hours on several possible policy options. Policymakers, those who will actually make final decisions, are watching the group via closed circuit television. They will have the advantage of hearing the values actually expressed by citizens as they talk. They will learn what is really important to the group, what their shared concerns are, what they most want, and what the true differences are among them. In the deliberations, the advisors are encouraged to be critical, to explore the issue honestly, to disagree with one another, and to explore the pros and cons of each option. If they need more information, they can invite resource persons into the room to answer questions. In the end, the advisors are asked to generate a set of concrete recommendations for the policymakers. The recommendations may or may not conform to one of the preset options. They may include elements of several or something altogether new. John Gastil used this model in many communities throughout New Mexico on the issue of transportation, and the citizens and policymakers alike found the process refreshingly different, interesting, and very helpful.

Getting Personal:
Study Circles and Dialogue Groups

Although deliberations can and do occur in large public meetings, we think that smaller study circles are the best format for meaningful discussion. There are several reasons for this. First, small groups can meet regularly over a period of time and really get into the details of an issue in ways that are not possible in large groups. Second, a degree of trust can develop in an ongoing study circle, making true dialogue possible. Third, in small groups, participants can get to know one another, share their life experiences, and develop a level of understanding for differing perspectives not typically seen in large meetings. Finally, small groups can work creatively with an issue and customize the format of their own group.

The Israeli-Palestinian dialogue mentioned earlier featured several speakers on different sides of the issue. They gave presentations, answered questions, and interacted with one another for over 2 hours on a Sunday afternoon. At the end of the session, we held short discussion groups. Even though these groups were quickly organized and very brief, only half an hour, the quality of discussion was quite good in most of the groups, and well over half of the participants immediately signed up to participate in regular dialogue groups in the future.

There is no end to the ways in which small dialogue groups can be structured. In the model used by the NIF, the group meets for about 5 weeks. The first week, the group explores the issue in general. They then address the policy options, one option each of the following 3 weeks. In the 5th week, they harvest what they have learned.

The model of the Study Circle Resource Center is somewhat different. These groups meet weekly for about a month, and they divide their time according to dimensions or aspects of the problem. For example, in the conversations on violence, groups had four meetings, in which they discussed (1) how violence affects our lives, (2) the reasons for violence, (3) neighborhood solutions, and (4) school solutions.

We have had tremendous luck using the CVA model in small dialogue groups. Standing for *concerns, visions,* and *actions,* this model is easy to teach participants. The use of this process is almost universally successful. A group can enter the process at any point—discussing concerns, visions, or actions. The idea is that each of these three elements is related to the other two, as shown in Figure 7.1. Our concerns lead to visions, visions are motivated by concerns, and actions both achieve visions and mitigate concerns.

In a typical CVA session, we would ask participants to explore their concerns about some topic. Then, we would work with the group to help participants translate these concerns into visions. The operative question is, "If these concerns were eliminated, what would things be like?" The answer, of course, expresses the group's vision. Then, we typically go into a creative period of brainstorming and developing action plans for alleviating the concerns and achieving the visions.

As an example, we once sponsored a town hall meeting in Cupertino. We had about 150 participants working at tables of 8 in facilitated dialogues. Next to each table was a flip chart. The facilitator led the group through a discussion of concerns, visions, and actions. Then each group isolated one

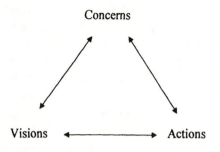

Figure 7.1. The CVA Model

shared concern it wished to share with other groups and, on the flip chart, drew a CVA triangle with the concern, the resulting vision, and one action that might be taken to help achieve the group's vision. Then in a plenary session, each group shared its "picture" of the CVA with the other groups. After about 18 presentations, participants had a rich set of concerns, visions, and actions. The ensuing discussion was wide-ranging and productive, and it led to concrete action within the community.

At a community-visioning event in Pasco, Washington, we used the CVA differently. In groups, participants brainstormed their concerns. After a brief round of reports, we asked participants what concerns they most wanted to explore and formed cluster groups around those concerns on the spot using an open-space method. The groups met in various locations around the room and explored their concern, the related vision, and potential actions. At various points during the day, we interrupted the groups for reports and asked groups to network with one another, to communicate between groups to discover how they might relate one concern or vision to another concern or vision and how they might support one another. We also gave the participants a chance to re-form groups, combine them, and switch from one group to another. It was interesting to watch this organic and fluid process evolve over the course of the event. In the end, there were three reconstituted groups, each presenting an elaborate and well-defined plan of action to achieve its desired visions.

Building Capacity: Public Training Events

In our work, the best outcome occurs when participants themselves learn constructive forms of communication and use these without the help of a third party. They carry forth the work on their own. This has happened in a variety of ways in Cupertino. The 5-C's, the self-formed group dedicated to improving communication, took up the banner and is sponsoring creative town hall meetings of its own. In addition, students in the high schools are teaching creative facilitation techniques to other students and sponsoring dialogue events.

There are many ways to help a community build the capacity to change its patterns of interaction on difficult issues. Certainly, one way is through modeling and practice. As more and more people participate in alternative processes, they begin to "get a feel for it," start advocating the use of these methods, and spearhead efforts to get community dialogue going. Often, we help by providing materials such as videos, training manuals, and issue booklets that groups can use on their own.

Training is one of the most direct methods of building capacity to change. One way we do this is to present "process tools" to participants during a public engagement event. Sometimes, we give the participants a handout with guidelines for communication. We always explain the processes we are using and often have "steps" on a flip chart or overhead transparency. Sometimes we actually demonstrate the process to be used. For example, if we ask participants to interview one another using appreciative inquiry, we might demonstrate the interview before having them do it. One of our most successful uses of process tools was a 2-day public meeting in Cupertino. The first day, a Friday afternoon, we presented training in dialogue methods to the citizens, about 100 individuals. We talked to them about how dialogue is different; we coached them on how to communicate in a dialogue; and we demonstrated actual techniques. Then, we spent all day Saturday in an actual community dialogue. The result was remarkable. The citizens developed a very good idea about how they should communicate during the event; they came to appreciate this; and many have become outspoken advocates for dialogue throughout the community.

Another approach is to have event-specific facilitator training. You begin by inviting interested individuals to be facilitators. They may or may not have previous experience, but they show up because they want to help promote dialogue in their community. After training, they then work as facilitators in an actual community event. In Waco, we trained 150 individuals, kids and adults, to help facilitate our youth summits there. We later followed up with additional training to help begin a facilitator corps that could be called upon in the future to facilitate various public meetings in and around Waco.

Event-specific training, as opposed to general training, can be especially effective because the trainees are highly motivated to use their new skills in the upcoming event. When we do this kind of training, we can tie the skills to the actual processes the trainees will use in the event itself. The advantage of this approach is clear: There is a concrete outcome that will have immediate effect. Once, we held a simultaneous community-visioning event and facilitator training. One of us met with the facilitator trainees in a nearby room, while the other directed the community event. We coordinated the training and event in such a way that the trainees could practice as small-group facilitators at the public event. The facilitators went back and forth from the training room to the event room. Although this design is more complex than most, it was amazingly successful. The trainees got good basic facilitation training; they were highly motivated to learn; they engaged in the best possible practice; and we gained an instant "staff" for the public event. The facilitators we trained at that time have remained very interested in alternative processes and have come back to facilitate other events in the community.

Occasionally after facilitating a public event, we receive a request by participants for training in our methods. This is one of the most gratifying rewards a facilitator can receive. Here, you have people who experienced an alternative process and were sufficiently impressed to want to learn how to do it themselves. We have offered public trainings ranging from 8 to 40 hours, depending upon available resources and the scope of the training desired. Most of our trainings are about 16 to 20 hours. Sometimes, we offer a two-part training in basic facilitation and advanced systemic techniques. In our longer trainings, we are able to include a segment on creative event design, in which participants enjoy working in groups to create public engagement processes of their own.

When we work in public settings, we are constantly reminded of the systemic nature of human life. The salient problems, themes, interaction patterns, and intervention methods are similar in all of the venues in which we work, whether they be private relationships, small groups, organizations, or communities. These processes may manifest themselves somewhat differently at various levels, but the communication perspective and systemic view bring them together in our theory and practice.

In the following chapter, the final chapter of the book, we expand our ongoing conversation to include several colleagues we greatly respect.

▪ Resources You Can Use

Cooperrider, D., & Srivastva, S. (Eds.). (1990). *Appreciative management in leadership: the power of positive thought and action.* San Francisco: Jossey-Bass.

Daggett, D. (1995). *Beyond the rangeland conflict: Toward a west that works.* Flagstaff, AZ: The Grand Canyon Trust.

Daitz, B. (1999). *Whose home on the range: A documentary about resolving environmental conflict* [Video]. (Available from New Mexico Center for Dispute Resolution, PO Box 25044, Albuquerque, NM 87125-5044)

Gastil, J. (2000). *By popular demand: Revitalizing representative democracy through deliberative elections.* Berkeley: University of California Press.

Gerzon, M. (1996). *A house divided: Six belief systems struggling for America's soul.* New York: Tarcher/Putnam.

Gutman, A., & Thompson, D. (1996). *Democracy and disagreement: Why moral conflict cannot be avoided in politics, and what should be done about it.* Cambridge, MA: Harvard University Press.

Kriesberg, L., Northrup, T. A., & Thorson, S. J. (1989). *Intractable conflicts and their transformation.* Syracuse, NY: Syracuse University Press.

National Issues Forums, 100 Commons Rd., Dayton, OH 45459-2777, www.nifi.org

Pearce, W. B., & Littlejohn, S. W. (1997). *Moral conflict: When social worlds collide.* Thousand Oaks, CA: Sage.

Pearce, W. B., & Pearce, K. A. (1999). Combining passions and abilities: Toward dialogic virtuosity. *Southern Communication Journal, 65,* 161-175.

Public Conversations Project, 46 Kondazian Street, Watertown, MA 02172. www.publicconversations.org

Public Dialogue Consortium, 504 Luna Blvd. NW, Albuquerque, NM 87102. www.publicdialogue.org

Smith, M. (1998). *The Catron County Citizens Group: A case study in community collaboration.* Albuquerque, NM: New Mexico Center for Dispute Resolution.

Spano, S. (2000). *Public dialogue and participative democracy: The Cupertino community project.* Cresskill, NJ: Hampton Press.

Study Circle Resource Center, PO Box 203, Promfret, CT 06258. www.studycircles. com

PART IV

Toward Better Social Worlds

A Conversation With Friends

Over the years, we have often referred to our work as an ongoing conversation. In our respective offices, in restaurants, on airplanes, over e-mail, and on the phone, our 7-year conversation has taken many turns and explored many topics. In this conversation, we have seen our learning intensify, our minds change, our perspectives expand, and our practices enlarge. In preparing this chapter, we sat down for a couple of hours to talk, with a tape recorder on the table between us, just to see where our conversation might lead next. In this section, we share the themes that emerged on that occasion.

By expanding our view of communication, our worlds have also grown. We began our discussion by looking back. We talked about our early communication work—long before we met one another—and how our field has moved through many stages to where it is today. Back then, 20 or 25 years ago, we began to sense that ideas about communication were limited. Both of us were somehow uneasy with the "hypodermic needle" model that seemed prevalent in those days. Communication was taught as a transmission: A speaker communicates something to a listener (receiver). Many communication researchers studied methods to decrease interference and ensure that intended messages got across. We appreciate those contributions to our field but have moved to a place in which communication takes on a much richer meaning—the way of constructing the very worlds in which we live.

In reflecting on these changes, Kathy commented on how the communication discipline seemed too inwardly focused when she first started her work: "After studying mediation and conflict, I was intrigued by the cross-cutting potential of the field of communication. Many other disciplines could learn from the communication perspective, and mediation could be one avenue for development of the communication discipline. I suggested we interact with psychology, political science, law, counseling, and sociology."

Along the same vein, Stephen recalled his early mediation work and the limited notion of communication in this new area: "I was at the University of Massachusetts doing some research on mediation when community mediation was new. We sat behind a one-way mirror and observed the sessions from a critical perspective and immediately noticed that the method used often reproduced the very division that brought the disputants there in the first place. Using a rather transmissional approach to communication, the mediators were like a conduit, going back and forth from one party to the other." Stephen commented that our practice of mediation today treats communication as the very medium in which new social worlds can be made. In retrospect, we can now see that our view of communication has expanded from a limited, linear, inward-looking perspective to a systemic, constructionist, and dynamic notion of what communication is and should be.

Communication has practical virtues in everyday life. As we talked, we discovered that our communication interest has paralleled most everything else going on in our world. For example, we thought about the ways we had used communication to build a functioning family, and Kathy told of her interest in communication skills in parenting: "I focused on communication to help my kids learn how to interact well in the world. I didn't know it then, but when I taught courses on 'How to talk so kids will listen and listen so kids will talk,' I was using the same perspective we offer in our work today. People support what they create. Involvement leads to commitment."

Stephen said he has come to realize lately that experiences in his teens and 20s profoundly affected his current orientation toward communication. As a debater in school, he learned to argue for any position: "Even during those years," he commented, "I was debating, and the Vietnam War was going on, and I was somehow getting a personal lesson that led me to take a multiperspective view of life. Even as a young professor, I found myself committed to helping young people understand a variety of different perspectives on human experience." Stephen added that his interest in conflict as a positive resource came naturally after those formative experiences.

By privileging the wisdom of ordinary people, we build more durable social worlds. As we explored these new ideas about communication, we realized that our conception of the role of "experts" in a dynamic communication system has surely evolved. Kathy recounted her attempts to empower mothers to make healthy relationships with their babies. The natural tendency was to ask the doctor what to do, but "if mothers are encouraged to parent a child in a way that's safe and instinctual, what results is a natural process that fulfills many important needs to both the baby and the mother. In this realm of life, the mother and baby are the experts!"

We recognized, of course, that experts in any field have an important role that needs to be clearly understood. We are convinced, however, that experts have a great deal to learn from citizens, community members, employees, and ordinary people who are doing what they do. Stephen called this learning "the wisdom of ordinary citizens." Kathy tied her work in parenting issues together with her work in conflict management. "Whether it is parenting, personal decision making, teaching, or mediating, I am committed to interacting rather than prescribing. I am glad we are committed to that 'high road' in our work also." So much communication consists of advice, suggestions, orders, and heavy-handed intervention, and in our discussion, we both expressed the desire to see more respectful interactions among all types of people.

There is truth in many positions on an issue. Stephen recently came to the realization that he is an "in-between" person, noting that "no matter what side of the issue you are on, you have a good reason for being there." He added, "I always had trouble understanding people who were so self-identified with one side of an issue that they could not see the good reasons one might have for holding a different view. Over the years, I have very consciously made the choice to be *in-between* and help transform differences that are otherwise adversarial."

He remarked that there are constraints to deliberately taking the in-between space, including the potential confusion of not knowing what you stand for. At the same time, however, that in-between space can be a foundation, a basis for work and life. The possibilities in constructing our social worlds seem to expand when we deliberately put ourselves there. As an in-between person, Stephen now believes he stands for something very important—bridging and co-constructing mutually beneficial realities.

Making a commitment is a way of marking moments in an evolving social reality. We have always emphasized commitment making in our work. During this conversation, we talked a bit about how this fits into our overall way of working. Whether brief and transitory or deep and longstanding, the commitments seem to act as a marker, a stop along the way to note a move forward in life's work.

Kathy first began emphasizing the need for deliberate commitment steps in problem solving, planning, and conflict management work. She noticed that people who are living and working together usually want a sense of accomplishment, a view of the next steps facing them. Having these conscious commitments as a reference point contributes to an ongoing construction of their workable world. "I remember a friend talking about how much he appreciated his staff taking time out of their hectic day to meet for 10 or 20 minutes for a staff meeting. They had decided that if they could take that time to make some deliberate decisions, some concrete steps on an issue or project, the whole staff would have a marker to refer back to during the week."

Stephen remarked that commitment markers essentially say, "Let's be clear about what we are making." Groups are always engaged in a process of making social worlds, but often, they are confused about what kind of world is actually being made. They may not know what is happening, and a commitment step is one way of tagging a moment in an ongoing social construction.

Peacemaking is more than ending wars. An extraordinary learning we have appreciated over the years is the multiple dimensions of peace. We call ourselves peacemakers and continue to explore the dimensions of that effort in our work and lives. We like to speculate about what we are constructing. Is respectful communication on difficult issues a form of peace? Is a community that decides together on how to use a parcel of its land engaged in peacemaking? Is training scientists in effective means of communicating with the public an example of peace? Is reframing an aggressive response in a workplace mediation also a contribution to peace?

Toward the end of our talk together, Kathy requested a deliberate exploration of our role as peacemakers in the early part of year 2000, "Does peacemaking mean more than the work we are doing right now? Can we create a process for ourselves to explore the dimensions of peace in our work and in our future work? This conversation is a marker, an anchor set in time, where we made a commitment to continue to explore our role as peace-makers."

▪ Expanding the Conversation

The conversation summarized above was both surprising and revealing, as we learned some new things and pinpointed some important insights. In the spirit of ongoing conversation, we thought it would be interesting to see what would happen as new voices entered the discussion. We invited several colleagues we greatly admire to join in. We met with most in person and had e-mail exchanges with others. We asked them about their work and philosophy but mostly listened to their stories. These turned out to be fascinating and exciting talks, and we would like to share them with you now.

Our conversation partners included 10 people: Anne Kass is the chief judge of the family division in the district court in Albuquerque. Rick Sallee attends Cibola High School and works with a peer counseling program called Natural Helpers. Kim Pearce is a professor of speech communication at De Anza College and a principal of Pearce Associates, Inc., in San Mateo, California. Saul (Coco) Fuks is a clinical psychologist on the faculty of the National University in Rosario, Argentina. SanJuanita (Janie) Cantu is an educator, mediator, and community leader living in the rural Hispanic community of Estancia, New Mexico. Robyn Penman is the executive and foundation director of the Communication Research Institute of Australia. Murray Anderson-Wallace is codirector of Inter~logics, in the United Kingdom. Carl Moore is a nationally known facilitator, leadership development trainer, and public participation practitioner. Melinda Smith, the former executive director of the New Mexico Center for Dispute Resolution, is a mediator and adjunct professor of public administration at the University of New Mexico, where she teaches dispute systems design and mediation. Pace VanDevender is the chief information officer at Sandia National Laboratories.

On Self-Insight

Besides her duties on the "bench," **Anne Kass** practices early intervention processes with her clients in the form of settlement conferences and mediations. She is always willing to speak to classes, groups, and individuals who are interested in exploring humane and creative means of managing conflict, and we have enjoyed observing her conflict management processes. We once had a group of visiting Argentine mediators scheduled to observe one of her settlement conferences, but it was cancelled because of a huge snowstorm. Anne came to our home that day and explored mediation with these fellow peacemakers, and this turned out to be the best session of the entire visit. In our inspiring interview with Anne, we asked what she would most want readers of our book to remember from her words. She encouraged readers to *"Be curious about yourself. Take the time to discover your interests, values, and experience leading to them. Ask yourself in every situation, 'What am I bringing to this process?'"*

Many of our conversation partners talked about their own self-insights. For instance, Janie, our teacher friend from Estancia, New Mexico, told us how looking inward has helped in her life. She learned to accept responsibility for her own disabilities and move through the anger associated with her situation. "Being a mediator is therapeutic. I am able to look at situations and understand the necessity of taking responsibility for your actions," Janie observed.

Pace reflected on his self-awareness developed while working at the National Laboratories. He told us, "There are three things that drive people. One is the impact they can make. Second is money, and third is freedom. In my world, the number one motivator should be impact. I wish to make an impact."

Rick told us about his experience in the high school peer counseling program and how he saw the need to do self-reflection, always inquiring about his own motives and values. Rick relies on many others as sounding boards to help him see his options and actions more clearly, "I lean on a variety of people, such as . . . sponsors, my parents, people at church, anyone else I can talk to."

On Self-Trust

Rick Sallee, 17, attends Cibola High School and works with a program there called Natural Helpers, where he is available to assist his peers when they are experiencing tough situations. Using constructive communication skills, Rick helps students, his school, his church, his family and friends, and himself. We learned from Rick the value of internal conversations, of thinking about problem areas in our lives and trusting that the solution will arise. We have enjoyed watching Rick contribute to the world and look forward to including him in more of our work. Rick advises our readers to *"trust yourself. When you get into talking about problems and thinking about them, most of the time, the problem solves itself."* You can help others by knowing what you have to offer and building skills to continue to contribute to helping relationships.

In our conversation with Anne, she addressed the question of honesty quite directly. She sees that when you are working with someone in therapy (or in Rick's Natural Helper program), the clients usually are being honest with themselves, as they want to make a personal change. In an evaluative situation such as a judicial hearing, on the other hand, the clients and their advocates rarely are honest. In fact, they often are trying to convince the judge to exercise power to their own benefit. Anne concluded that in processes where dominant power is minimized, people are more apt to be honest and truthful in their communication with themselves and others.

On Self and Other

Kim Pearce is a professor of speech communication at De Anza College and a principal of Pearce Associates, Inc., in San Mateo, California, where she does communication consulting. As one of the founders of the Public Dialogue Consortium, Kim privileges dialogue in her work with communities, groups, and individuals. We have learned much from Kim, as she encourages and models a kind of peaceful, respectful, and attentive communication. Kim invited us to *"stay in the tension between our own perspective and that of others. This commitment will invite curiosity, wonder, respect, and compassion, enriching us all."*

Coco, our Argentine friend, says that this kind of "relational positioning contributes among people to improved connections that appreciate difference, respectful curiosity opened to surprise." Such connections further "allow different ways to explore reality and promote a playful attitude in life."

Anne talked about the difficulty of this tension in her role as a judge: "One of the things I've learned about myself is how difficult it is to get people to believe that even if I don't seem to agree with a perspective or an opinion in my courtroom, I am not judging that person." When we asked Anne how she is able to live and work in this tension, she answered, "I do a lot more meditation. I breathe more deeply. Owning a cat is very helpful."

Pace gave us a personal example of just the sort of tension Kim referred to. He recalled a "catharsis" time in his work as a director at Sandia National Labs. He called in a consultant to meet with him and 40 leaders from his group to diagnose certain organizational problems they were having. Within the first hour, the consultant was telling the group what was wrong, but Pace could tell from their body language that the participants did not agree with what the consultant was saying. Pace excused the consultant, and asked his employees to open up. They told him that, basically, he was the problem. Pace recalled their comments, "They were made to follow orders and not able to engage with their heart and intellectual and emotional capacity which they were capable of. We changed our management style and I was no longer the center of this large organization. I began to trust them to make decisions and facilitate approaches without my intervention."

Rick talked about the importance of this same kind of tension in internal conversations: "I catch myself doing it when I'm helping somebody with a problem. I'll be talking to them about one thing and helping them out; my body will be telling me another thing, and my heart telling me another. It's like those cartoons you see when people have little bubbles on each side of your head. Back-and-forth communication inside of you."

On Coherence

Saul (Coco) Fuks is a clinical psychologist on the faculty of the National University in Rosario, Argentina. Coco is also director of the Centro de Asistencia a la Comunidad (Center for Community Assistance) there. He has contributed immensely to the field of community psychology and serves communities in South America, Europe, and the United States, working to improve life conditions. We have worked with Coco in Argentina and the United States, and he inspires us to empower people, regardless of their resources, to build the world they desire. When Coco helped us teach a course in Communication and Community Development in 1998, we were struck by the projects he inspired in our students. For months, they reported to us on the results of Coco's teaching and encouragement. Coco encourages readers of this book to *value coherence between your work and your relationship with others.* As for himself as a peacemaker, family therapist, and community psychologist, *"I am interested in maintaining a resonance between my 'scientific' productions and this way of 'being in the world.'"*

We heard this theme also in our conversation with Pace about his work in national security. For Pace, coherence is a way of building trust and collaborative relations with others. Janie talked about a reciprocal relationship between what she has learned about herself and how she relates to the disabled children in her classroom. For Janie, knowing yourself and knowing others goes hand in hand.

Our conversation with Carl provides a living example of the kind of life coherence advocated by Coco. Carl was a professor at Kent State University at the time of the shootings there in 1970. That event and his work on the establishment of the Center for Peaceful Change launched a 30-year career of working to equalize privilege and achieve balance and fairness among all people. Today, he works throughout the nation to help communities find their vision. Always, his way of working is to build processes whereby community members themselves can achieve voice and vision for the future.

On Human Potential

SanJuanita (Janie) Cantu lives in a rural Hispanic area where she is a mediator and educator. She mediates victim-offender cases in Spanish and teaches young children the value of communication skills that can prevent conflict. As a community leader, Janie helps her small town address tough issues in land use, water, family, and safety. Janie talked about her experience mediating cases between juvenile offenders and their victims. She told how the victims came in to the mediation session very angry, not open to discussion. They wanted the child to be punished but, instead, heard the stories from the young individuals (the "offenders"): why they made the choices they did and what the environment they came from was like. The human side of these young people was revealed. Many participants in the mediation processes go away changed and softened, seeing all of the different aspects of the choices people make. Janie wants most to inspire us to *"see the goodness and the potential of everyone, no matter who they are, what limitations they have. Trust in the potential of every person. Expect the best in everyone."*

Kim agreed and told us how she does this in practical ways by listening to stories people tell about their experiences and inviting them to explore untold, unheard, and unknown stories. She described this process: "We help them explore the significance among the stories they live, the stories they tell, and the way they tell their stories." Melinda, who established the victim-offender mediation program in Albuquerque, also emphasizes the importance of stories in her work. Melinda offers a new view of kids in society, especially those in some kind of trouble. She suggests, "We need to build proactive programs to build upon these kids' strengths."

When our friend from the United Kingdom, Murray, discussed with us the importance of building meaning by respecting the stories of others, he told about a time in his work with a social service organization providing mental health assistance to families and children. We were really inspired by the dedication Murray brought to the fragmented clinical, professional, and managerial relationships of mistrust he found in this organization. Murray told of how he and his partner began this work, "We began gently to inquire into the stories that were being told around the organization. . . . We carefully, deliberately, separately, and purposefully dealt with the various stakeholders, acknowledging and validating their differences." How amazing to have Janie "gently" listening to stories of children in Estancia, New Mexico, with the same passion as Murray has listening to workplace stories in Leeds, in the United Kingdom!

On Ordinary Experience

Robyn Penman is the executive and foundation director of the Communication Research Institute of Australia. Robyn looks carefully at the quality of communication in courts of law and the relationship between legislation, language, and the citizen's capacity to act. Robyn lights up a room with her intensity and bright laugh. Her stories about privileging communication in Australia encouraged us all. She has set high standards in her country for people discussing important national and international issues. Robyn tells us that *"communicating matters. Attend to the minutia of the everyday experiences of communication, acting in good faith with both the process and the participants in it."*

Murray also sees the great importance of every speech act. He sees that "language plays a constitutive role in human existence, rather than having a purely representational function." He has learned that realities are created in language and that expression organizes our experience, not the other way around. What a responsibility we have as communicators!

Carl, our New Mexico facilitation colleague, also wants to privilege the communication for participants in sessions he is facilitating. He gives the participants time to think before speaking and then records their actual language to honor all the differences in the room.

We appreciated, too, Melinda's story of her work in Catron County, New Mexico, where she designed processes for the people to explore the severe conflict among the forest service, loggers, environmentalists, and residents.

She says her work there was like a marriage: "You have the highs, the abso-
lute inspiration in terms of communication, incredible civility, and insight.
You also have the same old acrimony and bitterness. I've seen those two
walk hand in hand for over four years."

Kim added to this discussion by telling us of her intent to stay in the tension between expressing one's views and remaining profoundly open to the
other's perspective. She attempts to integrate this into all aspects of her life;
it's a way of being and acting: "For example, I find myself in *daily* situations
with my 10-year-old son and my college students who see the world and act
in ways quite foreign and baffling to me (and I to them). Instead of trying to
make them more like me, I consciously choose to stay in the tension with
them, to learn from them, and to invite them into my worldview."

On Language and Action

Murray Anderson-Wallace is codirector of Inter~logics, an association
based in the United Kingdom dedicated to the development of collaborative
and knowledge management tools for complex business environments.
Much of his work focuses on relationships between groups of professionals,
agencies, and stakeholders. His approach is not to create "harmonious"
relationships but to acknowledge differences and discover what the people
want to do together. Working to construct contexts in which more useful and
generative relationships occur, Murray sees that conversations and changes
can emerge over time. We have worked with Murray both in the United
States and in the United Kingdom, and of the many valuable insights we
have learned from him, one that we use often is the value of transitioning
from the term *strategic planning* to *strategic relationship development.*
Murray offers this thought to readers as they ponder how to create meaning
in their conversational worlds: *"We only own half of what we say. Any sense
of shared meaning depends on the level of mutual cooperation between us."*
Murray sees that there is a great deal to be gained by *viewing language and
conversation as that which builds joint spaces for action.*

As a case in point, Rick described the helping language he uses at his high
school. He says, "We don't give them a solution, though we might give them
different choices. We ask them what they'd like to do about their situation.
We are basically just there to guide them along. They make their own decision." Rick's conversation joins that of the person he is helping, building the
basis for action.

In the same spirit, Melinda sees it as absolutely essential to compare her work with that of other colleagues and talk about the processes to be used. "Otherwise," she points out, "we're working in a tunnel, working in some kind of black box." When she reaches out to other cultures and joins in diverse conversations, Melinda is creating these "joint spaces for action" that Murray describes.

Robyn explores the question of what constitutes good communication practices in the book she is just finishing at home in Australia. She takes dialogue in the Buberian sense as an exemplar form of good communication and says, "I see my responsibility as a primary researcher as one of setting up the conditions for the possibility of dialogue and of making offerings to the collaborative process that further enhance that possibility." Robyn's role and commitment is focused on the *how* of communication. She leaves it up to the other participants to offer the *what*. "I provide *how*/process tools to help them construct a better *what*." We thank Robyn for reminding us that "there is usually not a 'truth' out there to be discovered; rather what we have is a 'trueing' process that requires us to act in good faith with the process of communicating and with the participants in the communication."

On Democracy

Carl Moore is a facilitator, leadership development trainer, and public participation practitioner who for 26 years was professor of communication at Kent State University. His primary emphasis in consulting has been coaching communities in how to conduct communitywide goal setting and visioning, facilitating organizational decision making, directing the development of strategic plans, and conducting retreats and evaluations for community leadership programs. We love Carl's concept of the "Community Store," the name of his consulting practice. The "store" creates spaces where community people can come and gather and become empowered in participative processes. "Customers" in the store can also acquire community-building resources. Carl practices those same principles in his work with the New Mexico Consensus Council, an organization that was created to help governmental entities interact with citizens in addressing vexing public issues and enabling communities to respond to deeply rooted problems. Carl dreams of the *renewed vitalization of democracy*. He sees that people have been *dulled away* from participating in issues that concern them. He wants to welcome greater varieties of people into decision making. *Ask the citizens what they want to do; ask the leaders how they want to get it done.*

Robyn joins Carl's search for "important voices." She told us that "most of the voices I help are not important in the everyday sense. They are the voice of the ordinary citizen or community group, the voice of the HIV/ AIDS patients, of the career for the elderly and disabled, of the construction worker or the small-business person, of the osteoporosis sufferer. These are not usually heard in discussions." We imagine these voices could be visitors to Carl's "community store."

One of the features of Murray's work in Europe is to help parties do things in ways that make sense to them. He emphasizes the importance of "treating all parties as resourceful and knowledgeable, so to design conversational architectures which help to develop an appreciation of the intercontextual logic." Hence the name of Murray's company: Inter~logics.

On Time

Melinda Smith is a mediator and adjunct professor of public administration at the University of New Mexico, where she teaches dispute systems design and mediation. Melinda was founding executive director of the New Mexico Center for Dispute Resolution, where she developed mediation systems in organizational, community, justice, educational, and social service settings. She is currently a coordinator of the New Mexico Consensus Council. She has extensive cross-cultural experience, having lived and worked in Native American communities and conducted training in the Middle East, Africa, and Central Asia. When we asked Melinda what she would most want our readers to gain from her interview, she encouraged, *"Take time. Intervenors have a responsibility to offer passion, commitment, creativity, and time to address issues that face us."*

How did our other interviewees discuss this responsibility? Anne told about her work in the past 10 years dealing with family disputes in her court. She takes time with these families, asking them to think back to early experiences, hoping they can recognize some patterns in their behavior and life. Anne recounts, "I try to establish a safe setting so people can talk, and as they talk, they hear themselves and they should hear the other person in a new way." Rick takes time in his busy school day to help his peers with problems: "It is extremely hard, I've had a couple of students come in to me talking about suicide." Janie sees that giving time to her "exceptional" students helps them "to feel better about themselves and then in turn they can start to learn more."

Kim told us of working for 4 years with the city of Cupertino. As she committed this time to the city, residents began, over the years, "to talk meaningfully together about their hopes and fears and to develop action steps to move the community forward."

Carl has contributed much time to his work in the community of Chattanooga, Tennessee. He tells us how he "played a large role in helping to think through and design a vision to begin change in the community. There is almost a 'Chattanooga Approach' that occurs whenever there is a mix of people working on an issue."

In Pace's work serving the U.S. interests in security and safety, he still takes time to build trust. On any scale—interpersonal, national, international—Pace tries to make a positive difference and do so "in a way that builds trust and rapport with those I work with. If we temporarily make a positive difference, it can destroy the relationship. In our world, that's fatal. So, the difference we make has to build trust in the relationship."

Murray takes time to help organizations recognize the diversity of views and relational vigor that are tangible parts of the reality of organizational life. The social service organization project he told us about earlier took much time. He recounts, "Of course, all this work took place slowly and painstakingly over a number of months and involved numerous setbacks as well as successes."

On Openness

Pace VanDevender is the chief information officer at Sandia National Laboratories, where they are "engaging people and dialoguing in the technical means by which trust can be built." Working with people and technologies in systems, he promotes open and respectful communication to foster productive working environments. We love Pace's story about his evolution as the creator of Prosperity Games™, a vehicle to explore difficult public issues facing our world. As the cold war was ending, Pace asked his boss, the president of Sandia National Labs, "What's my next job?" Al Narath answered, "To enhance the economic security of the United States." Since then, we have observed Pace address economic security with the same dedication and high principles that he brings to any situation dealing with people and important issues. What Pace most wanted for readers from our conversation with him is to embrace the notion that *"openness is the path to the future. Open and respectful communication builds trust. The protective mode will be death to our society. We must take these risks to establish communication with people in nontraditional ways. That personal vulnerability will serve our civilization very well."*

We think Pace would like Carl's dream of "community stores" throughout the world, where a critical mass of kids are coached and trained in capacities in public participation. The openness that Pace spoke of is also evident in Janie's stories about working with "exceptional" children. In her communication with those children, Janie says, "I let them know that no matter how insignificant they feel, anything they say has great importance."

Kim related aspects of her work to us that support openness in communication. One of her objectives is to "look at the kinds of patterns people make which create the social worlds in which they live and then coach/train them to create better patterns of information." Coco said the same thing in his typically poetic style: "I'm speaking about an attitude of life that positions me, even in hard and difficult situations, to do no other than look for possibilities, opportunities, apprenticeship, and alternatives for growing."

Melinda told us of the various programs she developed as the director of the New Mexico Center for Dispute Resolution. She was at the forefront of the mediation movement, reminding us of the nontraditional means of which Pace spoke. Melinda "did not want to do a program here and a program there, but to create a whole continuum so that all the institutions that work with kids and families can build on each other's strengths. This continuum helps us to really change the way we think about kids and conflict."

Robyn also caught Pace's enthusiasm for open and nontraditional communication with her comment, "I hope we can open our conversations up to more complex, more uncertain, more hardworking, and more joint action imaging."

What hope we find in these types of conversations!

- ## Joining the Conversation

It is somewhat tempting to draw grand conclusions from all this. If we were to do so, this would be the place where some kind of integrative summary would appear. In the spirit of the social construction of reality, however, we want to leave this conversation open. Rather than sum it up, we want to invite you, the reader, to join in.

We hope you have already joined this conversation and are responding right now to the conversation of this chapter. We hope you will continue to do so and will invite others to participate as well. We know that we will meet some of you personally and continue talking about whatever evolution of ideas is in the air at that time.

We are putting our finishing touches on this chapter on January 1, 2000. This seems quite appropriate as we recall the words of the Dalai Lama, interviewed by Larry King yesterday on New Year's Eve, the last day of the century. The Dalai Lama proposed that we no longer see other humans as adversaries. We are now entering a century of dialogue, with a focus on understanding of all others. Let us end with the words of our friend Coco Fuks: "My hope is that peace may be constructed along with justice and solidarity, that the new millennium will be an era where the bases for relationship among people, countries, and continents are love and honor."

APPENDIX

Principled Practice: On Theory-Based Intervention

■■■■■■■■■■■■■■■■■■■■■■■■■■■■■■■■■■■■

We have prepared this appendix for readers interested in the theoretical background of our work. Although this book was written from our experience, our practice is informed by a coherent set of theories well established in the academic literature. Our commitments have evolved from years of studying, teaching, and writing about communication theory (Littlejohn, 1999). Over time, we have come to employ a set of theories that provide us with a powerful way of understanding human communication and principles for working in the conflict management field.

A theory is a consistent way of understanding human experience, and *principled practice* is based on the careful consideration of perspective and the desire to work consistently with an appropriate mode of thought. Although we use an eclectic set of tools, our choices in how to act in any situation are guided by certain ways of understanding the human condition that are well worked out by scholars devoted to research and theory building. Theory does not so much determine *which* tools we use as definitely provide guidelines on *when* and *how* to use those tools.

Theory-driven practice is not a linear process. Indeed, the very theories we employ teach us that theory and practice have a reciprocal and circular relationship. Theory informs practice, but practice provides the basis for constructing theory. Consequently, the more work we do with individuals,

213

groups, and communities, the more insight we gain into human experience, which affects our view of theory.

We have organized this section around four important theoretical learnings. The theories presented in the following section are not really independent but actually quite connected with one another. In general, we group these theories under the rubric of *systemic social constructionism,* or the view that reality is constructed through patterns of interaction in human systems. In this text, we have referred to this more simply as *the communication perspective* (Pearce, 1994).

• Four Learnings

**From the theory of the Coordinated Management of
Meaning, we have learned that there is a reflexive
relationship between meaning and action.**

The theory of the Coordinated Management of Meaning (CMM) is a complex theory of communication going back to the 1970s. The theory was developed by W. Barnett Pearce, Vernon Cronen, and their colleagues at the University of Massachusetts (Pearce & Cronen, 1980) and still continues to evolve today (Pearce & Pearce, 2000). This theory is appealing because it integrates a variety of other work and presents a fresh and useful perspective. It is an especially useful theory because of its grounding in actual practice. Over the years, this theory has been refined and expanded by constant testing and application in the world of practice. For adherents to CMM, theory and practice cannot and should not be separated. The value of the theory is in its ability to help us work in practical situations, and that work in turn helps us to make better theory. For this reason, CMM has been called a *practical theory* (Cronen, 1995).

In CMM, communication is seen as a process of coordination in which the parties must make sense of and mesh their respective actions into a coherent whole. Each communicator may understand what is happening very differently, but the parties feel successful to the extent that their actions are perceived as organized.

When we human beings encounter any situation, we naturally assign meaning to what we experience. Objects, events, sounds, sights, images, and words are never just things in themselves. Rather, they represent, bring to mind, or elicit some second-order meaning. Meaning, however, is never singular; it is always multiple and continually embedded in context. In other words, any experience will have more than one possible meaning for us, and any given meaning arises from some context. The same word or action in a different context will have a different meaning.

Meanings are never inherent in the symbol but are worked out socially between people through interaction. Our meanings arise out of interaction with others over a lifetime. Because communicators have different interactional histories, their meanings may be quite different. We constantly find this in our conflict intervention practice. Disputants understand what is happening differently and assign different meanings to particular events and words.

CMM views contexts as hierarchical. In other words, one context is embedded in another, each context changing the meaning of other contexts. Take the case of an employee and manager involved in a conflict over a job reassignment. Within the *context of self-image*, the employee may see this action as rejection. We can better understand this reaction if we realize that the employee's self-image is affected by the *context of relationship with the manager*. The employee views the relationship as one of power in which the manager can make judgments and take action that can hurt people. If we take another step back, however, we can see something even bigger happening: The *context of culture* may be shaping the employees' view of relationship. Occurring in a rather egalitarian culture, a power relationship may be viewed quite negatively as inappropriate and potentially hurtful to persons.

In the above example, we see a hierarchy of three contexts operating to influence the employee's meaning for the reassignment. Culture affects the employee's views of relationship; his views of relationship affect self-image; and his self-image affects his meaning for the job reassignment. You cannot fully explain the employee's reaction without understanding the hierarchy of contexts operating for him at this moment. Figure A.1 illustrates this relationship.

It would come as no surprise that the manager would have an entirely different meaning for what happened. If you were to ask her why she reassigned the employee, she might say that he was not handling the stress very well and that his talents could be better used in a less stressful environment. Notice that the boss's meanings for what happened are embedded in a different set of contexts. For her, the employee's performance was understood within the *context of a stressful situation*. The reassignment was viewed within the *manager's self-image* as a caring person. Further, within *a cultural context of personal responsibility*, the manager feels that tough

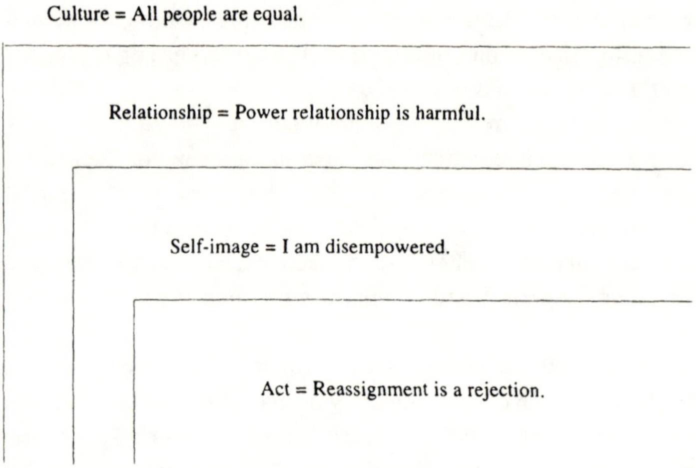

Culture = All people are equal.

Relationship = Power relationship is harmful.

Self-image = I am disempowered.

Act = Reassignment is a rejection.

Figure A.1. Employee's Hierarchy of Meaning

decisions need to be made to improve the organization. Thus, reassigning the employee was both a support act and a good management decision.

In CMM, the object of attention is called the *text* and the frame within which the object is understood is the *context*. In the above example, the act of reassigning the employee is the text. For the employee, this text is understood within the context of a low self-image, a power relationship, and an egalitarian culture. For the manager, it is understood within the context of a stressful situation, a self-image of caring, and a culture of personal responsibility. Notice that text and context are not reflections of some verifiable reality but reflections of how the communicators understand and act on their experience. So we are not saying that in some psychological sense, the employee has a true trait of low self-esteem or that good management inherently involves tough decision making, but that these communicators enact their conflict with these meaning structures in mind.

A person's meanings can be very powerful in determining how things are experienced. There seems to be a *logical force* that governs how a person will connect meaning and action in a particular situation. Sometimes, we do things out of a sense of *prefigurative, or causal, force*. Here, we see that our actions were forced, or caused, by previous events—sort of as in the statement, "My behavior was caused by things outside my control." Sometimes, we view our actions as leading to desired outcomes. CMM calls this *practi-*

cal force, acting to accomplish something: "If I want to get X, I better do Y."
Other times, an individual may feel something called *contextual force,* a
feeling that he or she must do something just because the context demands
it, something like, "In situations like this, a person like me just must act in
this way." Finally, we sometimes understand our actions as an attempt to
influence the context itself, *implicative force.* Here, the reasoning goes: I
want to change the very context that controls what is happening ("I am not
willing to accept a power relationship and will act to define our relationship
in different terms").

CMM is a circular, rather than a linear, theory. In other words, it puts faith
in reciprocal relationships among elements of a system. The relationship
between text and context is a good example of the circular principle. A
frame that may serve as context at one point in time may become the text at
another point in time. Texts and contexts switch back and forth, each reproducing or changing the meaning of the other. Stated in slightly more sophisticated terms, the relationship is reflexive, each part forming the other.

This is a difficult concept to grasp at first, so let's return to the example of
the manager and employee. Having a low self-image makes it easier for the
employee to feel that the reassignment was a personal attack, and being
reassigned makes it easier for him to have a low self-image. Seeing herself
as a caring person makes it easier for the manager to view the reassignment
as a supportive act, and the act makes it easier for her to view herself as a
supportive person.

When they are self-reinforcing, these reciprocal relationships are called
charmed loops, and when they are self-contradictory, they are called
strange loops. The employee in our workplace case seems to be involved
in a strong, self-reinforcing charmed loop. Perhaps the manager's position
is a bit more complex. The manager may feel both caring and tough-minded.
*"As a caring manager, I will avoid hurting employees, but when I avoid
hurting employees, I cannot make the tough decisions that will improve the
organization. So I will make tough decisions like reassignment. Yet reassignment may hurt an employee."* Strange loops like this often happen as a
person switches from one context or logic to another. The meanings for a
particular act will shift along with the context, which explains why good,
intelligent people sometimes become confused. In a complex world,
strange loops are inevitable. They can actually be beneficial, because they
can lead to new ways of understanding experience and to flexibility in
thought and action. Charmed loops, in contrast, have the benefit of clarity
and consistency, but they may seal a person off from productive change.

If we think of ways of understanding as *resources* and ways of acting as *practices,* we can employ the text-context loop to connect the two. CMM says that there is an inextricable connection between resources and practices, that how we think affects how we act and how we act affects how we think. This idea has been immensely helpful in our conflict intervention work. People's stories reveal how they understand events in context. As we invite participants to expand and develop their stories, they become more aware of their own meanings and the multiple contexts in which actions might be understood. An action that once looked hateful within the confines of a particular context may come to have new, more constructive meanings as contexts expand. By scoping out and scoping in, participants can expand their awareness and change their behaviors and their ways of understanding events. As they behave in new ways, they may come to see actions differently. As horizons expand, resources grow, and positive system change becomes more likely. Even in single mediations, we have seen these kinds of changes happen many times. Dialogue is really a process of exploring the inevitable link between meaning and action.

> From system theory, we have learned that
> human experience consists of
> dynamic interactional patterns.

System theory has been popular in one form or another throughout the 20th century. Although several variations of system theory exist (Bahg, 1990), they all share the idea that things work by virtue of dynamic interaction. Interactional patterns constitute forces above and beyond the characteristics of individual elements. In other words, the whole is more than the sum of its parts. A family is a good example. The dynamics of interaction within the family give the family itself a "character" that is more than and different from the "personalities" of the individual family members. We have often observed in our teaching that college classes differ significantly from one another, even sections of the same course, not only because they consist of different people but also because the class dynamics are always different. In our mediation trainings, we will divide the participants into several role-playing groups, give each group the same case, and have them play it out. Always, the results vary from group to group, even though the case is the same.

Systems by nature are constantly moving and therefore shifting from one state to another. In complex systems, the parts interact with one another within a network of relationships, and there may be many pathways from any one point to any other point in the system. Therefore, the ways in which one part of a system interacts with another part can change from moment to moment. However, systems are not chaotic. They have a set of self-organizing forces that keep the system on track, and there is usually sufficient redundancy so that if one stabilizing force fails, another takes over. For this reason, systems tend to have staying power.

Cybernetics is that feature of systems leading to self-influence. If you imagine a system as a complex set of interactions, you can see many "loops" from one element to another. The loops are lines of effect, such that when one thing happens at point A, events are triggered at point B, and what happens at B comes back to affect A again. This is feedback. Some *feedback loops* are *positive,* meaning that they accelerate a tendency: The more the boss gives orders, the more the employee withdraws, and the more the employee withdraws, the more the boss gives orders. Other feedback loops are *negative,* or self-correcting, and perpetuate a steady state: The boss sees that an employee needs direction and gives an order; the employee complies with the order, and the boss, seeing no need for further direction, stops giving orders.

In the realm of human life, systems are *open,* meaning that there is an interchange with the *environment.* The system takes in *input* from outside and discharges *output* into the environment. Open systems must constantly adapt to their environment and do so by feedback loops with the environment. Inputs provide new resources for the system to change, and the system is able to gauge the effects of its output. In order to maintain structure and stability, then, a system must have some balance, or *homeostasis,* which is achieved by self-correction, but it must also have the ability to change, or undergo *morphogenesis.* Both stability and change are made possible by the patterns of interaction within the system and between the system and other systems.

In old-style system theory (e.g., Buckley, 1968), it is believed possible for someone outside a system to observe it objectively. The observer sees the boundaries of the system, sees how the system interacts with its environment, and watches the internal adjustments that the system makes. Using classical system theory, for example, a mediator might treat the disputants as a system, diagnose what is going on between them, and intervene to fix the problem.

In order for system theory to work for us, however, we must incorporate a more recent generation of work, known as *second-order cybernetics* (von Foerster, 1981). Here, the boundary between system and environment is highly permeable, perhaps even nonexistent. As we observe a system interacting with its "environment," we are really just scoping out into a larger system. As we focus on "internal" patterns, we are scoping in to a smaller one. We come to realize when we do this kind of context shifting that the system is not really anything in and of itself, but that we as observers are actually defining what we wish to treat as a system.

If this is the case—if we as mediators, for example, construct or create boundaries for useful purposes—then we must acknowledge our own involvement with this system—the system-as-defined-by-us. In other words, we become part of a system whenever we act on or even just "observe" it. Observing is a kind of interaction. You *cannot not* be part of the system you are looking at. This does not mean that a family therapist becomes part of the family, but he or she does become part of the system of "family-in-therapy."

For this reason, we never view our work as benign. Indeed, how and when we interact with the system assumes major importance. We must take every intervention seriously, from the moment of first contact to the final good-bye. Using this perspective, too, we never view ourselves as *doing something to* the system but rather as *interacting with the system.*

Second-order system theory teaches us not to use an objectivist model of intervention: (1) diagnose, (2) prescribe, (3) evaluate. We are not confident in this method because it would lead us to push against the force of the system. We know that when that happens, homeostatic loops will push back, or resist. In other words, the system's desire for balance will cause it to resist forces of change from outside. This is why we are extremely reluctant to make suggestions in a mediation. Even though we are part of the *mediation system,* we are still outsiders to the ongoing system of the disputants.

System theory encourages us to view the system as a complex set of interactional patterns and a rich fund of resources with which the system can change. Intervention is essentially a *perturbation* of the system that can elicit new forms of interaction and a restructuring. When clients ask us to intervene, they are really asking for some kind of expanded cybernetic mechanism that will help them overcome a stuck spot or achieve some set of desired goals. Our role in the newly established loop is to ask certain kinds of questions that help participants reflect on their system of interaction and to say what we see so that they might adjust or create new avenues and patterns.

In many ways, the idea of collaboration is an application of second-order cybernetics. Rather than prescribe what a system should do, we invite parties into an interaction that may allow the system to restructure itself to some extent. This is why we are so intent on concentrating on and asking questions about interactional patterns rather than individual characteristics. A system in distress is one in which the patterns are not working very well, and good intervention merely invites new patterns that in turn can lead to new outcomes and new, more functional, cybernetic loops.

From social constructionism,
we have learned that reality is
co-constructed through communication.

Social constructionism, popular today in many social sciences, is a body of theory based on the premise that our experience of reality is a product of social interaction (Gergen, 1985, 1999). More literally, reality is formed or created by persons-in-interaction.

This line of thought goes back to the old philosophies of American pragmatism (Cronen & Lang, 1994) and symbolic interactionism (Lal, 1995). Pragmatism builds on the idea that understanding is tied to action—What we do determines how we think. Symbolic interactionism, a long-standing school of thought still very much alive today in sociology, teaches that our personal meanings for objects, persons, and the self are developed through a process of interaction with other people: We internalize meanings worked out over a lifetime of social relations. Contemporary social constructionism probably owes its most recent and direct debt to the well-known works *The Social Construction of Reality* by Peter Berger and Thomas Luckmann (1966) and *The Phenomenology of the Social World* by Alfred Schutz (1967). Over the past 20 years, constructionism has undergone considerable development on several fronts (Pearce, 1995).

Constructionism imagines that we are primarily social creatures and that communication, more than a tool for transmitting information, is the very medium in which we construct reality as we know it (Pearce, 1989). This is a radical idea. Most people think that reality is objective, that it is separate from the observer; but constructionism teaches that reality is actually made in communication and that it changes from community to community, from time to time, and from situation to situation (Gergen, 1973). This theory does not deny material fact, but it does show that human beings have no way of knowing other than through the categories or meaning structures built within social communities. From the time we are born, our worlds are structured through talk, words, and gestures. We can sense the materiality of a thing, but we can never conceive of it outside of social categories. For all intents and purposes, then, reality is socially constructed.

Eschewing an individualistic focus, constructionists take interaction as the basic unit of analysis. The questions are always

What is being made within a particular interaction?

Over time, what is being made through a series of interactions?

And on the macro level, what is being made within any entire community?

Even on the widest level of society, broadly shared realities are nothing more or less than institutionalized ways of packaging experience.

As a result of this orientation, constructionists are not very interested in what any one person says or does in isolation. Instead, they want to look at how others respond to what is said and done, to look at the pattern that develops between actions over time, and to question what meanings are being created within those patterns. The meaning of an act is negotiated or worked out by a kind of back-and-forth "conversation." We construct our meanings in the process of talking about things, and often those meanings come clear only retrospectively. When a person confronts a situation or object, he or she will assign certain meanings to the experience based on what has been in previous interactions with others.

Our connections between things, our concepts, the rules we employ to relate one object or category to another, and the logic we use to "reason" our way through a series of thoughts are all social arrangements. These ways of structuring reality work to the extent that they have led to a coherent pattern of action or understanding in the past. As people encounter new conversational partners, new communities, and new contexts, their meanings of experience migrate and often change. Other aspects of our reality remain essentially unchanged because those ways of understanding are highly cultural, widespread, institutionalized, durable, and workable. These realities are socially constructed nonetheless.

This theory has sensitized us to important dynamics of conflict. We know that disputants approach a conflict with rich social realities that arise from their experience over a lifetime. Although disputants themselves may dismiss an "opponent's" view, we know that each person's views are part of a complex set of social arrangements and must be taken seriously. What may appear misguided, uninformed, immoral, or downright stupid to one party is the essence of another party's experience. People are so serious about their positions, interests, values, goals, and feelings because these seem so very real to them. And they are real, socially real. As our friend Anne Kass the judge has told us, two parties with categorically opposing views can both be right.

Social constructionism moves us to place value on stories as the essential material in conflict interventions. This is why we think good dialogue is a process of sharing and hearing stories. Stories reveal not only what a communicator believes to be important but also the contextual reality within which that position, idea, or feeling assumes importance. If we can help parties listen deeply to one another's stories, a new level of understanding may begin to develop. We are not so concerned that parties understand literally what others want but that parties develop a coherent idea of the story as lived by that person (Pearce, 1994). Hearing stories told and stories lived is not meant to change minds but to broaden perspective and open up the potential for new patterns of communication and, thereby, new and better social realities.

It should come as no surprise, then, that language assumes immense importance in social constructionism. To constructionists, language is more than a medium for the expression of meaning. It is the medium in which reality is made. Words and grammar determine how experience is packaged and therefore understood. At the same time, however, language is not an external, immutable structure. By itself, language is not reality; rather by *using* language, we mold the ways of connecting things, labeling things, and thereby understanding things. Language is inherently malleable. It is true that basic language structure comes to us culturally, perhaps even biologically, but the myriad ways in which we can modify, adapt, and use it make language a natural means for making social worlds.

Interaction, especially in language, enables people and groups to establish difference. Human beings use language in ways that establish distinctions, and these distinctions define a person's orientation toward conflict. We might call these orientations *conflict patterns*. Such patterns define how we understand and react to people different from ourselves. Constructionism, understood in these terms, makes the work of conflict intervention extremely important, for intervention engages a "reality-in-the-making." Done awkwardly and without an awareness of co-construction, intervention can contribute to, even strengthen, inhumane and destructive notions of difference. Done wisely and skillfully in the spirit of making a better world, interventions can invite new patterns that may lead to understanding conflict as a positive resource. If it is hard for parties in conflict to change the realities they are making, perhaps third parties invited into the conversation can move it to new visions and vistas.

> From the theory of transcendent discourse,
> we have learned the value of changing
> contexts of communication.

When people are communicating, they generally have a clear idea of what they are doing. They see themselves as *explaining, persuading,* or perhaps *negotiating.* They will feel satisfied or disappointed in their performance as a speaker, their effectiveness in influencing others, or their skill in fending off an enemy. The study of discourse is the study of what people *do* when they communicate. Different discourses do different kinds of things (Ellis & Donohue, 1986).

Over the past two decades or so, Stephen Littlejohn and Barnett Pearce have done considerable research on conflict. This work is explained in their book *Moral Conflict: When Social Worlds Collide* (1997). In this book, Pearce and Littlejohn present the makings of a theory of discourse in conflict. Actually, this work is firmly embedded in the tradition of the theory of the Coordinated Management of Meaning, and it incorporates a good dose of system theory and constructionism as well.

In their case studies, Pearce and Littlejohn observed a variety of *discourses* of conflict. Ordinarily, people in conflict are struggling to prevail, perhaps to win a point, meet an interest, or achieve a goal. Here, disputants tend to use discourses of persuasion and influence. The parties to ordinary disputes gather their best arguments and evidence to show the truth and value of what they believe and want. Occasionally, one party prevails by persuading others that they are wrong. More often, the appeal is won with a third-party decision maker such as a judge, manager, arbitrator, policy officer, or parent or a decision-making body such as a legislature, board of directors, jury, or electorate.

Often, too, disputants settle their differences through a discourse of negotiation. Here, they compromise or even collaborate to solve problems and make decisions. Indeed, society is able to maintain order largely through a highly developed system of dispute resolution that relies on persuasion, negotiation, adjudication, and decision making.

Often, however, these forms of ordinary discourse fail. They fail because the parties cannot agree to a method of resolution, a standard of argument, or a rule of decision. They fail because basic identities are at issue. They fail also because the social realities of the parties clash on a very deep level and reflect incommensurate moral orders. In these cases, normal appeals to persuasion and negotiation lead only to frustration and ultimately degrade to the discourses of diatribe and violence.

Yet, as many of the examples from the previous chapters show, it is possible to get past some of these most difficult conflicts. They are hard but not impossible, especially if the participants are willing to redefine their discourse, or what they believe they are doing when they communicate. For this reason, Pearce and Littlejohn identify a different form of communication, which they call *transcendent discourse.*

A transcendent discourse acknowledges the failure to achieve *first-order change;* the parties understand that they will not change one another's views on the subject at hand. Instead, they go for *second-order change* (Littlejohn, 2000), or a realignment of their orientation toward one another and toward communication itself. The question is this: Can we find a frame in which to make a positive social reality within which we can (and should) disagree? Or can we make something bigger and better than a polarizing dispute? Or again, can we redefine the meaning of *winning?*

Such discourse is transcendent because it breaks free from and transforms old unworkable patterns of communication. It is transcendent because it employs new categories of conversation in which the parties can find constructive collaboration. It is transcendent because it overcomes polarized debate. There are many potential forms, but, in general, transcendent discourse embodies the values of dialogue outlined in Chapter 2 and has two important qualities.

First, it creates new frames in which old differences can be transformed. Using a metaphor from language, transcendent discourse establishes a new *grammar* that enables parties to reconceptualize their differences while finding an area of common ground. The new categories of conversation constitute a creole of sorts, making it possible for parties to have a coherent dialogue across otherwise incommensurate worldviews (Stout, 1988). You have heard the expression "I don't want to go there," meaning "I don't want to get into that subject." In transcendent discourse, the parties agree to take the stand "We don't want to go there." If parties are unable to talk constructively and respectfully within a particular context, perhaps they can find a context of dialogue by going somewhere else.

Second, transcendent discourse is a form of communication that redefines the relationship between the parties. Instead of viewing one another as enemies on an issue, they define themselves as fellow travelers in search of a context for productive conversation. Instead of viewing the relationship as one of struggle, they redefine it as a relationship of creative collaboration, and what they create together are transcendent contexts in which new frontiers can be co-constructed. The participants decide mutually to transcend old patterns of simple polarization and commit jointly to explore complexity. In the process, they learn that we live in a multivalued world, that every value or position—even their own—has both powers and limits, and that new fusions are possible.

The theory of transcendent discourse has made us aware of the need for creativity in conflict intervention. Rarely do traditional methods of dispute resolution lead to the kind of discourse that can transcend. Indeed, disputants and third parties interested in transforming old patterns of communication must search for new ways of doing so. Engaging in discourses that transcend is a foray into new territory and is inherently creative. There is no canon of transformative methods. They are worked out anew whenever and wherever the challenge is experienced. We hope our practice as described in this book provides some measure of how this work might proceed.

■ Resources You Can Use

Bahg, C.-G. (1990). Major systems theories throughout the world. *Behavioral Science, 35,* 79-107.

Berger, P., & Luckmann, T. (1966). *The social construction of reality: A treatise in the sociology of knowledge.* Garden City, NY: Doubleday.

Buckley, W. (Ed.). (1968). *Modern systems research for the behavioral scientist.* Chicago: Aldine.

Cronen, V. (1995). Practical theory and the tasks ahead for social approaches to communication. In W. Leeds-Hurwitz (Ed.), *Social approaches to communication* (pp. 217-242). New York: Guilford.

Cronen, V., & Lang, P. (1994). Language and action: Wittgenstein and Dewey in the practice of therapy and consultation. *Human Systems: The Journal of Systemic Consultation and Management, 5,* 5-43.

Ellis, D. C., & Donohue, W. A. (Eds.). (1986). *Contemporary issues in language and discourse processes.* Hillsdale, NJ: Erlbaum.

Gergen, K. (1973). Social psychology as history. *Journal of Personality and Social Psychology, 26,* 309-320.

Gergen, K. (1985). The social constructionist movement in modern psychology. *American Psychologist, 40,* 266-275.

Gergen, K. (1999). *An invitation to social construction.* London: Sage Ltd.

Lal, B. B. (1995). Symbolic interaction theories. *American Behavioral Scientist, 38,* 421-441.

Littlejohn, S. W. (1999). *Theories of human communication.* Belmont, CA: Wadsworth.

Littlejohn, S. W. (2000, February). *Challenging discourse in a diverse society.* Paper presented at the Western States Communication Association, Sacramento, CA. (Request a copy from littlej@unm.edu)

Pearce, W. B. (1989). *Communication and the human condition.* Carbondale: Southern Illinois University Press.

Pearce, W. B. (1994). *Interpersonal communication: Making social worlds.* New York: HarperCollins.

Pearce, W. B. (1995). A sailing guide for social constructionists. In W. Leeds-Hurwitz (Ed.), *Social approaches to communication* (pp. 88-113). New York: Guilford.

Pearce, W. B., & Cronen, V. (1980). *Communication, action, and meaning.* New York: Praeger.

Pearce, W. B., & Littlejohn, S. W. (1997). *Moral conflict: When social worlds collide.* Thousand Oaks, CA: Sage.

Schutz, A. (1967). *The phenomenology of the social world* (G. Walsh & F. Lehnert, Trans.). Evanston, IL: Northwestern University Press.

Schutz, A. (1970). *On phenomenology and social relations.* Chicago: University of Chicago Press.

Stout, J. (1988). *Ethics after Babel: The languages of morals and their discontents.* Boston: Beacon.

von Foerster, H. (1981). *Observing systems: Selected papers of Heinz von Foerster.* Seaside, CA: Intersystems Publications.

Bibliography

■■■■■■■■■■■■■■

Arnett, R. C., & Arneson, P. (1999). *Dialogic civility in a cynical age.* Albany: State University of New York Press.

Bahg, C.-G. (1990). Major systems theories throughout the world. *Behavioral Science, 35,* 79-107.

Barker, J. R. (1999). *The discipline of teamwork: Participation and concertive control.* Thousand Oaks, CA: Sage.

Barker, J. R., & Domenici, K. L. (2000). Mediation practices for knowledge-based teams. In M. M. Beyerlein, D. A. Johnson, & S. T. Beyerlein (Eds.), *Product development teams: Vol. 5. Advances in interdisciplinary studies of work teams.* Stamford, CT: JAI.

Berger, P., & Luckmann, T. (1966). *The social construction of reality: A treatise in the sociology of knowledge.* Garden City, NY: Doubleday.

Brandenburger, A., & Nalebuff, B. (1996). *Co-opetition.* Garden City, NY: Doubleday.

Buber, M. (1958). *I and thou.* New York: Scribner.

Buckley, W. (Ed.). (1968). *Modern systems research for the behavioral scientist.* Chicago: Aldine.

Bush, R. A. B., & Folger, J. P. (1994). *The promise of mediation: Responding to conflict through empowerment and recognition.* San Francisco: Jossey-Bass.

Campbell, D., Draper, R., & Huffington, C. (1989). *A systemic approach to consultation.* London: D.C. Publishing.

Constantino, C. A., & Merchant, C. S. (1996). *Designing conflict management systems: A guide to creating productive and healthy organizations.* San Francisco: Jossey-Bass.

Cooperrider, D., & Srivastva, S. (Eds.). (1990). *Appreciative management in leadership: the power of positive thought and action.* San Francisco: Jossey-Bass.

Cronen, V. (1995). Practical theory and the tasks ahead for social approaches to communication. In W. Leeds-Hurwitz (Ed.), *Social approaches to communication* (pp.217-242). New York: Guilford.

Cronen, V., & Lang, P. (1994). Language and action: Wittgenstein and Dewey in the practice of therapy and consultation. *Human Systems: The Journal of Systemic Consultation and Management, 5,* 5-43.

Crum, T. F. (1987). *The magic of conflict.* New York: Simon & Schuster.

Daggett, D. (1995). *Beyond the rangeland conflict: Toward a west that works.* Flagstaff, AZ: The Grand Canyon Trust.

Daitz, B. (1999). *Whose home on the range: A documentary about resolving environmental conflict.* [Video]. (Available from New Mexico Center for Dispute Resolution, PO Box 25044, Albuquerque, NM 87125-5044)

Davis, M. (1970). *Game theory: A non-technical introduction.* New York: Basic Books.

Domenici, K. (1996). *Mediation: Empowerment in conflict management.* Prospect Heights, IL: Waveland.

Domenici, K., & Littlejohn, S. W. (1998). *The team mediation system: Effective communication in teams* [Video]. (Available from Domenici Littlejohn, 504 Luna Blvd. NW, Albuquerque, NM 87102, 505-246-9890)

Ellis, D. C., & Donohue, W. A. (Eds.). (1986). *Contemporary issues in language and discourse processes.* Hillsdale, NJ: Erlbaum.

Fagre, Leslie. (1995, February). *Recognizing disputants' face-needs in community mediation.* Paper presented at Western States Communication Association Conference, Portland, OR.

Fisher, R., & Ury, W. (1991). *Getting to yes: Negotiating agreement without giving in.* New York: Penguin.

Folger, J. P., & Jones, T. S. (Eds.). (1994). *New directions in mediation: Communication research and perspectives.* Thousand Oaks, CA: Sage.

Foss, S. K., & Foss, K. A. (1994). *Inviting transformation: Presentational speaking for a changing world.* Prospect Heights, IL: Waveland.

Gastil, J. (2000). *By popular demand: Revitalizing representative democracy through deliberative elections.* Berkeley: University of California Press.

Gergen, K. (1973). Social psychology as history. *Journal of Personality and Social Psychology, 26,* 309-320.

Gergen, K. (1985). The social constructionist movement in modern psychology. *American Psychologist, 40,* 266-275.

Gergen, K. (1999). *An invitation to social construction.* London: Sage Ltd.

Gerzon, M. (1996). *A house divided: Six belief systems struggling for America's soul.* New York: Tarcher/Putnam.

Gleason, S. (Ed.). (1997). *Workplace dispute resolution: Directions for the twenty-first century.* East Lansing: Michigan State University Press.

Gutman, A., & Thompson, D. (1996). *Democracy and disagreement: Why moral conflict cannot be avoided in politics, and what should be done about it.* Cambridge, MA: Harvard University Press.

Kayser, T. A. (1994). *Building team power: How to unleash the collaborative genius of work teams.* New York: Irwin.

Kegan, R. (1994). *In over our heads: The mental demands of modern life.* Cambridge, MA: Harvard University Press.

Kolb, D. M. (1994). *When talk works: Profiles of mediators.* San Francisco: Jossey-Bass.

Kriesberg, L., Northrup, T. A., & Thorson, S. J. (1989). *Intractable conflicts and their transformation.* Syracuse, NY: Syracuse University Press.

Lakoff, G., & Johnson, M. (1980). *Metaphors we live by.* Chicago: The University of Chicago Press.

Lal, B. B. (1995). Symbolic interaction theories. *American Behavioral Scientist, 38,* 421-441.

Littlejohn, S. W. (1999). *Theories of human communication.* Belmont, CA: Wadsworth.

Littlejohn, S. W. (2000, February). *Challenging discourse in a diverse society.* Paper presented at the Western States Communication Association, Sacramento, CA. (Request a copy from littlej@unm.edu)

Lumsden, G., & Lumsden, D. (1993). *Communicating in groups and teams: Sharing leadership.* Belmont, CA: Wadsworth.

Matson, F. W., & Montagu, A. (1967). *The human dialogue: Perspectives on communication.* New York: Free Press.

McDaniel, G. L. (1999). Designing a team management system that really works. In *The Best of Teams 99* (pp. 248-262). Lexington, MA: Linkage, Inc.

McKinney, B. C., Kinzey, W. D., & Fuller, R. M. (1995). *Mediator communication competencies: Interpersonal communication and alternative dispute resolution.* Edina, MN: Burgess.

Moore, C. W. (1996). *The mediation process: Practical strategies for resolving conflict.* San Francisco: Jossey-Bass.

National Issues Forums, 100 Commons Rd., Dayton, OH 45459-2777, www.nifi.org

Nicotera, A. M. (1995). *Conflict and organizations: Communicative processes.* Albany: State University of New York Press.

Papa, M. J., & Canary, D. J. (1995). *Conflict in organizations: A competence-based approach.* In A. M. Nicotera (Ed.), *Conflict and organizations: Communicative processes* (pp. 154-179). Albany: State University of New York Press.

Pearce, W. B. (1973). *Interpersonal communication: Making social worlds.* New York: HarperCollins.

Pearce, W. B. (1989). *Communication and the human condition.* Carbondale: Southern Illinois University Press.

Pearce, W. B. (1994). *Interpersonal communication: Making social worlds.* New York: HarperCollins.

Pearce, W. B. (1995). A sailing guide for social constructionists. In W. Leeds-Hurwitz (Ed.), *Social approaches to communication* (pp. 88-113). New York: Guilford.

Pearce, W. B., & Cronen, V. (1980). *Communication, action, and meaning.* New York: Praeger.

Pearce, W. B., & Littlejohn, S. W. (1997). *Moral conflict: When social worlds collide.* Thousand Oaks, CA: Sage.

Pearce, W. B., & Pearce, K. A. (1999). Combining passions and abilities: Toward dialogic virtuosity. *Southern Communication Journal, 65,* 161-175.

Program on Negotiation, Harvard Law School, 513 Pound Hall, Cambridge, MA 02138. www.pon.harvard.edu

Prosperity Games™ Design Manual. (1997). (Available from Prosperity Institute, 7604 Lamplighter Lane NE, Albuquerque, NM 87109)

Public Conversations Project, 46 Kondazian Street, Watertown, MA 02172. www.publicconversations.org

Public Dialogue Consortium, 504 Luna Blvd. NW, Albuquerque, NM 87102. www.publicdialogue.org

Rapoport, A. (1960). *Fights, games, and debates.* Ann Arbor: University of Michigan Press.

Rapoport, A. (1967). Strategy and conscience. In F. Matson & A. Montagu (Eds.), *The human dialogue: Perspectives on communication* (pp. 79-96). New York: Free Press.

Schutz, A. (1967). *The phenomenology of the social world* (G. Walsh & F. Lehnert, Trans.). Evanston, IL: Northwestern University Press.

Schutz, A. (1970). *On phenomenology and social relations.* Chicago: University of Chicago Press.

Shailor, J. G. (1994). *Empowerment in dispute mediation: A critical analysis of communication.* Westport, CT: Praeger.

Slaikeu, K. A. (1996). *When push comes to shove: A practical guide to mediating disputes.* San Francisco: Jossey-Bass.

Smith, M. (1998). *The Catron County Citizens Group: A case study in community collaboration.* Albuquerque, NM: New Mexico Center for Dispute Resolution.

Spano, S. (2000). *Public dialogue and participative democracy: The Cupertino community project.* Cresskill, NJ: Hampton Press.

Steinfatt, T., & Miller, G. (1974). Communication in game theoretic models of conflict. In G. R. Miller & H. Simons (Eds.), *Perspectives on communication in conflict* (pp. 14-75). Englewood Cliffs, NJ: Prentice Hall.

Stout, J. (1988). *Ethics after Babel: The languages of morals and their discontents.* Boston: Beacon.

Study Circle Resource Center, PO Box 203, Promfret, CT 06258. www.studycircles. com

von Foerster, H. (1981). *Observing systems: Selected papers of Heinz von Foerster.* Seaside, CA: Intersystems Publications.

von Neumann, J., & Morgenstern, O. (1944). *The theory of games and economic behavior.* Princeton, NJ: Princeton University Press.

Index

■ ■ ■ ■ ■ ■ ■

About the Authors
■■■■■■■■■■■■■■■■■■■■■■■

Stephen W. Littlejohn is a mediator and communication consultant in Albuquerque, New Mexico. He has been a professor of communication for 30 years and has written widely on communication and conflict. His book *Moral Conflict: When Social Worlds Collide,* co-authored with Barnett Pearce, presents a groundbreaking theory of social conflict based on ten years of research. His textbook *Theories of Human Communication* is now in its sixth edition. He is President of the Public Dialogue Consortium. He received his Ph.D. in communication from the University of Utah.

Kathy Domenici is the manager of Communication Services and an Associate of the Public Dialogue Consortium. As a conflict management consultant, mediator, facilitator, and trainer, she founded the Mediation Clinic at the University of New Mexico. She has helped design and facilitate high-level strategy and leadership games for such clients as Eastman Kodak, the President's Commission on Critical Infrastructure, Sandia National Laboratories, and Lockheed Martin. She is the author of *Mediation: Empowerment in Conflict Management* (1996) and coauthor of "Mediation Practices in Knowledge-Based Teams," in *Product Developement Teams: Vol. 5. Advances in Interdisciplinary Studies of Work Teams* (2000). With 10 years of academic work in conflict and communication and 15 years' experience in mediation and public issue management, She concentrates on conflict system design and innovative methods in alternative dispute resolution. She received her master's degree in communication from the University of New Mexico.

Kathy Domenici and Stephen Littlejohn are co-principals in Domenici Littlejohn, Inc., an organization dedicated to planning and facilitating processes involving high-quality communication. They work with individuals, groups, organizations, and communities throughout the United States and abroad to promote constructive conflict management. Dedicated to improving human relationships, they use a systems approach and emphasize communication in their work. They regularly offer trainings in mediation, public issue facilitation, and conflict management. Among their recent clients are the Equal Employment Opportunity Commission, New Mexico Human Rights Division, Advanced Micro Devices, U.S. Postal Service, and the White House Initiative on Tribal Colleges and Universities.

Printed in the United States
78352LV00004B/132